AF886649

Think, Code, Create

Advanced Python Programming Series

A companion volume to the twelve-book advanced series.

Can be used independently or alongside the series.

Northward House Publishing
Brisbane, Queensland, Australia
www.northwardhouse.com.au

Think, Code, Create
Advanced Python Programming Series

Think Before You Code

Planning, Pseudocode & Program Design for Better Python

M. North
BEd. (Sec), BSc, MInfoTech

Northward House Publishing
Brisbane, Queensland, Australia
2026

Prerequisite:

Think, Code, Create — A Python Programming Journey for Students

ISBN 978-1-7640698-0-9

This book is a companion to the Think, Code, Create Advanced Python Programming Series. It can be studied at any point after completing the foundation text, and can be used independently of the twelve-book advanced series. It does not assume knowledge of any particular advanced topic — only the foundation concepts covered in the prerequisite text.

Teachers may choose to use this book as a preparatory resource before students begin the advanced series, or as a supplementary planning and design reference throughout.

Designed for Years 9–12 — Australian Curriculum Version 9 — Digital Technologies.

About the Author

M. North holds a Bachelor of Education (Secondary), a Bachelor of Science, and a Master of Information Technology. He has worked as a secondary school teacher of Digital Technologies, Mathematics, and Science across Queensland, Australia, before turning to educational publishing full time.

His teaching practice has centred on making abstract computational thinking concrete and accessible for students at every level — from those encountering programming for the first time to advanced students pursuing algorithmic thinking and software engineering. The Think, Code, Create series grew directly from classroom experience: the need for structured, curriculum-aligned materials that treat secondary students as capable thinkers, not passive recipients of watered-down content.

The foundation text, Think, Code, Create — A Python Programming Journey for Students (ISBN 978-1-7640698-0-9), established the pedagogical approach: clear explanations, worked examples with annotated code, guided exercises with hints, and challenge tasks for extension. The twelve-book advanced series extends that approach through specialised programming domains.

Think Before You Code grew from a gap observed consistently in classroom practice: students who understood Python syntax well but struggled to plan, structure, and verify their programs before writing code. The skills of pseudocode writing, flowcharting, structured decomposition, and desk checking are rarely taught explicitly — yet they underpin everything that makes the difference between code that works and code that almost works. This book addresses that gap directly.

M. North is based in Brisbane, Queensland, Australia, and publishes through Northward House Publishing.

Northward House Publishing
Brisbane, Queensland, Australia
www.northwardhouse.com.au

Feedback, corrections, and curriculum enquiries are welcome. Contact the publisher via the website above.

Publication Information

First published 2026

Published by Northward House Publishing, Brisbane, Queensland, Australia

This book is a companion volume to the Think, Code, Create — Advanced Python Programming Series.

ISBN: 978-1-7640698-7-8

Foundation text (2025)**, ISBN:** 978-1-7640698-0-9

Acknowledgements

The author and publisher gratefully acknowledge the contribution of all teachers and students who provided feedback during the development of this series. The Python programming language is created and maintained by the Python Software Foundation (python.org).

Disclaimer

The information in this book is provided in good faith and is accurate to the best of the author's knowledge at the time of publication. Programming languages, libraries, and tools change over time. The publisher and author accept no liability for errors, omissions, or outcomes arising from the use of code or information in this publication.

All example programs are written for educational purposes. Any resemblance to real persons, organisations, or events in example scenarios is coincidental.

The Think, Code, Create Advanced Series

Think Before You Code can be used alongside any book in the series below, or independently after completing the foundation text.

Chapter 01 **Object-Oriented Programming in Python**
Design and build programs using classes, objects, and the four pillars of OOP
Prerequisite: Foundation text Chapters 14–15 **Audience:** Years 9–12

Chapter 02 **File Handling & Exception Management**
Read, write, and manage data files; handle errors gracefully in real-world programs
Prerequisite: Foundation text Chapters 3–4, 11–12 **Audience:** Years 9–12

Chapter 03 **Modules, Packages & the Python Ecosystem**
Organise, share, and reuse code with modules, packages, and the broader Python library
Prerequisite: Foundation text Chapters 14–15 **Audience:** Years 9–12

Chapter 04 **Data Structures & Algorithms**
Understand, implement, and analyse core data structures and fundamental algorithms
Prerequisite: Foundation text Chapters 11–13 **Audience:** Years 10–12

Chapter 05 **Functional Programming & Advanced Iterables**
Master Python's functional tools — generators, comprehensions, closures, and more
Prerequisite: Foundation text Chapters 14–15 **Audience:** Years 10–12

Chapter 06 **Regular Expressions & Advanced Text Processing**
Search, validate, and transform text data using Python's powerful re module
Prerequisite: Foundation text Chapter 10 **Audience:** Years 10–12

Chapter 07 **Database Programming with Python**
Store and retrieve data persistently using SQLite, SQL queries, and Python ORMs
Prerequisite: Books 01–02 recommended **Audience:** Years 10–12

Chapter 08 Web Scraping & Working with APIs
Collect real-world data from websites and web services using Python
Prerequisite: Books 02–03 recommended **Audience:** Years 10–12

Chapter 09 Data Analysis with Python
Explore, clean, and visualise real-world datasets using NumPy, Pandas, and Matplotlib
Prerequisite: Book 03; spreadsheet literacy **Audience:** Years 11–12

Chapter 10 GUI Programming with Tkinter
Design and build graphical desktop applications using Python's built-in GUI toolkit
Prerequisite: Book 01 (OOP) **Audience:** Years 10–12

Chapter 11 Testing, Debugging & Code Quality
Write reliable, maintainable code using testing frameworks, debugging tools, and style standards
Prerequisite: Books 01 and 03 **Audience:** Years 11–12

Chapter 12 Concurrency, Networking & Automation
Write programs that do multiple things at once, communicate over networks, and automate tasks
Prerequisite: Books 01, 02, and 03 **Audience:** Years 11–12

How to Use This Book

Think Before You Code is designed to be read and worked through sequentially, from Chapter 1 to Chapter 8. Each chapter builds on the tools introduced in previous chapters, and Chapter 8 draws on all of them in a single extended worked example. That said, individual chapters can also be used as standalone reference material: Chapter 2 (Pseudocode) and Chapter 7 (Desk Checking) are particularly useful as reference chapters that can be returned to throughout any programming project.

Placement in a Course

This book is most effective when studied before or alongside any of the twelve advanced series books. Students who work through Think Before You Code first will find that every book in the advanced series is easier to plan, design, and debug. It is equally effective as a concurrent resource: students who have started the advanced series but are finding it difficult to manage program complexity will benefit from returning to this book for its structured design tools.

Chapter Structure

Every chapter opens with a blockquote describing what the chapter covers and connecting it to what you already know. This is followed by seven numbered sections, each with worked examples, a Note callout for important tips or warnings, and closing paragraphs that lead to the next concept.

At the end of each chapter you will find:

- **Chapter Summary** — Eight bullet points summarising the key concepts from the chapter.
- **Guided Exercises** — Five hands-on tasks with hints to help you get started. Complete these before moving on.
- **Challenge Tasks** — Three open-ended tasks with no hints. These require independent problem-solving and are suitable for extension or assessment.

The Tools Introduced in This Book

Each of the following tools is introduced in its own chapter and then used in combination throughout the book:

Pseudocode (Ch 2)	Expresses logic in plain English before a line of code is written
Flowcharts (Ch 3)	Makes control flow — branching, loops, module calls — visually clear
UML Diagrams (Ch 4)	Documents object-oriented structure: classes, relationships, and interactions
Structure Charts (Ch 5)	Maps a decomposed design: which functions call which, and what data flows between them
Logic Error Prevention (Ch 6)	A checklist of the most common errors and how planning catches each one
Desk Checking (Ch 7)	Traces pseudocode step by step with test data to verify correctness before coding
The Full Workflow (Ch 8)	All tools applied in sequence to a single, complete problem from specification to code

Code Examples

All pseudocode and Python code is shown in shaded blocks. Pseudocode uses the keyword conventions established in Chapter 2 and maintained consistently throughout the book. Python code is written for Python 3.10 or later. Each worked example is introduced, varied, and then applied to a realistic context — school, finance, or commerce — drawn from Australian settings where they naturally fit.

Prior Knowledge

This book assumes you have completed Think, Code, Create — A Python Programming Journey for Students. Foundational concepts (variables, data types, loops, functions, lists, dictionaries) are not re-explained. Chapters 2 through 8 build on each other; reading them in order is recommended for first-time readers.

Contents

Why Plan Before You Code? — *1*

1 The Cost of Jumping Straight In — 1

2 The Myth of 'Just Start Coding' — 2

3 What Professional Programmers Actually Do — 4

4 The Design-First Workflow — 6

5 Introducing the Four Planning Tools — 8

6 A Taste of Planning in Action — 10

7 How This Book Is Organised — 11

Guided Exercises — 14

Challenge Tasks — 15

Writing Pseudocode — *17*

1 What Pseudocode Is (and Isn't) — 17

2 Standard Pseudocode Keywords and Conventions — 19

3 Expressing Sequences and Input/Output — 22

4 Expressing Decisions — IF, ELSE IF, ELSE, and CASE — 24

5 Expressing Repetition — WHILE, FOR, and REPEAT ... UNTIL — 26

6 Procedures, Functions, and Modular Pseudocode — 28

7 Translating Pseudocode to Python — 30

Guided Exercises — 33

Challenge Tasks — 34

Flowcharts and Flow Diagrams — *36*

1 What Flowcharts Are and Why They Matter — 36

2 Standard Flowchart Symbols — 38

3 Flowcharts for Sequential Logic — 41

4 Flowcharts for Decision Logic — 44

5 Flowcharts for Loops — 47

6 Flowcharts for Modular Programs — 50

7 Flowcharts and Pseudocode — Choosing and Combining — 53

Guided Exercises — 56

Challenge Tasks — 57

UML Diagrams for Program Design — *58*

1 What UML Is and Why It Matters — 58

2 Use Case Diagrams — 60

3 Class Diagrams — Attributes, Methods, and Visibility 62
4 Class Relationships — Inheritance, Association, and Multiplicity 65
5 Sequence Diagrams 68
6 Activity Diagrams 70
7 Keeping UML Practical — Just Enough Modelling 73
Guided Exercises 77
Challenge Tasks 78
Decomposition and Structured Design *80*
1 What Decomposition Is and Why It Matters 80
2 Top-Down Design and Stepwise Refinement 82
3 Structure Charts and Hierarchy Diagrams 84
4 From Structure Chart to Python Functions 87
5 Cohesion — Designing Modules That Do One Thing Well 90
6 Coupling — Designing Modules That Depend on Each Other as Little as Possible 93
7 A Complete Worked Example — The Student Records Application 96
Guided Exercises 100
Challenge Tasks 101
Common Logic Errors and How to Prevent Them *103*
1 Why Logic Errors Are Different from Other Errors 103
2 Off-by-One Errors in Loops 105
3 Boundary Condition Errors in Decisions 108
4 Assuming Input Is Always Valid — Defensive Design 110
5 Infinite Loops and Missing Termination Conditions 113
6 Scope and Uninitialised Variable Errors 115
7 A Planning Checklist for Logic Error Prevention 118
Guided Exercises 122
Challenge Tasks 123
Desk Checking and Algorithm Tracing *125*
1 What a Desk Check Is and Why It Works 125
2 Setting Up a Trace Table 127
3 Tracing Sequential Pseudocode 129
4 Tracing Conditional Logic 131
5 Tracing Loops and Iterative Algorithms 133
6 Choosing Meaningful Test Data 135
7 Desk Checking a Complete Algorithm — Finding and Fixing a Bug 138
Guided Exercises 142

Challenge Tasks 143

From Design to Code — A Complete Worked Example *145*

1 The Problem and the Process 145

2 Step 1 — Understand 147

3 Step 2 — Plan 148

4 Step 3 — Design 151

5 Step 4 — Desk Check 154

6 Step 5 — Code 156

7 Step 6 — Reflect 160

Guided Exercises 163

Challenge Tasks 164

Why Plan Before You Code?

> This chapter introduces the central idea of this book: that time spent planning a program is never wasted. You will explore what goes wrong when programmers skip the planning stage, discover how professional developers approach a new problem, and meet the four tools — pseudocode, flowcharts, UML diagrams, and desk checking — that form the foundation of good program design. By the end of this chapter, you will understand why thinking carefully before you type a single line of code leads to cleaner, more correct, and more maintainable programs.

1 The Cost of Jumping Straight In

When you first learn to programme, the temptation is to open your editor and start writing code immediately. The problem is interesting, the solution feels obvious, and typing something — anything — feels like progress. This instinct is understandable. It is also one of the most common reasons programs contain bugs, miss requirements, and become difficult to maintain.

Consider what happens when a builder constructs a house without a plan. Walls go up in the wrong places. Wiring is added after plasterboard is installed. Rooms end up too small. Every fix costs far more than it would have if the problem had been identified on paper first. Programming is no different. A function written without a clear understanding of what it must do is a function that will almost certainly need to be rewritten.

Research consistently shows that errors caught during the planning stage cost almost nothing to fix — you simply cross out a line and rewrite it. The same error caught during testing costs hours. The same error discovered after a program has been deployed can cost significant time and effort to resolve. Planning is not a bureaucratic formality. It is the most cost-effective step in any programming project.

Example 1.1 Introduction — The Averaging Program

A student is asked to write a program that reads a list of scores from the user and calculates the average. Without planning, the student begins writing code immediately. Twenty minutes later, the program crashes when the user enters zero scores. A fix is added. Then it crashes when someone enters a non-numeric value. Another fix. Then the client mentions the program also needs to ignore scores below zero. More fixes. Each patch introduces the possibility of a new error.

The original problem could have been stated clearly in one sentence before any code was written: 'Read a list of numbers from the user and return their average, handling empty lists, non-numeric input, and negative values.' Had this been written down first, the student would have known exactly what to code before writing a single line.

Example 1.2 Variation — When Requirements Change

Six weeks after submitting the averaging program, the student is asked to extend it: scores now come from a file rather than the keyboard. Without any planning document to refer back to, the student must re-read the original code from scratch to understand how it works. Functions that mixed input and calculation are now impossible to separate cleanly. The entire program must be rewritten.

Had the student planned the program using a simple structure diagram — separating the input step from the calculation step from the output step — extending it would have required modifying only one function. The rest of the program would have remained untouched.

Example 1.3 Real-world application — The Canteen Ordering System

A school canteen asks a student to build a basic ordering system. The student starts coding immediately, building a menu display, a price lookup, and a total calculator. The program is demonstrated to canteen staff, who immediately point out that it does not handle meal deals (a drink and a sandwich at a reduced combined price), does not apply the staff discount, and crashes if an item is out of stock.

Each of these requirements was discoverable before coding began — simply by asking. A five-minute conversation and a brief written description of what the system needed to do would have prevented three days of rework. The time spent coding was not wasted because the programmer was slow; it was wasted because the programmer built the wrong thing.

> ▶ **NOTE** Errors caught during planning cost almost nothing to fix. The same error caught after code is written costs significantly more time and effort. Every minute spent planning can save ten minutes of debugging.

The examples above share a common theme: the programmer began solving the problem before fully understanding it. The next section examines why this happens so often — and why experience alone does not prevent it.

2 The Myth of 'Just Start Coding'

There is a persistent belief in programming communities that experienced programmers do not need to plan — that planning is training wheels for beginners, and that real developers simply sit down and write. This belief is false, and it is worth examining exactly why it persists.

What actually happens is that experienced programmers plan quickly and mentally, often without consciously labelling the process. A senior developer who appears to 'just start coding' has already reasoned through the problem, identified the major components, and resolved key design decisions in their head. That mental reasoning is planning. The difference between a beginner and an expert is not that the expert skips planning — it is that the expert's planning is faster and more automatic.

The danger for students is misreading this behaviour and concluding that planning is unnecessary. Without years of experience to support rapid mental planning, jumping straight into code leads directly to the problems described in Section 1. The tools in this book — pseudocode, flowcharts, UML diagrams, and desk checking — give you a structured way to do externally what experienced programmers do internally.

Example 2.1 **Introduction — Two Students, One Problem**

Two students are given the same task: write a program that reads a student's name and five test scores, then prints their average and a letter grade (High Distinction, Distinction, Credit, Pass, or Fail).

Student A opens their IDE immediately and begins coding. After 40 minutes they have a working program for most inputs, but it crashes on empty names and returns the wrong grade when the average sits exactly on a boundary value — 50 or 75 — because they had not thought about boundary conditions before writing the comparison logic.

Student B spends 10 minutes writing pseudocode first, listing the inputs, the grade boundaries, and the steps in order. They identify the boundary conditions during planning and decide how to handle them. After 30 minutes of coding they have a complete, correct program. Total time: 40 minutes, the same as Student A. Errors: zero.

Example 2.2 **Variation — The Illusion of Speed**

When a programmer begins coding without a plan, the early stages feel fast. Code appears on screen quickly. The program works for the first test case tried. This creates a false sense of progress. The slowdown arrives when edge cases and unexpected requirements reveal gaps in the original design.

Planning appears to slow you down at the start. In practice, it moves the inevitable thinking from the middle of the coding stage — where changing your mind is expensive — to the beginning, where it is free. The total time from problem to working program is consistently shorter with planning than without it.

Example 2.3 **Real-world application — Professional Software Development**

In professional software development, planning and design typically account for between 20 and 30 per cent of a project's total effort. Organisations that skip this phase do not save that time — they typically spend two to three times longer overall, because rework during or after development is far more expensive than design work completed before it begins.

This is why every major software development methodology — from traditional waterfall approaches to modern agile frameworks — includes an explicit planning phase. The names and levels of formality differ; the underlying principle does not. Planning is not optional in professional practice. It is standard.

> ▶ **NOTE** Even a small amount of planning produces a measurable improvement in code quality. You do not need a perfect plan before you begin — a rough pseudocode sketch or a simple flowchart is enough to clarify your thinking and surface hidden complexity before it becomes a bug.

If experienced programmers plan — even informally — and planning consistently reduces errors and rework, the natural question becomes: what does that planning actually look like in practice? The next section provides a concrete answer.

3 What Professional Programmers Actually Do

Professional programmers do not approach a new problem by guessing what to type. They read the requirements carefully — often more than once. They ask questions. They identify inputs and outputs. They think about what can go wrong. Only then do they begin writing anything resembling code.

The specific techniques vary by context, team, and project size. A solo developer working on a small utility might jot pseudocode in a notebook. A team building enterprise software might produce formal UML diagrams and detailed design documents. The level of formality differs; the underlying discipline is the same: understand the problem completely before committing it to code.

Professional programmers also revisit their plans as they code. A plan is not a contract — it is a starting point. When the plan meets reality and adjustments are needed, updating the plan first (rather than simply patching the code) keeps the design coherent and the program readable long after it is written.

Example 3.1 **Introduction — Reading and Restating the Problem**

Before writing any pseudocode or code, a professional programmer's first step is to restate the problem in their own words and check that restatement against the original requirements. This simple act catches a surprising number of misunderstandings before they become errors.

```
PLANNING STEP - Restate the problem

  Original requirement:
    'Write a program that processes student enrolment data.'

  Restated by the programmer:
    'The program reads a list of student names and subject selections
     from a file, checks that each student is enrolled in between
     4 and 6 subjects, and outputs a report listing any students
     whose enrolment is incomplete or exceeds the maximum.'

  Questions raised during restatement:
```

```
    - What file format is the input? (CSV? Plain text?)
    - What should happen if the file does not exist?
    - What format should the output report take?
    - Are subject codes case-sensitive?
```

Notice that the restatement is far more specific than the original requirement. The questions it raises are all things that must be answered before any code is written — and all of them are easier to answer now than after the code exists.

Example 3.2 **Variation — Identifying Inputs and Outputs Explicitly**

A useful and underused habit is to explicitly list a program's inputs and expected outputs before designing any logic. This sounds almost trivially simple. It is frequently skipped — and its absence is often the source of later confusion.

```
PLANNING STEP — Inputs, outputs, and constraints

  Program: Student Enrolment Checker

  INPUTS:
    - A CSV file: each row contains student_name, subject_code
    - Each student may appear on multiple rows (one per subject)

  OUTPUTS:
    - A printed report listing:
        * Students enrolled in fewer than 4 subjects (under-enrolled)
        * Students enrolled in more than 6 subjects (over-enrolled)
    - A summary count: valid / under-enrolled / over-enrolled

  CONSTRAINTS:
    - Handle a missing or empty file gracefully (no crash)
    - Treat subject codes as case-insensitive
    - Ignore blank lines in the input file
```

Example 3.3 **Real-world application — Agile Sprint Planning**

In agile software development, each two-week work cycle (called a sprint) begins with a planning session. The team reviews the requirements for that sprint — called user stories — and breaks each one into specific, testable tasks. These tasks are effectively pseudocode at the project level: plain-language descriptions of what needs to happen, in what order, under what conditions.

The planning session typically takes a few hours. The alternative — letting each developer interpret requirements individually without coordination — leads to inconsistent implementations, conflicting assumptions, and integration problems that can take days to resolve. The planning session is the cheaper option, every time.

> ▶ **NOTE** Professional programmers do not plan because they are required to — they plan because experience has taught them that it is faster overall. Adopt this habit now and you will write better programs in less time, from the very beginning of your career.

With a clear picture of what professional planning involves, it is time to examine the specific workflow this book recommends: a structured sequence of steps that takes you from a problem statement to a working, tested program.

4 The Design-First Workflow

The design-first workflow is a simple, repeatable process for approaching any programming problem. It does not require special software or formal training. It requires only discipline — the willingness to think before you type.

The workflow consists of six stages, applied in order for the first attempt at a problem and revisited as understanding develops. The stages are: Understand, Plan, Design, Code, Test, and Refine.

```
THE DESIGN-FIRST WORKFLOW

  1. UNDERSTAND    Read the problem carefully. Restate it in your own
                   words. Identify inputs, outputs, and constraints.
                   Ask questions before assuming.

  2. PLAN          Write pseudocode. Express the major steps in plain
                   English. Do not worry about Python syntax yet.

  3. DESIGN        Draw a flowchart or UML diagram for complex logic.
                   Decompose the problem into functions or classes.

  4. CODE          Translate your plan into Python, following your
                   pseudocode step by step. Revise the plan — not
                   just the code — if adjustments are needed.

  5. TEST          Run the program with normal, boundary, and
                   erroneous input. Compare outputs against the
                   expected results from your desk check.

  6. REFINE        Fix any errors found during testing. Update your
                   plan to reflect any changes made. Review code
                   quality and clarity.
```

This is not a rigid, one-way process. You will often loop back — discovering during coding that your plan needs adjustment, or finding during testing that a requirement was misunderstood. The important thing is that each loop back begins with updating the plan, not simply patching the code.

Example 4.1 Introduction — Applying the Workflow to a Simple Problem

Problem: Write a program that asks the user to enter a temperature in Celsius and displays the equivalent temperature in Fahrenheit.

```
STAGE 1 — UNDERSTAND

  Input:       A temperature in Celsius (numeric, may be a decimal)
  Output:      The equivalent temperature in Fahrenheit
  Formula:     fahrenheit = (celsius × 9 / 5) + 32
  Constraints: Handle non-numeric input gracefully

STAGE 2 — PSEUDOCODE

  BEGIN
    DISPLAY 'Enter a temperature in Celsius: '
    INPUT celsius
    IF celsius is not a valid number THEN
      DISPLAY 'Error: please enter a numeric value'
      STOP
    END IF
    SET fahrenheit = (celsius × 9 / 5) + 32
    DISPLAY celsius, '°C is equal to', fahrenheit, '°F'
  END
```

With this pseudocode written, the Python code almost writes itself. Every line of pseudocode corresponds directly to one or two lines of Python, and every decision has already been made.

Example 4.2 **Variation — Looping Back to the Plan**

Partway through coding the temperature converter, the student realises the program should allow multiple conversions in a loop rather than terminating after a single result. Rather than changing the code directly, the student returns to the pseudocode and revises it first:

```
STAGE 2 — REVISED PSEUDOCODE

  BEGIN
    REPEAT
      DISPLAY 'Enter a temperature in Celsius (or Q to quit): '
      INPUT celsius
      IF celsius = 'Q' OR celsius = 'q' THEN
        STOP
      END IF
      IF celsius is not a valid number THEN
        DISPLAY 'Error: please enter a numeric value'
      ELSE
        SET fahrenheit = (celsius × 9 / 5) + 32
        DISPLAY celsius, '°C is equal to', fahrenheit, '°F'
      END IF
    UNTIL user quits
  END
```

Updating the pseudocode first ensures the revised logic is sound before any code is changed. It also means the pseudocode remains an accurate description of how the program works — useful for anyone who reads it later, including your future self.

Example 4.3 **Real-world application — A School Grade Calculator**

A teacher asks a student to create a grade calculator for a class assessment. The student follows the design-first workflow. During the Understand stage, they identify the grade boundaries, the weighting between assessment tasks, and the fact that any student with a documented medical absence should receive an 'Incomplete' result rather than a Fail.

Had the student started coding immediately, the 'Incomplete' case would almost certainly have been missed — it was mentioned only briefly in the original requirements. The Understand stage, with its deliberate focus on inputs, outputs, and constraints, surfaces it before a single line of code is written. A five-minute planning step prevents a significant rework later.

> ▶ **NOTE** The design-first workflow is not a suggestion — it is a professional standard. Every time you bypass it, you trade a small amount of planning time for a much larger amount of debugging and rework time later. The trade is never worth it.

The workflow refers to four planning tools — pseudocode, flowcharts, UML diagrams, and desk checking. The next section briefly introduces each one so you can see the full toolkit before learning each tool in detail in the chapters that follow.

5 Introducing the Four Planning Tools

This book uses four complementary planning tools. Each one expresses program logic in a different way, and each has situations in which it communicates more clearly than the others. You will learn each tool in depth in subsequent chapters. This section gives you a brief preview of all four.

The four tools are pseudocode, flowcharts, UML diagrams, and desk checking. They are not competing approaches — they work together. A well-planned program might use pseudocode for the overall logic, a flowchart to clarify a complex decision, a class diagram to plan its object-oriented structure, and a desk check to verify the logic before coding begins.

Example 5.1 **Introduction — Pseudocode**

Pseudocode is a way of expressing a program's logic in plain English, using a loose but consistent structure. It is not Python. It is not any specific programming language. It is an intermediate step between a problem description and real code — precise enough to be translated directly into Python, but readable by anyone regardless of programming experience.

```
PSEUDOCODE – Find the largest number in a list

  BEGIN
    INPUT numbers                  ← A list of numbers from the user
    SET largest = numbers[0]       ← Assume the first is the largest
    FOR EACH number IN numbers DO
      IF number > largest THEN
```

```
      SET largest = number    ← Update if a larger number is found
    END IF
  END FOR
  OUTPUT 'The largest number is', largest
END
```

Pseudocode is covered in full in Chapter 2, including a standard set of keywords and conventions that make pseudocode consistent and readable across different problems and contexts.

Example 5.2 Variation — Flowcharts

A flowchart expresses the same logic visually, using standard symbols connected by arrows. Flowcharts are particularly useful when a program has complex branching logic that is difficult to follow in a linear pseudocode listing. Standard symbols include: a rounded rectangle for START and END, a parallelogram for INPUT and OUTPUT, a rectangle for a process step, and a diamond for a decision.

For the 'find the largest number' example, the flowchart would show a START terminal, an input parallelogram, a process box setting the initial value, a decision diamond at each comparison, an update box on the YES path, a loop arrow returning to the next number, and a final output parallelogram followed by the END terminal. The loop structure and the branching decision are both immediately visible in the diagram. Flowcharts are covered in full in Chapter 3.

Example 5.3 Real-world application — Choosing the Right Tool

```
TOOL SELECTION GUIDE

  Use PSEUDOCODE when:
    - Planning the overall logic of a function or program
    - Communicating your plan to another person in writing
    - Translating a problem statement into ordered steps

  Use a FLOWCHART when:
    - The program has complex branching or looping logic
    - You need to visualise the flow of control clearly
    - You are presenting a design to a non-technical audience

  Use a UML DIAGRAM when:
    - Designing an object-oriented program with multiple classes
    - Planning how objects interact with each other over time
    - Documenting the structure of an existing system

  Use a DESK CHECK when:
    - Verifying that pseudocode is logically correct
    - Testing boundary conditions before writing any code
    - Tracing through an algorithm step by step with sample data
```

> ▶ **NOTE** You do not need to use all four tools for every program. A short script might need only pseudocode. A complex object-oriented application might benefit from all

four. Use the minimum set of tools required to clearly understand and communicate your design.

Each of the four tools is explored in full in the chapters that follow. Before turning to those chapters, Section 6 demonstrates what it looks like to apply these tools together on a single, realistic example.

6 A Taste of Planning in Action

The best way to appreciate the value of planning is to see it applied from start to finish on a realistic problem. This section walks through a short but complete planning exercise: reading a list of item prices, applying a discount where applicable, and printing a formatted receipt. The Python code comes last — and when it does, it is almost effortless.

Example 6.1 Introduction — From Problem to Pseudocode

Problem: A small business wants a program that reads a list of item prices, applies a 10 per cent discount to any item over $50.00, and prints a receipt showing each item's original price, the discounted price where applicable, and the final total.

```
STAGE 1 — UNDERSTAND

  Inputs:      A list of item prices (decimal numbers, in AUD)
  Output:      A formatted receipt showing:
               - Each item's original price
               - The discounted price (only if a discount applies)
               - The final total of all adjusted prices
  Rules:       Apply 10% discount only if price > $50.00
               Discounted price = original price × 0.90
  Constraints: Prices will always be non-negative
```

```
STAGE 2 — PSEUDOCODE

  BEGIN
    SET prices = [list of item prices]
    SET total = 0
    DISPLAY receipt header
    FOR EACH price IN prices DO
      IF price > 50.00 THEN
        SET final_price = price × 0.90
        DISPLAY price, '→', final_price, '(10% discount applied)'
      ELSE
        SET final_price = price
        DISPLAY price, '(no discount)'
      END IF
      SET total = total + final_price
    END FOR
    DISPLAY '----------------------------'
    DISPLAY 'Total: $', total
  END
```

Example 6.2 Variation — Desk Checking the Pseudocode

Before writing any Python, a desk check is performed using sample data: prices of $29.95, $75.00, and $12.50. The trace table below records the value of each variable at each step of the pseudocode, confirming the logic is correct before a single line of Python is written.

Item processed	price	final_price	total
`$29.95 → no discount`	`$29.95`	`$29.95`	`$29.95`
`$75.00 → 10% discount`	`$75.00`	`$67.50`	`$97.45`
`$12.50 → no discount`	`$12.50`	`$12.50`	`$109.95`

The desk check confirms the logic is correct. The final total of $109.95 is verified by hand: $29.95 + $67.50 + $12.50 = $109.95. With the pseudocode validated, the program is ready to be translated into Python. There are no surprises waiting.

Example 6.3 Real-world application — Notice How the Code Writes Itself

With verified pseudocode in hand, the translation to Python is a straightforward mechanical process. Every line of pseudocode maps directly to Python. There are no structural rethinks, no logic errors to hunt down, and no late discoveries of missing cases. The programmer's attention during the coding stage is focused entirely on Python syntax — not on working out what the program should do, because that decision was made during planning.

This is the fundamental advantage of the design-first approach: coding becomes a translation exercise, not a problem-solving exercise. Problem-solving happens at the pseudocode stage, where it is fast and cheap. Coding happens when the solution is already known.

> ▶ **NOTE** When your Python code closely mirrors your pseudocode, that is a sign your planning was thorough. If you find yourself writing code that has no corresponding pseudocode step, stop and update the pseudocode first. The code and the plan should always agree.

You have now seen the problem that planning solves, the workflow that structures it, the four tools it draws on, and a demonstration of those tools working together. The final section of this chapter explains how the rest of the book is organised.

7 How This Book Is Organised

This book follows the same structure as every other book in the Think, Code, Create series. Each chapter contains seven numbered sections, three worked examples per section (Introduction, Variation, and Real-world application), a Note callout, a

Chapter Summary, five Guided Exercises with hints, and three Challenge Tasks without hints.

The chapters build on each other in a logical sequence, but each chapter also functions as a standalone reference. If you need to review pseudocode conventions, you can turn directly to Chapter 2. If you are working on an object-oriented design problem and need UML guidance, Chapter 4 is your reference. You do not need to read the book linearly, though doing so will give you the most complete understanding of how the tools work together.

Example 7.1 Introduction — Chapter-by-Chapter Overview

```
BOOK STRUCTURE – Think Before You Code

  Chapter 1   Why Plan Before You Code?
              (This chapter – the why and the workflow)

  Chapter 2   Writing Pseudocode
              (Conventions, keywords, expressing logic in plain
English)

  Chapter 3   Flowcharts and Flow Diagrams
              (Standard symbols, drawing tools, representing complex
logic)

  Chapter 4   UML Diagrams for Program Design
              (Use case, class, sequence, and activity diagrams)

  Chapter 5   Decomposition and Structured Design
              (Top-down design, structure charts, cohesion and
coupling)

  Chapter 6   Common Logic Errors and How to Prevent Them
              (Off-by-one, boundary conditions, defensive design)

  Chapter 7   Desk Checking and Algorithm Tracing
              (Trace tables, test data selection, verifying logic)

  Chapter 8   From Design to Code – A Complete Worked Example
              (All four tools applied to a single realistic problem)
```

Example 7.2 Variation — How to Use the Exercises

At the end of each chapter, five Guided Exercises are provided with hints to help you get started. Complete all five before moving on — they are designed to consolidate the key concepts from the chapter. After the Guided Exercises, three Challenge Tasks are provided without hints. These require independent thinking and are suitable for assessment or extension work.

The most valuable thing you can do with the exercises in this book is actually write the pseudocode, draw the flowcharts, and complete the trace tables — on paper if possible. Reading about planning is informative. Practising planning is transformative. The exercise where you produce a real plan for a real problem is the exercise that will stick.

Example 7.3 Real-world application — Connecting to Your Digital Technologies Course

The planning skills in this book are directly relevant to the Australian Curriculum Version 9 — Digital Technologies. The curriculum explicitly requires students to plan, design, and evaluate digital solutions, not merely implement them. The tools in this book — pseudocode, flowcharts, UML diagrams, and desk checking — are the standard tools used to demonstrate these design skills in both classroom assessments and industry practice.

If you are preparing for a Digital Technologies assessment task that includes a design or planning component, this book will help you produce work that meets the curriculum's expectations for structure, justification, and rigour in the design phase.

> ▶ **NOTE** You can read this book from start to finish, or return to individual chapters as your current project requires. Either way, begin with Chapters 2 and 3 — pseudocode and flowcharts are the foundation on which all the other tools rest.

This chapter has introduced the why and the what of program planning. The remaining chapters give you the how — in detail, with worked examples drawn from realistic contexts, and with exercises that develop real planning skill. Begin with Chapter 2.

Chapter Summary

- Planning before coding consistently leads to fewer errors, less rework, and cleaner, more maintainable programs.
- Errors caught during planning cost almost nothing to fix; the same errors caught after coding can cost significant time and effort to correct.
- The belief that experienced programmers skip planning is a myth — they plan quickly and mentally, drawing on accumulated experience.
- The design-first workflow has six stages: Understand, Plan, Design, Code, Test, and Refine. These stages may be revisited as understanding develops.
- Pseudocode expresses program logic in plain English, independent of any specific programming language or syntax.
- Flowcharts express program logic visually using standard symbols; they are particularly effective for representing complex branching and looping structures.
- UML diagrams describe the structure of object-oriented programs; class diagrams, use case diagrams, and sequence diagrams each serve a different design purpose.
- A desk check traces through pseudocode manually using sample data, verifying that the logic is correct before any code is written.

Guided Exercises

Complete all five exercises before moving on to Chapter 2. Each exercise includes a hint to help you get started.

Exercise 1

A student is asked to write a program that asks the user for their age and reports how many years remain until they turn 100. List at least three questions that should be answered during the Understand stage before any pseudocode is written.

Hint: Think about what can go wrong with the input. What if the user is already over 100? What if they enter a decimal? What if they enter a negative number or a non-numeric value?

Exercise 2

Apply the design-first workflow to the following problem: 'Write a program that reads five temperatures and reports the highest, the lowest, and the average.' Produce a clear Understand stage (inputs, outputs, and constraints) and a complete pseudocode plan.

Hint: Start by listing the inputs and expected outputs. Then write the pseudocode one step at a time, beginning with how the temperatures are read and stored.

Exercise 3

Using the tool selection guide from Section 5 (Example 5.3), identify which planning tool or tools you would use for each of the following: (a) planning a function that sorts a list using bubble sort; (b) designing a banking application with Account, SavingsAccount, and Transaction classes; (c) verifying that a while loop terminates correctly for all input values.

Hint: Refer to Example 5.3. More than one tool can be appropriate for a single scenario. For (b), think about which tool is designed to represent the relationship between classes.

Exercise 4

Perform a desk check on the pseudocode below using the test values x = 10, x = 0, and x = −5. Record your trace in a table with three columns: Step, x, result. The pseudocode to trace is as follows:

```
BEGIN
  INPUT x
  IF x > 0 THEN
    SET result = x × 2
  ELSE IF x = 0 THEN
    SET result = 0
  ELSE
    SET result = x × -1
  END IF
  OUTPUT result
END
```

Hint: Draw a table on paper with three columns: Step, x, result. Trace through the pseudocode once for each test value, recording the variable state after every step that changes a value.

Exercise 5

Reflect on a program you have previously written — from the Think, Code, Create foundation text, another subject, or your own projects. Identify one error or design problem in that program that would have been caught if you had written pseudocode before coding. Explain clearly what the pseudocode would have revealed and why.

Hint: Think about boundary conditions, missing cases, or structural problems that only became apparent when you tested the program or tried to extend it.

Challenge Tasks

These tasks have no hints. They require independent thinking and are suitable for extension or assessment. Complete the Guided Exercises before attempting these.

Challenge Task 1

Design the planning process — not the code — for a student library borrowing system. The system must allow students to borrow books (up to a maximum of three at a time), return books, and check which books they currently have on loan. Produce a complete Understand stage (all inputs, outputs, and constraints) and a full pseudocode plan covering all three operations. Identify at least three edge cases that your plan must address and explain how each one is handled.

Challenge Task 2

A classmate argues that planning is unnecessary for small programs: 'If the program is short enough to fit on one screen, there is no point planning it. You can just write it and fix any bugs.' Write a structured rebuttal of this position, using specific examples from this chapter and your own experience to support your argument. Your rebuttal should address at least three distinct reasons why planning benefits even small programs.

Challenge Task 3

Select any real-world digital system you use regularly — a school timetabling system, a transport app, an online ordering platform, or similar. Apply the Understand stage of the design-first workflow to one specific feature of that system. Produce a complete list of inputs, outputs, and constraints for that feature, then write pseudocode that describes how the feature works at a high level. Your pseudocode should be readable by someone who has never used the system.

Writing Pseudocode

> This chapter teaches you to write pseudocode: the single most important planning tool available to a programmer. You will learn what makes pseudocode different from both natural language and real code, master a standard set of keywords and conventions, and practise expressing sequences, decisions, loops, and modular structure in pseudocode form. By the end of this chapter, you will be able to translate any problem description into clear, consistent pseudocode, and translate that pseudocode directly into Python with confidence.

1 What Pseudocode Is (and Isn't)

Pseudocode sits between a problem description and real code. It is precise enough to express a program's logic step by step, but relaxed enough to be written quickly and read easily by anyone, regardless of which programming language they know. The word 'pseudo' means false or imitation — pseudocode imitates the structure of real code without being bound by its syntax rules.

Pseudocode is not English prose. Prose is too vague: 'calculate the result' tells you nothing about how. Pseudocode is also not Python. Python is too specific: writing Python is coding, not planning. Pseudocode occupies the middle ground — specific enough to think clearly about logic, loose enough to think freely about design.

There is no single official standard for pseudocode. Different textbooks, examination bodies, and organisations use slightly different conventions. What matters is not which set of conventions you use, but that you use them consistently within a document. The conventions used throughout this book are introduced in Section 2 and are aligned with common practice in Australian Digital Technologies education.

Example 2.1 Introduction — The Three Levels of Description

Consider this problem: 'Calculate a student's letter grade from their percentage score.' The same logic can be expressed at three different levels of precision, and understanding the difference between them is the key to writing good pseudocode.

✗ Prose — too vague

```
Too vague (prose):

  Work out what grade the
  student gets based on their
  score. High scores get better
  grades.
```

✗ Python — too specific

```
Too specific (Python):

  if score >= 85:
    grade = 'HD'
  elif score >= 75:
    grade = 'D'
  elif score >= 65:
    grade = 'C'
  ...
```

```
✓  Pseudocode – the right level of precision

BEGIN
  INPUT score
  IF score >= 85 THEN
    SET grade = 'High Distinction'
  ELSE IF score >= 75 THEN
    SET grade = 'Distinction'
  ELSE IF score >= 65 THEN
    SET grade = 'Credit'
  ELSE IF score >= 50 THEN
    SET grade = 'Pass'
  ELSE
    SET grade = 'Fail'
  END IF
  OUTPUT 'Grade:', grade
END
```

The pseudocode is readable without Python knowledge, yet precise enough that the translation to Python is straightforward and unambiguous.

Example 2.2 **Variation — What Makes Pseudocode Too Python-Like?**

A common mistake is writing pseudocode that is simply Python with slightly relaxed syntax. This defeats the purpose: it forces you to think about Python details (colons, indentation rules, method names) when you should be thinking about logic.

✗ Avoid: Python in disguise

```
Too Python-like:

  scores = []
  for i in range(5):
    scores.append(
      int(input('Score: ')))
  avg = sum(scores) / len(
    scores)
  print(f'Avg: {avg:.2f}')
```

✓ Prefer: language-neutral logic

```
Good pseudocode:

  SET scores = empty list
  FOR i FROM 1 TO 5 DO
    INPUT score
    ADD score TO scores
  END FOR
  SET avg = SUM(scores)
          / COUNT(scores)
  OUTPUT 'Average:', avg
```

The right-hand version can be translated into Python, Java, C#, or any other language with equal ease. It expresses what the program does, not how Python does it.

Example 2.3 **Real-world application — A Login System**

A school IT system requires a student login. The pseudocode below describes the authentication logic clearly and completely, without committing to any specific implementation. Any developer, regardless of their background, could implement this from the pseudocode alone.

```
BEGIN
  SET attempts = 0
  SET max_attempts = 3
  SET authenticated = FALSE
  WHILE attempts < max_attempts AND authenticated = FALSE DO
    INPUT username
    INPUT password
    IF username AND password match a valid account THEN
      SET authenticated = TRUE
      DISPLAY 'Login successful. Welcome, ', username
    ELSE
      SET attempts = attempts + 1
      DISPLAY 'Invalid credentials. Attempts remaining:',
              max_attempts - attempts
    END IF
  END WHILE
  IF authenticated = FALSE THEN
    DISPLAY 'Account locked. Contact your administrator.'
  END IF
END
```

Notice the phrase 'match a valid account'. Pseudocode is allowed to leave implementation details abstract when those details are not yet decided. The logic is clear; the specifics of how passwords are stored and compared can be resolved later.

> ▶ **NOTE** Pseudocode should be readable by a non-programmer and translatable by a programmer. If a non-programmer cannot follow your pseudocode, it is too technical. If a programmer cannot translate it into code, it is too vague. Aim for the middle ground.

Now that you understand what pseudocode is and what level of precision it aims for, the next step is to establish a consistent set of keywords and conventions. Consistency is what makes pseudocode a reliable communication tool rather than an informal scribble.

2 Standard Pseudocode Keywords and Conventions

The power of pseudocode as a communication tool depends on consistency. When everyone working on a project uses the same keywords in the same way, pseudocode becomes a shared language — precise enough to communicate intent without ambiguity, readable enough to be checked by anyone on the team.

The keyword set below is used throughout this book. It is aligned with common practice in Australian Digital Technologies courses and with widely used international conventions. Each keyword is capitalised, making it visually distinct from variable names and data values, which are written in lowercase or mixed case.

Example 2.4 Introduction — The Standard Keyword Reference

The table below lists the complete set of pseudocode keywords used in this book, grouped by category. You do not need to memorise these immediately — familiarity will develop with practice. Refer back to this table whenever you are unsure which keyword to use.

Category	Keyword(s)	Purpose
Program structure	`BEGIN / END`	Mark the start and end of a pseudocode block
Input	`INPUT / READ`	Accept a value from the user or a data source
Output	`OUTPUT / DISPLAY / PRINT`	Send a value or message to the screen
Assignment	`SET variable = value`	Store a value in a named variable
Selection	`IF / THEN / ELSE IF / ELSE / END IF`	Choose between alternative paths
Multiple selection	`CASE / OF / OTHERWISE / END CASE`	Select one path from several named options
Count-controlled loop	`FOR / TO / STEP / END FOR`	Repeat a block a known number of times
Condition-controlled	`WHILE / DO / END WHILE`	Repeat while a condition remains true
Post-condition loop	`REPEAT / UNTIL`	Repeat until a condition becomes true
Subprograms	`CALL / PROCEDURE / FUNCTION`	Define or invoke a named block of logic
Return value	`RETURN value`	Send a result back from a function
Comments	`← or // or (* ... *)`	Annotate pseudocode for the reader

Two conventions are observed throughout all pseudocode in this book. First, keywords are always written in UPPERCASE. Second, the body of every block (IF, FOR, WHILE, PROCEDURE, and so on) is indented by two or four spaces. These conventions make the structure of the pseudocode visible at a glance.

Example 2.5 Variation — Why Indentation Matters

Indentation in pseudocode serves the same purpose as indentation in Python: it makes the structure of nested blocks immediately visible. Without consistent indentation, even simple pseudocode becomes difficult to follow. Compare the two versions below.

✗ Hard to follow	✓ Structure is clear
Without indentation:	With indentation:

✗ **Hard to follow**

Without indentation:

```
FOR i FROM 1 TO 10 DO
IF i MOD 2 = 0 THEN
OUTPUT i, 'is even'
ELSE
OUTPUT i, 'is odd'
END IF
END FOR
```

✓ **Structure is clear**

With indentation:

```
FOR i FROM 1 TO 10 DO
  IF i MOD 2 = 0 THEN
    OUTPUT i, 'is even'
  ELSE
    OUTPUT i, 'is odd'
  END IF
END FOR
```

The right-hand version makes it immediately clear that the IF block is inside the FOR loop, and that the OUTPUT statements are inside the IF block. This visual clarity is essential when pseudocode becomes longer and more complex.

Example 2.6 Real-world application — Annotating Pseudocode with Comments

Comments in pseudocode are written after a left arrow (←) or double slash (//). They explain the reasoning behind a step, not just what the step does. Well-placed comments turn pseudocode into a design document that another person can read and understand without explanation.

```
PROCEDURE calculate_final_mark(assignments, exam)
  // assignments is a list of marks out of 100
  // exam is a single mark out of 100

  SET assignment_avg = SUM(assignments) / COUNT(assignments)
  ← Weight: 60% assignments, 40% exam
  SET final_mark = (assignment_avg * 0.60) + (exam * 0.40)

  IF final_mark < 45 THEN
    ← Students must achieve at least 45 overall to pass
    RETURN 'Fail (Below Minimum)'
  END IF

  RETURN final_mark
END PROCEDURE
```

Comments answer the question 'why?' rather than 'what?'. The reader can see that the next line sets the final mark; the comment explains why the weights 0.60 and 0.40 were chosen.

> ▶ **NOTE** Use keywords consistently and capitalise them. Indent every block body. Add comments to explain decisions, not just actions. These three habits will make your pseudocode clear to read, straightforward to check, and easy to translate into code.

With a consistent set of keywords and conventions established, the next four sections practise applying them. We begin with the simplest structure in any program: the sequence.

3 Expressing Sequences and Input/Output

A sequence is the most fundamental structure in programming: a set of steps executed one after another, in order. Every program contains sequences, and writing them in pseudocode is the foundation on which decisions and loops are built.

In pseudocode, a sequence is simply a list of statements written top to bottom. Each statement either reads data (INPUT or READ), stores or transforms data (SET), or sends data to the user (OUTPUT, DISPLAY, or PRINT). The order of statements matters — you cannot use a variable before you have assigned it a value, and you cannot output a result before you have calculated it.

When writing a sequence, ask yourself: 'Does each step have everything it needs from the steps above it?' If the answer is yes, the sequence is correct. If any step relies on a value that has not yet been established, the sequence has an ordering error — one that is trivial to fix at the pseudocode stage and potentially expensive to find after the code is written.

Example 2.7 Introduction — Area of a Rectangle

This example demonstrates a simple sequential program: read two values, compute a result, and display it. Every step builds on the one before it.

```
BEGIN
  DISPLAY 'Area of a Rectangle Calculator'
  DISPLAY '--------------------------------'
  INPUT length      ← Read the length from the user (metres)
  INPUT width       ← Read the width from the user (metres)
  SET area = length * width            ← Calculate area
  SET perimeter = 2 * (length + width) ← Calculate perimeter
  OUTPUT 'Area:       ', area, 'm²'
  OUTPUT 'Perimeter: ', perimeter, 'm'
END
```

Notice that area and perimeter are calculated only after both inputs have been read. Attempting to calculate area before width is read would produce an ordering error. Writing the sequence in pseudocode makes this dependency visible before any code is written.

Example 2.8 Variation — Multiple Inputs and Intermediate Calculations

Many programs require several inputs and multiple intermediate calculations before producing a final output. Pseudocode keeps the sequence visible and verifiable at each step.

```
BEGIN
  ← Read student results for three assessment tasks
  INPUT task1_mark    ← Out of 100
  INPUT task2_mark    ← Out of 100
  INPUT exam_mark     ← Out of 100

  ← Apply weightings: Task 1 = 30%, Task 2 = 30%, Exam = 40%
```

```
    SET weighted_t1    = task1_mark * 0.30
    SET weighted_t2    = task2_mark * 0.30
    SET weighted_exam = exam_mark  * 0.40
    SET final_mark     = weighted_t1 + weighted_t2 + weighted_exam

    OUTPUT 'Task 1 contribution: ', weighted_t1
    OUTPUT 'Task 2 contribution: ', weighted_t2
    OUTPUT 'Exam contribution:   ', weighted_exam
    OUTPUT '----------------------------'
    OUTPUT 'Final mark: ', final_mark, '/100'
  END
```

Each intermediate result is stored in a named variable before it is needed. This makes each calculation step independently verifiable — you can check the value of weighted_t1 without needing to know anything about the other weightings.

Example 2.9 Real-world application — A Point-of-Sale Receipt

A small retail business needs a program to calculate and print a receipt for a single purchase. The sequence reads the item details, calculates the total with GST, and prints a formatted receipt.

```
  BEGIN
    DISPLAY 'Northward Book Shop'
    DISPLAY '==================='
    INPUT item_name
    INPUT unit_price       ← Price excluding GST
    INPUT quantity

    SET subtotal  = unit_price * quantity
    SET gst       = subtotal * 0.10     ← GST is 10% in Australia
    SET total     = subtotal + gst

    OUTPUT item_name, ' x', quantity
    OUTPUT 'Subtotal (excl. GST): $', subtotal
    OUTPUT 'GST (10%):            $', gst
    OUTPUT '----------------------------'
    OUTPUT 'Total (incl. GST):    $', total
  END
```

This sequential pseudocode is ready to be desk checked and translated. Every value used in a calculation has been established by an earlier INPUT or SET statement. The ordering is unambiguous.

> ▶ **NOTE** When writing a sequence, ensure that every variable is assigned a value before it is first used. Read the pseudocode from top to bottom and ask: 'Does each line have what it needs?' If the answer is no, reorder or add a missing step.

Sequences execute every step unconditionally. Most real programs need to choose between different paths depending on the data they receive. The next section introduces the pseudocode structures for expressing decisions.

4 Expressing Decisions — IF, ELSE IF, ELSE, and CASE

A decision structure allows a program to follow different paths depending on a condition. In pseudocode, decisions are expressed using IF … THEN … ELSE IF … ELSE … END IF for two or more alternatives, and CASE … OF … END CASE for selecting from a set of named options.

Every decision structure has three components: a condition that evaluates to TRUE or FALSE, a block of steps to execute when the condition is true, and optionally a block of steps to execute when it is false. Nested decisions — an IF block inside another IF block — are common in real programs, and consistent indentation is what makes nested structures readable.

A critical habit when writing decision pseudocode is to consider every possible path before writing the code. Ask: 'What happens if this condition is true? What happens if it is false? Are there edge cases that fall between conditions?' These questions are cheap to answer during planning and expensive to discover during testing.

Example 2.10 Introduction — Simple IF/ELSE

The simplest decision structure has two paths: one taken when the condition is true, and one taken when it is false. This example classifies a temperature reading as hot or not hot.

```
BEGIN
  INPUT temperature     ← Temperature in degrees Celsius
  IF temperature >= 35 THEN
    OUTPUT 'It is a hot day. Stay hydrated.'
  ELSE
    OUTPUT 'Temperature is ', temperature, '°C.'
  END IF
END
```

The END IF keyword closes the decision block explicitly. This is important in pseudocode because, unlike Python, we do not rely on indentation alone to show where a block ends. The explicit END IF makes the boundary unambiguous.

Example 2.11 Variation — IF / ELSE IF / ELSE Chains

When there are more than two possible outcomes, ELSE IF branches extend the decision chain. Each condition is checked in order; the first condition that evaluates to TRUE determines the path taken. The ELSE branch at the end catches any case not handled by earlier conditions.

```
BEGIN
  INPUT score     ← A percentage score from 0 to 100
  IF score < 0 OR score > 100 THEN
    OUTPUT 'Error: score must be between 0 and 100'
  ELSE IF score >= 85 THEN
    OUTPUT 'High Distinction'
  ELSE IF score >= 75 THEN
    OUTPUT 'Distinction'
```

```
    ELSE IF score >= 65 THEN
      OUTPUT 'Credit'
    ELSE IF score >= 50 THEN
      OUTPUT 'Pass'
    ELSE
      OUTPUT 'Fail'
    END IF
  END
```

Notice that the validation check (score < 0 OR score > 100) comes first. This is defensive design: always check that your inputs are valid before processing them. In pseudocode, this pattern is easy to include; in code written without planning, it is frequently forgotten.

Example 2.12 Real-world application — A Menu System with CASE

When a decision must select from a set of clearly named options, CASE … OF … END CASE is cleaner than a long chain of ELSE IF statements. This example processes a canteen menu selection.

```
BEGIN
  DISPLAY 'School Canteen Menu'
  DISPLAY '1. Meat pie     - $4.50'
  DISPLAY '2. Sandwich     - $5.00'
  DISPLAY '3. Sausage roll - $3.50'
  DISPLAY '4. Water        - $2.00'
  INPUT choice

  CASE choice OF
    1: SET item = 'Meat pie'     SET price = 4.50
    2: SET item = 'Sandwich'     SET price = 5.00
    3: SET item = 'Sausage roll' SET price = 3.50
    4: SET item = 'Water'        SET price = 2.00
    OTHERWISE:
      OUTPUT 'Invalid selection. Please choose 1 to 4.'
      STOP
  END CASE

  OUTPUT 'You selected: ', item, ' ($', price, ')'
END
```

The OTHERWISE branch handles any input that does not match one of the listed cases. Without it, an unexpected input would silently fall through to the OUTPUT statement, producing incorrect results. Planning with pseudocode makes this omission visible before any code is written.

> ▶ **NOTE** Always include an ELSE or OTHERWISE branch in your decision structures, even if you believe the input will always be valid. Defensive programming — handling unexpected inputs gracefully — is a habit that saves significant debugging time.

Decisions allow a program to choose between paths. Repetition allows a program to execute the same path multiple times. The next section introduces the three pseudocode structures for expressing loops.

5 Expressing Repetition — WHILE, FOR, and REPEAT … UNTIL

Repetition, or looping, is the third fundamental control structure. A loop executes a block of statements multiple times, either for a known number of iterations or until a condition changes. Choosing the right loop structure for a situation makes pseudocode clearer and reduces the risk of logic errors such as infinite loops or off-by-one errors.

Three loop structures are used in this book. The WHILE loop checks its condition before each iteration and is used when the number of repetitions is not known in advance. The FOR loop iterates a fixed number of times and is used when the count is known. The REPEAT … UNTIL loop checks its condition after each iteration, guaranteeing that the loop body executes at least once.

When writing a loop in pseudocode, always identify three things before writing a single line: the loop's starting condition, what changes inside the loop to eventually make the condition false, and what should happen after the loop ends. If you cannot answer all three, the loop design is not complete.

Example 2.13 Introduction — WHILE Loop for Input Validation

A WHILE loop continues as long as its condition remains true. It is well suited to input validation: keep asking until valid input is received. The loop may execute zero times if the first input is already valid.

```
BEGIN
  INPUT age    ← Read the user's age
  WHILE age < 0 OR age > 120 DO
    ← Keep asking until a realistic age is entered
    OUTPUT 'Invalid age. Please enter a value between 0 and 120.'
    INPUT age
  END WHILE
  OUTPUT 'Age accepted: ', age
END
```

The WHILE condition is checked before the loop body runs. If the first value entered is valid, the loop body never executes and the program moves straight to the OUTPUT. This is the correct behaviour for validation: do not display an error message if no error has occurred.

Example 2.14 Variation — FOR Loop for Processing a Fixed List

A FOR loop is used when the number of iterations is known at the time the loop begins. This example reads five test scores and accumulates their total.

```
BEGIN
  SET total = 0
```

```
    FOR i FROM 1 TO 5 DO
      OUTPUT 'Enter score ', i, ' of 5:'
      INPUT score
      IF score < 0 OR score > 100 THEN
        OUTPUT 'Warning: score ', score, ' is outside range 0-100'
      END IF
      SET total = total + score
    END FOR
    SET average = total / 5
    OUTPUT 'Total: ', total
    OUTPUT 'Average: ', average
  END
```

The variable i counts from 1 to 5. Each iteration reads one score and adds it to the running total. After the loop ends, the average is calculated using the accumulated total. Note that the average is calculated after the loop, not inside it — only a final total is useful inside the loop.

Example 2.15 Real-world application — REPEAT ... UNTIL for a Menu-Driven Program

A menu-driven program should always display the menu at least once. The REPEAT ... UNTIL structure guarantees this by executing the loop body before checking the exit condition.

```
BEGIN
  REPEAT
    DISPLAY '=============================='
    DISPLAY 'Student Records System'
    DISPLAY '  1. View all records'
    DISPLAY '  2. Add a new record'
    DISPLAY '  3. Search by name'
    DISPLAY '  4. Exit'
    DISPLAY '=============================='
    INPUT choice

    CASE choice OF
      1: CALL display_all_records()
      2: CALL add_record()
      3: CALL search_by_name()
      4: DISPLAY 'Goodbye.'
      OTHERWISE: DISPLAY 'Please enter 1, 2, 3, or 4.'
    END CASE

  UNTIL choice = 4
END
```

The loop body always executes at least once because the exit condition (choice = 4) is checked after the menu and the CASE block have already run. CALL statements in the CASE block refer to separate procedures that are defined elsewhere — this is the basis of modular pseudocode, introduced in the next section.

▶ **NOTE** Choose the right loop for the situation. Use WHILE when the loop might not execute at all. Use FOR when you know exactly how many times to iterate. Use

REPEAT … UNTIL when the loop must execute at least once. The wrong loop structure is a source of subtle logic errors that planning can prevent.

Loops and decisions operating on sequences of statements give you the three fundamental building blocks of any program. The next step is learning to organise those building blocks into named, reusable units — procedures and functions.

6 Procedures, Functions, and Modular Pseudocode

A real program is not one long sequence of statements. It is a collection of named, purposeful units — called procedures and functions — each of which does one job. This decomposition of a program into smaller units is called modular design, and it is one of the most important skills in programming.

In pseudocode, a procedure is a named block of steps that performs an action. It may accept input parameters but does not return a value. A function is a named block that accepts parameters and returns a result to its caller. The distinction matters because it determines how the unit is used: procedures are CALLED, and functions are used as values in expressions.

When writing modular pseudocode, the main program describes the overall flow at a high level, using CALL statements to invoke procedures and functions. Each procedure and function is then defined separately. This separation mirrors the structure of a well-designed Python program, where the main script calls functions rather than containing all the logic inline.

Example 2.16 Introduction — Defining and Calling a Procedure

A procedure is defined using PROCEDURE … END PROCEDURE and called using CALL. This example separates the display of a report header into its own procedure, keeping the main program clean.

```
PROCEDURE display_header(title)
  ← Print a formatted header to the screen
  DISPLAY '=============================='
  DISPLAY title
  DISPLAY '=============================='
END PROCEDURE

BEGIN   ← Main program
  CALL display_header('Student Results Report')
  ← ... rest of the main program ...
  CALL display_header('Summary Statistics')
  ← ... summary output ...
END
```

The procedure is defined once and called twice. If the header format ever needs to change, it is changed in one place. This is the modularity principle: write once, use everywhere.

Example 2.17 Variation — A Function with Parameters and a Return Value

A function accepts inputs, performs a calculation, and returns a result. The result can be used anywhere a value is needed: in a SET statement, an IF condition, or an OUTPUT call.

```
FUNCTION calculate_bmi(weight_kg, height_m)
  ← Body Mass Index = weight (kg) / height (m)²
  SET bmi = weight_kg / (height_m * height_m)
  RETURN bmi
END FUNCTION

FUNCTION classify_bmi(bmi)
  IF bmi < 18.5 THEN
    RETURN 'Underweight'
  ELSE IF bmi < 25.0 THEN
    RETURN 'Healthy weight'
  ELSE IF bmi < 30.0 THEN
    RETURN 'Overweight'
  ELSE
    RETURN 'Obese'
  END IF
END FUNCTION

BEGIN
  INPUT weight_kg
  INPUT height_m
  SET bmi    = calculate_bmi(weight_kg, height_m)
  SET class  = classify_bmi(bmi)
  OUTPUT 'BMI: ', bmi
  OUTPUT 'Classification: ', class
END
```

Each function has a single, clear responsibility: calculate_bmi computes the value, classify_bmi interprets it. Neither function does the other's job. This separation makes each function independently testable and independently reusable.

Example 2.18 Real-world application — A Modular Student Records System

A complete pseudocode design for a student records system uses multiple procedures, each responsible for one operation. The main program acts as a controller — it calls procedures rather than containing logic directly.

```
FUNCTION load_records(filename)
  ← Read all student records from file and return as a list
  SET records = empty list
  OPEN filename FOR READING
  WHILE file has more lines DO
    READ line FROM file
    ADD line TO records
  END WHILE
  CLOSE file
  RETURN records
END FUNCTION

PROCEDURE display_records(records)
```

```
  FOR EACH student IN records DO
    OUTPUT student.name, student.grade, student.score
  END FOR
END PROCEDURE

FUNCTION find_by_name(records, search_name)
  FOR EACH student IN records DO
    IF student.name = search_name THEN
      RETURN student
    END IF
  END FOR
  RETURN NOT FOUND   ← Signal that no match was found
END FUNCTION

BEGIN   ← Main program
  SET records = load_records('students.csv')
  CALL display_records(records)
  INPUT search_name
  SET result = find_by_name(records, search_name)
  IF result = NOT FOUND THEN
    OUTPUT 'No student found with name: ', search_name
  ELSE
    OUTPUT 'Found: ', result.name, result.grade
  END IF
END
```

The main program is brief and readable. Anyone reading it can understand what the program does without reading the procedure and function definitions. Those details are available when needed, but they do not clutter the high-level view.

▶ **NOTE** Each procedure or function should do one job and do it completely. If you find yourself writing a procedure that does two distinct things, split it into two procedures. The single-responsibility principle makes code easier to test, debug, and reuse.

You can now express any program logic in pseudocode: sequences, decisions, loops, and modular structure. The final section brings these skills together by practising the translation from pseudocode to Python — the moment when planning pays off.

7 Translating Pseudocode to Python

Translating well-written pseudocode into Python is a systematic, low-risk process. Because the logic has already been designed and verified, the translation step is concerned only with Python's syntax, not with the program's design. This is precisely the separation of concerns that planning is intended to achieve.

The translation follows a direct keyword mapping: INPUT becomes input() or a file read; OUTPUT becomes print(); SET becomes an assignment statement; IF … THEN becomes if; FOR … FROM … TO becomes a for loop with range(); WHILE becomes while; PROCEDURE becomes def (with no return); FUNCTION becomes def (with return). Each pseudocode keyword has a natural Python equivalent.

When a direct one-to-one mapping does not exist — for example, when the pseudocode says 'IF input is a valid number' — you need to decide how to implement that check in Python. This is not a failure of the pseudocode; it is a design detail that can reasonably be left abstract during planning and resolved during the coding step.

Example 2.19 Introduction — Direct Mapping: Pseudocode to Python

The table below shows how each major pseudocode structure maps to Python. These mappings are consistent and predictable, which is what makes the translation straightforward.

Pseudocode	Python equivalent
`INPUT x`	`x = input('Enter value: ')`
`INPUT x (numeric)`	`x = float(input('Enter value: '))`
`OUTPUT 'Hello,', name`	`print('Hello,', name)`
`SET total = total + score`	`total = total + score`
`IF x > 0 THEN ... END IF`	`if x > 0:\n ...`
`ELSE IF x = 0 THEN`	`elif x == 0:`
`ELSE`	`else:`
`FOR i FROM 1 TO 5 DO ... END FOR`	`for i in range(1, 6):\n ...`
`WHILE x < 10 DO ... END WHILE`	`while x < 10:\n ...`
`REPEAT ... UNTIL x = 0`	`while True:\n ...\n if x == 0: break`
`PROCEDURE name(params) ... END`	`def name(params):\n ...`
`FUNCTION name(params) ... RETURN val`	`def name(params):\n ...\n return val`
`CALL procedure_name(args)`	`procedure_name(args)`

Example 2.20 Variation — When Pseudocode Doesn't Map One-to-One

Some pseudocode statements describe behaviour at a level of abstraction that does not translate directly to a single Python statement. This is intentional — pseudocode describes what to do; Python describes how to do it. Consider this example:

Pseudocode (abstract)

```
Pseudocode:

  IF input is a valid
     positive integer THEN
    SET n = input
  ELSE
    OUTPUT 'Invalid input'
  END IF
```

Python (concrete)

```
Python (one approach):

  raw = input('Enter: ')
  if raw.isdigit() and
       int(raw) > 0:
    n = int(raw)
  else:
    print('Invalid input')
```

The pseudocode correctly identifies what needs to happen. The Python translation makes the specific implementation decision: use isdigit() and a range check. If a different validation approach were chosen, the pseudocode would remain unchanged — it describes the requirement, not the implementation.

Example 2.21 Real-world application — A Full Translation with Annotations

This example shows a complete pseudocode design and its Python translation side by side. Each Python line is annotated to show which pseudocode line it corresponds to.

```
  FUNCTION is_prime(n)                                    ← def is_prime(n):
    IF n < 2 THEN                                         ←   if n < 2:
      RETURN FALSE                                        ←     return False
    END IF                                                ←
    FOR i FROM 2 TO SQRT(n) DO                           ←   for i in range(2,
int(n**0.5)+1):
      IF n MOD i = 0 THEN                                ←     if n % i == 0:
        RETURN FALSE     ← divisible, not prime ←       return False
      END IF                                              ←
    END FOR                                               ←
    RETURN TRUE          ← no divisor found      ←   return True
  END FUNCTION

  BEGIN                                                   ← (main script body)
    INPUT n                                               ← n = int(input('Enter a
number: '))
    IF is_prime(n) THEN                                   ← if is_prime(n):
      OUTPUT n, 'is prime'                               ←   print(n, 'is prime')
    ELSE                                                  ← else:
      OUTPUT n, 'is not prime'                           ←   print(n, 'is not
prime')
    END IF                                                ←
  END
```

Every line of pseudocode has a direct Python counterpart. The translation is mechanical and fast because all the design decisions — the algorithm, the loop bounds, the return values — were made during the pseudocode stage. Coding is simply transcription.

> ▶ **NOTE** When you sit down to code from pseudocode, work through it line by line. Do not read ahead and improvise. If you find yourself wanting to deviate from the pseudocode, stop, update the pseudocode, then continue coding. The pseudocode is your source of truth.

You have now mastered the full toolkit of pseudocode writing: what it is, how to use it consistently, how to express sequences, decisions, loops, and modular structure, and how to translate it into Python. The skills practised in this chapter underpin everything that follows in this book. Chapter 3 introduces flowcharts — a visual complement to pseudocode that makes complex control flow immediately apparent.

Chapter Summary

- Pseudocode sits between natural language and real code — precise enough to express logic step by step, relaxed enough to be written and read without knowledge of any specific programming language.
- Pseudocode keywords should always be CAPITALISED and block bodies should be consistently indented. Comments, written with ← or //, explain the reasoning behind a step rather than simply restating what it does.
- A sequence is a list of steps executed in order. Every variable must be assigned a value before it is first used; reading pseudocode top to bottom reveals any ordering errors before coding begins.
- The IF … THEN … ELSE IF … ELSE … END IF structure expresses two or more alternative paths. CASE … OF … END CASE is cleaner when selecting from a named set of options. Always include an ELSE or OTHERWISE branch.
- Use WHILE when a loop might not execute at all; use FOR when the number of iterations is known in advance; use REPEAT … UNTIL when the loop must execute at least once. Choosing the wrong loop structure is a common source of logic errors.
- Procedures (defined with PROCEDURE … END PROCEDURE) perform actions and do not return values. Functions (defined with FUNCTION … END FUNCTION) return a result using the RETURN keyword.
- Modular pseudocode keeps the main program short and readable by delegating logic to named procedures and functions. Each unit should have a single, clearly defined responsibility.
- Translating pseudocode to Python is a direct keyword-mapping process. When a pseudocode step does not map one-to-one, the pseudocode correctly describes the requirement; the Python implementation fills in the concrete detail.

Guided Exercises

Complete all five exercises before moving on to Chapter 3. Each exercise includes a hint to help you get started.

Exercise 1

Write pseudocode for a program that reads a user's name, age, and favourite subject, then displays a formatted greeting: for example, 'Hello, Amelia! You are 16 years old and you enjoy Mathematics.' Your pseudocode must use INPUT for each value and OUTPUT for the greeting.

Hint: Start with BEGIN and list the three INPUT statements first. Then write the SET or OUTPUT statement that constructs the greeting. Make sure you use the values that were input, not literal text.

Exercise 2

Write pseudocode for a program that reads a whole number and determines whether it is positive, negative, or zero. Use an IF … ELSE IF … ELSE … END IF structure. Include an input validation check: if the input is not a number at all, display an error message and stop.

Hint: Begin with the validation check — handle the invalid input case first, before the positive/negative/zero logic. Use ELSE IF for each case and make sure your END IF closes the structure.

Exercise 3

Write pseudocode for a program that reads integer values from the user one at a time, accumulating a running total, until the user enters 0. When the user enters 0, display the total and the count of values entered (not counting the 0 itself). Use a WHILE loop.

Hint: Initialise total and count to 0 before the loop. The WHILE condition should check that the input is not 0. Read the first input before the loop begins, and read the next input at the end of each loop iteration.

Exercise 4

Write modular pseudocode for a simple bank account system. Define three functions: deposit(balance, amount) which returns the new balance, withdraw(balance, amount) which returns the new balance (or an error if funds are insufficient), and display_balance(balance) which outputs the current balance. Then write a main program that calls these functions.

Hint: Write each FUNCTION separately with its own RETURN statement. In the withdraw function, use an IF statement to check whether amount > balance and handle it with an appropriate message. The main program should use SET to capture the returned values.

Exercise 5

Translate the following pseudocode into Python exactly. Do not change the logic — your Python should produce the same results as the pseudocode for all inputs.

```
FUNCTION sum_of_digits(n)
  SET total = 0
  WHILE n > 0 DO
    SET total = total + (n MOD 10)
    SET n = n // 10    ← Integer division removes the last digit
  END WHILE
  RETURN total
END FUNCTION

BEGIN
  INPUT n
  OUTPUT 'Sum of digits: ', sum_of_digits(n)
END
```

Hint: Map each pseudocode keyword directly to its Python equivalent using the table in Section 7. Use int(input(...)) for numeric input, range(1, n+1) for FOR loops, and def for FUNCTION definitions.

Challenge Tasks

These tasks have no hints. They require independent thinking and are suitable for extension or assessment. Complete the Guided Exercises before attempting these.

Challenge Task 1

Write complete modular pseudocode for a quiz program that asks the user five multiple-choice questions on any topic of your choice. Each question should have four options (A, B, C, D). The program should accept the user's answer for each question, compare it to the correct answer, track the score, and at the end display the total score and a summary of which questions were answered correctly and which were not. Use at least two procedures or functions in your design.

Challenge Task 2

A student submits the following pseudocode for a program that finds the smallest value in a list of numbers. Identify every error in the pseudocode — logic errors, ordering errors, and structural errors — and write a corrected version. Explain each error you found and why it would cause the program to produce incorrect results.
BEGIN FOR i FROM 1 TO COUNT(numbers) DO IF numbers[i] < smallest THEN SET smallest = numbers[i] END IF END FOR INPUT numbers OUTPUT smallest END

Challenge Task 3

Write pseudocode for a number guessing game. The program selects a random whole number between 1 and 100. The user is given up to 10 guesses. After each guess, the program tells the user whether their guess was too high, too low, or correct. If the user guesses correctly, the program congratulates them and displays the number of guesses used. If the user runs out of guesses, the program reveals the correct answer. Your pseudocode must use a WHILE or REPEAT loop, an IF structure for the feedback logic, and at least one function.

Flowcharts and Flow Diagrams

> This chapter introduces flowcharts: a visual planning tool that makes program logic immediately apparent to anyone who reads it. You will learn the standard symbols used in flowcharts worldwide, and practise drawing flowcharts for sequential programs, decision structures, loops, and modular designs that call subprograms. By the end of this chapter, you will understand when a flowchart communicates more clearly than pseudocode, how to draw one accurately using standard conventions, and how to use flowcharts and pseudocode together as complementary planning tools.

1 What Flowcharts Are and Why They Matter

A flowchart is a diagram that uses standard symbols and connecting arrows to represent the steps and decisions in a program or process. Where pseudocode expresses logic in words, a flowchart expresses the same logic as a picture. Both tools describe the same thing; each does so in a way that reveals certain aspects of the design more clearly than the other.

The central advantage of a flowchart over pseudocode is that the flow of control — which steps lead where, how decisions branch, how loops cycle back — is immediately visible as a visual structure rather than something the reader must infer from indentation and keywords. For programs with complex branching or multiple exit points, this visual clarity is invaluable.

Flowcharts have been in use since the 1940s and are standardised internationally by ISO 5807. The symbols used in this chapter follow that standard, which is the same set taught in Digital Technologies courses in Australia and used in professional software documentation worldwide. Learning these symbols gives you a universal visual language for describing program logic.

Example 3.1 Introduction — The Same Logic Two Ways

Consider a program that checks whether a number is even or odd. The pseudocode on the left and the flowchart on the right express exactly the same logic. Notice how the flowchart makes the two paths immediately visible, while the pseudocode requires you to read and interpret the ELSE structure.

Pseudocode

```
PSEUDOCODE:

  BEGIN
    INPUT number
    IF number MOD 2 = 0 THEN
      OUTPUT 'Even'
```

Flowchart equivalent

```
FLOWCHART (described):

  START
    ↓
  INPUT number
    ↓
```

```
    ELSE
      OUTPUT 'Odd'
    END IF
  END
```

```
number MOD 2 = 0?
YES ↓          NO →
OUTPUT           OUTPUT
'Even'           'Odd'
  ↓                ↓
    STOP ←————
```

Both representations are equally correct. A planner would often write both: the pseudocode to plan the logic in detail, and the flowchart to verify that the branching structure is sound and to communicate it to others.

Example 3.2 **Variation — When a Flowchart Reveals What Pseudocode Hides**

For simple linear programs, pseudocode and flowcharts are equally clear. As branching complexity increases, flowcharts have a distinct advantage: they make it impossible to lose track of paths. In the pseudocode below, a reader must carefully trace the ELSE IF chain to understand every possible outcome. The equivalent flowchart makes every path — and every dead-end — visible at a glance.

Consider a program with four possible outcomes: a student who passes both theory and practical components, one who passes theory but fails practical, one who fails theory but passes practical, and one who fails both. A flowchart with two sequential decision diamonds makes all four outcomes visible as four distinct paths with no ambiguity. The pseudocode equivalent requires careful reading to verify that all four cases are covered.

This is not a weakness of pseudocode — it is a strength of flowcharts. Use the tool that best reveals the aspect of the design you need to verify.

Example 3.3 **Real-world application — Where Flowcharts Are Used Professionally**

Flowcharts appear in many professional contexts beyond software development. Hospital admission processes, legal decision procedures, manufacturing quality-control checks, and customer service escalation procedures are all commonly documented as flowcharts. Their value in each case is the same: anyone who reads the flowchart understands the process immediately, without needing specialised knowledge.

In software engineering, flowcharts are most commonly used at the early design stage to map out a complex algorithm or business rule before any code is written, and in system documentation to explain how a deployed system makes decisions. Many automated tools can generate flowcharts from existing code, but the skill of drawing them from scratch — as a planning step before coding — remains essential for designing new systems.

> ▶ **NOTE** Flowcharts drawn on paper are just as valuable as those drawn with software. Keep a pencil and grid paper nearby when planning programs. A hand-drawn

> flowchart produced in two minutes can prevent an hour of debugging. Tools such as draw.io, Lucidchart, and diagrams.net are useful for producing final versions.

To draw a flowchart, you need to know its symbols. The next section introduces the complete standard symbol set used throughout this book and in international practice.

2 Standard Flowchart Symbols

Flowcharts use a small set of standardised symbols, each with a specific meaning. Using the correct symbol in the correct situation is not merely a convention — it is what makes a flowchart readable to anyone who knows the standard. A programmer in Brisbane and a developer in Helsinki will read the same flowchart the same way because the symbols are internationally agreed.

There are six core symbols plus the flow arrow. Learning these seven elements gives you everything you need to draw any flowchart, from a five-step sequence to a complex multi-branch algorithm. The full symbol reference is provided in the table below.

Example 3.4 Introduction — The Standard Symbol Reference

Symbol	Appearance	Purpose	When to use
`Terminal (Start / Stop)`	`START` (double-bordered box)	Marks the beginning or end of a flowchart. Every flowchart must have exactly one START terminal and at least one STOP terminal.	Always the first and last symbol in any flowchart.
`Process`	`SET x=0` (box)	Represents a processing step: an assignment, calculation, or any action that transforms data.	SET statements, arithmetic calculations, updating variables.

`Input / Output`	`/————————/`
	`/ INPUT x /`
	`/————————/`
		Represents data entering the program (INPUT) or leaving it (OUTPUT / DISPLAY). Drawn as a parallelogram.	Any INPUT, OUTPUT, DISPLAY, or PRINT statement.

`Decision`	`/————————\`
	`/ x > 0? \`
	`\ /`
	`\————————/`
		Represents a YES/NO question. Exactly two arrows leave the diamond — one	IF conditions, WHILE conditions, loop exit tests.

Symbol	Appearance	Purpose	When to use
		labelled YES, one labelled NO.	
`Connector`	`( A )`	Links two parts of a flowchart that cannot be connected by a direct arrow. A letter inside identifies the matching pair.	When a flowchart is too large to fit on one page, or when an arrow would cross other arrows.
`Predefined Process`	`[│CALL f()│]`	Represents a call to a named procedure or function defined elsewhere. The double vertical bars distinguish it from a regular process box.	CALL statements; invoking procedures or functions defined in a separate flowchart.
`Flow Arrow`	──► or ↓	Shows the direction of program flow. Arrows connect all symbols. Every symbol must have at least one incoming and one outgoing arrow (except terminals).	Between every pair of connected symbols in the flowchart.

Two rules govern the use of all symbols. First, every flowchart must begin with a START terminal and end with at least one STOP terminal — there are no exceptions. Second, every symbol except terminals must have both an incoming arrow and an outgoing arrow. A symbol with no outgoing arrow represents an unreachable dead end; a symbol with no incoming arrow cannot be reached by any path.

Example 3.5 **Variation — Common Symbol Errors**

The three most common mistakes when drawing flowcharts are: using a process box where a decision box is needed (because a YES/NO question looks like an action to a careless reader); forgetting to label the YES and NO branches of a decision diamond; and drawing arrows that flow upward without a good reason, which usually indicates a missing loop structure.

```
COMMON FLOWCHART ERRORS

ERROR 1 — Process box used for a decision:
 ✗  ┌──────────────────────┐
    │  Check if x > 0      │   ← This is a question, not an action.
    └──────────────────────┘     Use a decision diamond instead.

 ✓  /──────────────────────\
   /        x > 0?          \  ← Correct: decision diamond
```

```
      \                          /     with YES and NO branches.
       \________________________/

ERROR 2 — Unlabelled decision branches:
  ✗  Decision diamond with two arrows but neither labelled YES or NO.
  ✓  Always label both branches clearly. Ambiguous branches
     make the flowchart unreadable.

ERROR 3 — Missing START or STOP terminal:
  ✗  Flowchart begins with a process box (no START).
  ✓  Every flowchart must begin with a START terminal
     and end with at least one STOP terminal.
```

Example 3.6 Real-world application — Reading an Existing Flowchart

Before drawing your own flowcharts, practise reading one. The flowchart below describes the process of logging into a school system. Read it from START to STOP and identify each symbol by name as you encounter it.

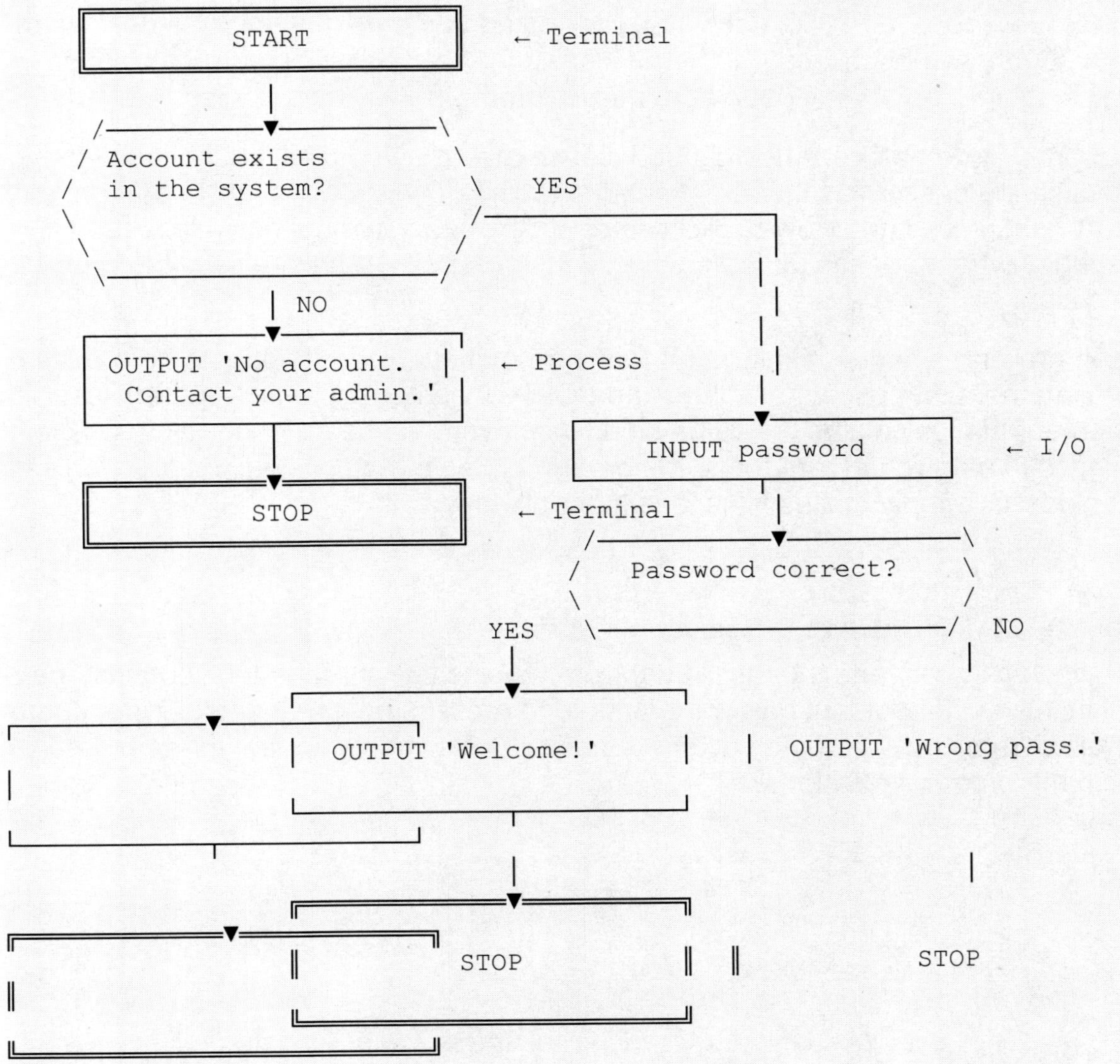

Notice that this flowchart has three STOP terminals: one for when the account does not exist, one for a successful login, and one for a failed login. Multiple STOP terminals are perfectly valid — they simply indicate that the program can end in more than one way.

> ▶ **NOTE** When reading a flowchart, trace every possible path from START to STOP. A correctly drawn flowchart should have no path that gets stuck (no outgoing arrow) and no path that loops forever without a way to exit.

With the standard symbols established, the next four sections practise using them. We begin with the simplest flowchart structure — a pure sequence with no branching.

3 Flowcharts for Sequential Logic

A sequential flowchart represents a program that executes every step in order, with no branches or loops. It is the simplest possible flowchart: a straight vertical path from START to STOP, with each step connected to the next by a single downward arrow. Every symbol except the terminals is either a process box (for calculations and assignments) or an input/output parallelogram (for reading or displaying data).

Sequential flowcharts are useful not because they are complex, but because they establish the basic rules that all flowcharts follow: flow is always top-to-bottom and left-to-right unless an arrow explicitly redirects it; every symbol has a label that describes what happens at that step; and the order of symbols reflects the order of execution.

When drawing a sequential flowchart, ensure that every input appears before the first statement that uses that value, and that every output appears after the last statement that calculates the value being displayed. These ordering rules, visible at a glance in a flowchart, are the same ordering rules that apply in pseudocode — the visual format simply makes violations more obvious.

Example 3.7 **Introduction — Temperature Conversion**

This flowchart converts a temperature from Celsius to Fahrenheit. It contains one terminal, two input/output parallelograms, one process box, and another input/output parallelogram, followed by a second terminal. The symbols appear in the order in which the program executes.

```
        ╔═══════════════════════════════╗
        ║             START             ║
        ╚═══════════════╤═══════════════╝
                        |
        ┌───────────────▼───────────────┐
       /  DISPLAY 'Enter temperature in   \
      /            Celsius:'                \
      \                                     /
```

```
\──────────────────────────────────────/
               │
   ┌───────────▼──────────────────────┐
  /         INPUT celsius              \
  \                                    /
   \─────────────┬────────────────────/
               │
   ┌───────────▼──────────────────────┐
   │ SET fahrenheit =                 │
   │    (celsius × 9 / 5) + 32        │
   └───────────┬──────────────────────┘
               │
   ┌───────────▼──────────────────────┐
  /  OUTPUT celsius, '°C =',           \
 /            fahrenheit, '°F'          \
 \                                      /
  \─────────────┬──────────────────────/
               │
   ╔═══════════▼══════════════════════╗
   ║            STOP                  ║
   ╚══════════════════════════════════╝
```

The input/output parallelograms are approximated here as angled shapes using / and \. In a drawn flowchart, these would be true parallelograms. The important point is that they are visually distinct from the rectangular process boxes. The separation between I/O and processing steps is a design principle, not just a drawing convention.

Example 3.8 **Variation — Multi-Step Sequence with Intermediate Results**

A slightly more complex sequential flowchart calculates a student's weighted final mark from three assessment components. Each intermediate result is a separate process step, making the order of operations clear and the flowchart independently checkable at each step.

```
   ╔══════════════════════════════╗
   ║           START              ║
   ╚═════════════╤════════════════╝
                 │
        /────────▼─────────────────\
       /  INPUT task1, task2,       \
       \       exam_mark            /
        \──────────────────────────/
                 │
   ┌─────────────▼──────────────────┐
   │ SET wt1  = task1 × 0.30        │
   │ SET wt2  = task2 × 0.30        │
   │ SET wexm = exam_mark × 0.40    │
   └─────────────┬──────────────────┘
                 │
   ┌─────────────▼──────────────────┐
   │ SET final = wt1 + wt2 + wexm   │
   └─────────────┬──────────────────┘
                 │
        /────────▼─────────────────────\
       / OUTPUT 'Weighted mark:',       \
```

```
        \           final              /
         \____________________________/
                      |
                      ▼
 ╔══════════════════════════════════════╗
 ║                 STOP                 ║
 ╚══════════════════════════════════════╝
```

Although this flowchart could place all three SET statements in a single process box, separating them into one box each makes each calculation independently readable and verifiable. In practice, closely related assignments (such as the three weighting calculations) are often grouped in one process box to keep the flowchart compact.

Example 3.9 Real-world application — A Payroll Calculation

A small business pays staff at their base hourly rate for the first 38 hours worked per week, and at 1.5 times the base rate for any additional hours. This sequential flowchart computes the gross pay for a single employee. All the steps are sequential because the business rule has no branches: both components are always calculated, and the total is always displayed.

```
 ╔════════════════════════════════════════╗
 ║                 START                  ║
 ╚════════════════════════════════════════╝
                     |
      /──────────────▼─────────────────\
     /  INPUT employee_name,            \
     \  hourly_rate, hours_worked       /
      \────────────────────────────────/
                     |
 ┌───────────────────▼─────────────────────┐
 │ SET standard_hours =                    │
 │   MIN(hours_worked, 38)                 │
 │ SET overtime_hours =                    │
 │   MAX(0, hours_worked - 38)             │
 └─────────────────────────────────────────┘
                     |
 ┌───────────────────▼─────────────────────┐
 │ SET standard_pay =                      │
 │   standard_hours × hourly_rate          │
 │ SET overtime_pay =                      │
 │   overtime_hours × hourly_rate × 1.5    │
 └─────────────────────────────────────────┘
                     |
 ┌───────────────────▼─────────────────────┐
 │ SET gross_pay =                         │
 │   standard_pay + overtime_pay           │
 └─────────────────────────────────────────┘
                     |
      /──────────────▼──────────────────────\
     /  OUTPUT employee_name,                \
     \          gross_pay                    /
      \─────────────────────────────────────/
                     |
 ╔═══════════════════▼═════════════════════╗
 ║                 STOP                    ║
 ╚═════════════════════════════════════════╝
```

> ▶ **NOTE** Keep process boxes short. If a single process box requires more than two or three lines of text, consider whether the step should be broken into smaller steps, or whether part of it should be moved to a subprogram (shown with a predefined process symbol).

Sequential flowcharts establish the foundations: symbols, arrows, and ordering. The next section introduces the decision diamond, which allows a flowchart to branch into two or more separate paths.

4 Flowcharts for Decision Logic

A decision diamond introduces a branch into the flowchart. Exactly two arrows leave each diamond: one labelled YES (the path taken when the condition is true) and one labelled NO (the path taken when it is false). The two paths typically rejoin at a later point in the flowchart, after each has performed its specific actions.

Multiple decision diamonds can be chained to represent ELSE IF logic: the NO path of the first diamond leads to the condition box of the second diamond, and so on. Each additional diamond adds one more path. For programs with many possible outcomes, this chaining of diamonds is what makes the flowchart comprehensive — every possible case is visible as a labelled path.

When drawing decision flowcharts, a useful habit is to count the paths. If your program has N possible outcomes, your flowchart should have exactly N paths from the last decision diamond (or set of diamonds) to a STOP terminal. Counting paths is a fast way to verify that no case has been forgotten.

Example 3.10 Introduction — A Simple Two-Way Decision

This flowchart checks whether a user is old enough to vote in Australia (18 or older). The decision diamond produces two paths: one for eligible voters and one for those not yet eligible. Both paths lead to the same STOP terminal.

```
         ╔════════════════════════╗
         ║         START          ║
         ╚════════════════════════╝
                    |
    /───────────────▼───────────────\
   /  DISPLAY 'Enter your            \
   \          age:'                  /
    \───────────────────────────────/
                    |
    /───────────────▼───────────────\
   /          INPUT age              \
   \                                 /
    \───────────────────────────────/
                    |
     /──────────────▼──────────────\
    /       age >= 18?              \
    \                               /
```

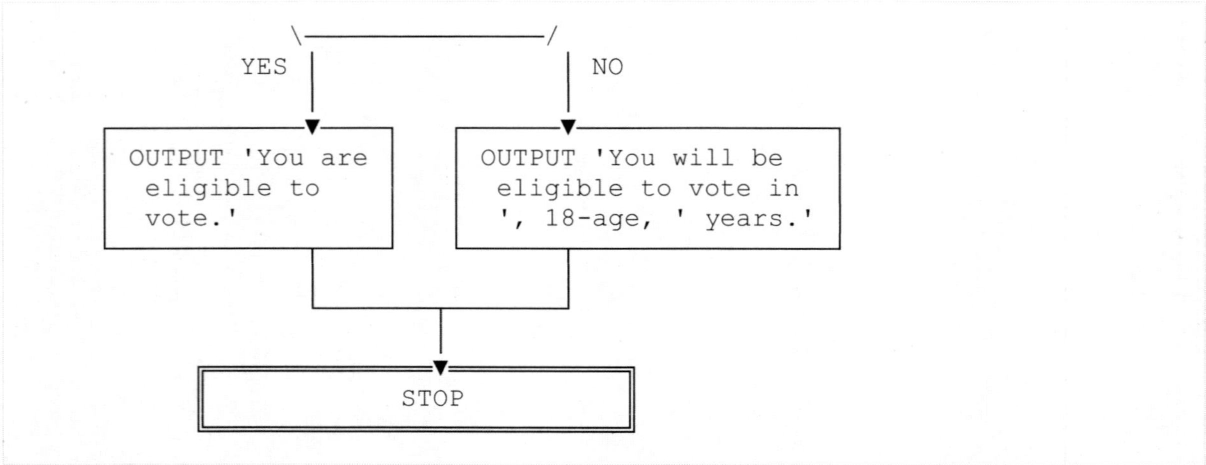

The YES branch goes left (or right — the direction is a layout choice, not a convention). Both branches converge before the STOP terminal. Convergence is shown by two arrows meeting at the same point and continuing as one.

Example 3.11 **Variation — Chained Decisions for Grade Classification**

Chaining decision diamonds creates an ELSE IF structure. Each NO branch leads to the next condition check. The YES branch at each diamond produces a specific outcome. This flowchart classifies a percentage score into five grade bands.

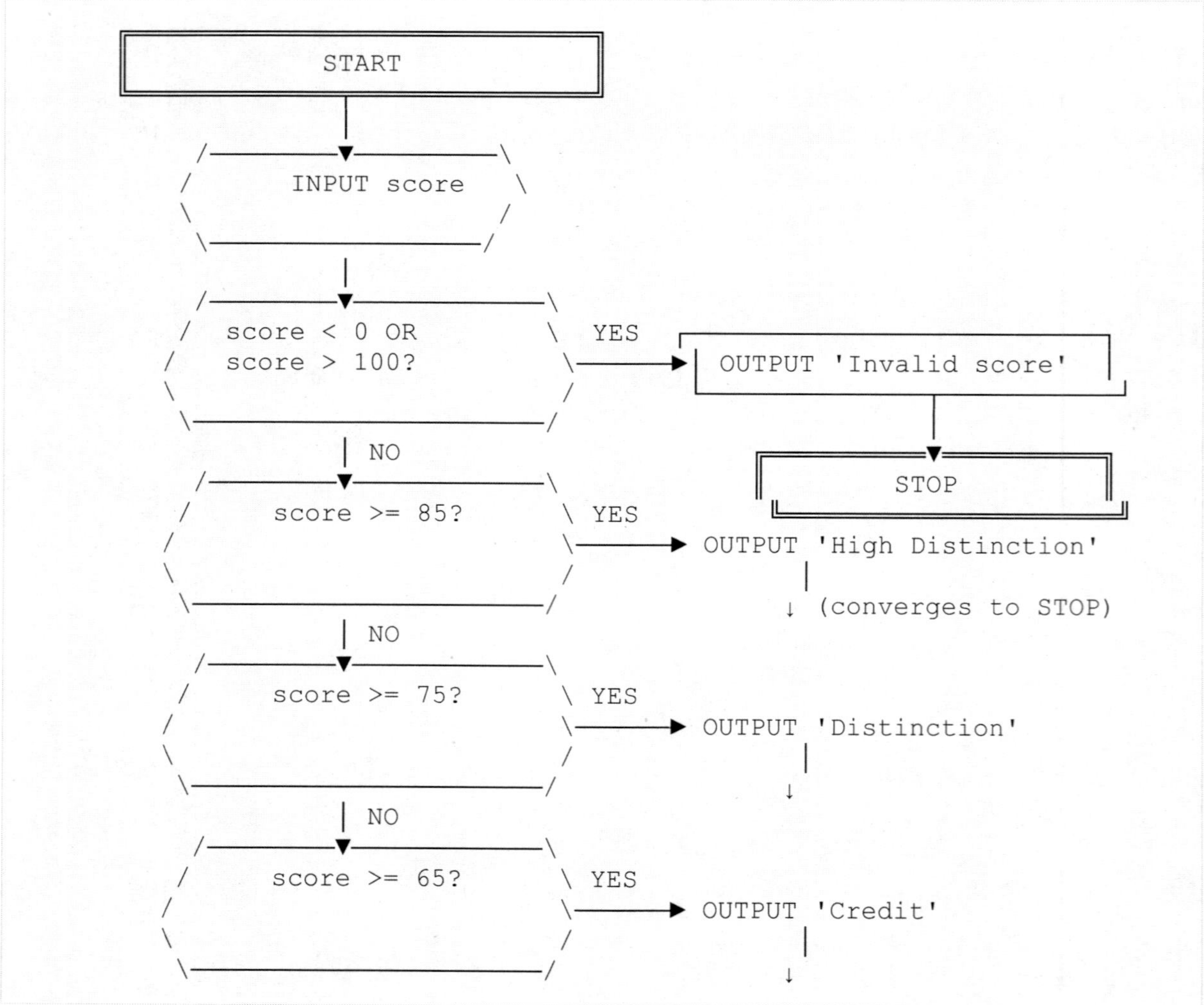

```
                | NO
       /--------▼--------------\
      /     score >= 50?        \ YES
     /                           \-------► OUTPUT 'Pass'
     \                           /                |
      \-------------------------/                 ↓
                | NO                              |
  OUTPUT 'Fail' |                                 |
                |                                 |
                └─────────────────────────────────┘
                               |
                 ┌=============▼=============┐
                 |           STOP            |
                 └===========================┘
```

Each output on the right side eventually converges to the single STOP terminal at the bottom. In a full drawn flowchart, connector symbols (lettered circles) would be used where arrows need to travel long distances to avoid crossing other lines.

Example 3.12 Real-world application — A Login System with Lockout

This flowchart represents a login process with a maximum of three attempts. It combines a decision diamond (password check) with a counter-based lockout decision. Two separate STOP terminals represent the two ways the program ends: successful login and account lockout.

```
 ┌===========================┐
 |          START            |
 └===========================┘
              |
 ┌────────────▼────────────┐
 | SET attempts = 0        |
 | SET max = 3             |
 └─────────────────────────┘
              |
 ┌────────────▼────────────┐ ◄──────────────────────────┐
 | SET attempts = attempts |                            |
 |          + 1            |                            |
 └─────────────────────────┘                            |
              |                                         |
     /--------▼-----------\                             |
    /   INPUT username,    \                            |
    \      password        /                            |
     \--------------------/                             |
              |                                         |
    /---------▼--------------\                          |
   /  Credentials valid?  \  YES  ┌──────────────────┐  |
  /                        \─────►| OUTPUT 'Welcome!'|  |
  \                        /      └──────────────────┘  |
   \----------------------/                |            |
              | NO              ┌==========▼==========┐ |
    /---------▼--------------\  |   STOP (success)    | |
   /  attempts >= max?        \ └=====================┘ |
  /                            \                        |
  \                            /                        |
   \--------------------------/                         |
      YES |              | NO                           |
```

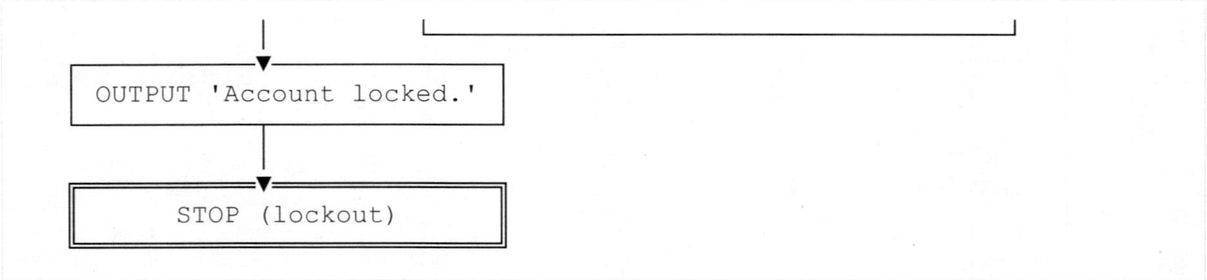

The back-arrow on the right side of the flowchart shows the loop: if credentials are invalid and the maximum attempts have not been reached, the flowchart cycles back to the INPUT step for another try. This is the first hint of loop structure in a flowchart — treated fully in the next section.

> ▶ **NOTE** Every decision diamond must have exactly two labelled exit arrows. If you find yourself drawing a diamond with three or more exits, replace it with nested or chained diamonds. Each diamond answers exactly one YES/NO question.

Decision diamonds allow programs to branch. When combined with back-arrows that return flow to an earlier point in the diagram, they create loops. The next section shows how to represent the three loop structures from Chapter 2 as flowcharts.

5 Flowcharts for Loops

A loop in a flowchart is created by drawing an arrow that flows backward — from a later point in the diagram to an earlier one. This back-arrow, combined with a decision diamond that tests the loop condition, produces the three loop structures introduced in Chapter 2: the pre-test loop (WHILE), the count-controlled loop (FOR), and the post-test loop (REPEAT … UNTIL).

The key visual difference between the three loop types lies in the position of the decision diamond relative to the loop body. In a pre-test loop, the diamond appears before the loop body: the condition is checked first, and the body may never execute at all. In a post-test loop, the diamond appears after the loop body: the body always executes at least once. In a count-controlled loop, a counter variable and an increment step are added, and the diamond tests whether the counter has reached its limit.

When drawing a loop flowchart, always identify the back-arrow explicitly — draw it on the left side of the diagram, running upward from the bottom of the loop body to the top of the condition diamond or to the first step inside the loop. This consistent placement makes the loop structure immediately recognisable.

Example 3.13 **Introduction — Pre-Test Loop (WHILE) for Input Validation**

This flowchart validates a score input. The condition is checked before the loop body runs. If the first input is valid, the loop body never executes and the program continues immediately.

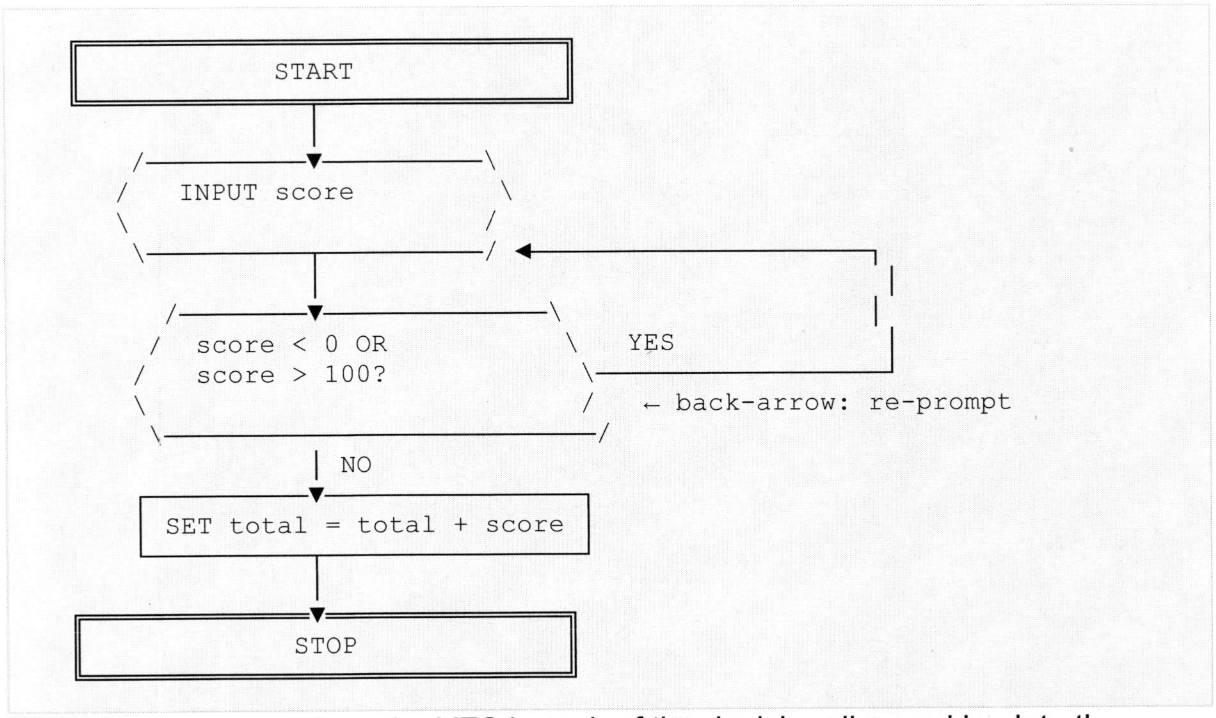

The back-arrow runs from the YES branch of the decision diamond back to the INPUT step. If the score is invalid, the program asks again. If it is valid (NO branch), the program continues to the process step and then to STOP. This is the pre-test pattern: check before acting.

Example 3.14 **Variation — Count-Controlled Loop (FOR) Accumulating Scores**

A count-controlled loop requires three extra elements compared to a simple WHILE loop: an initialisation step (setting the counter to its starting value), a condition diamond (checking whether the counter has exceeded its limit), and an increment step (increasing the counter at the end of each iteration). The back-arrow connects the increment step back to the condition diamond.

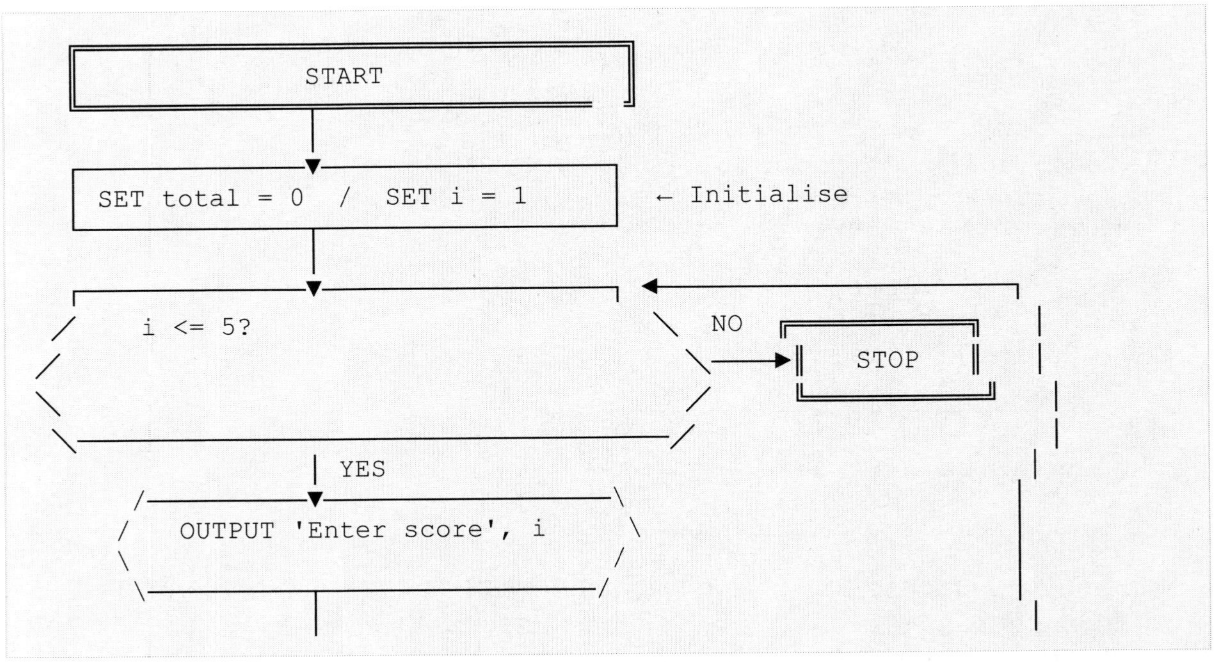

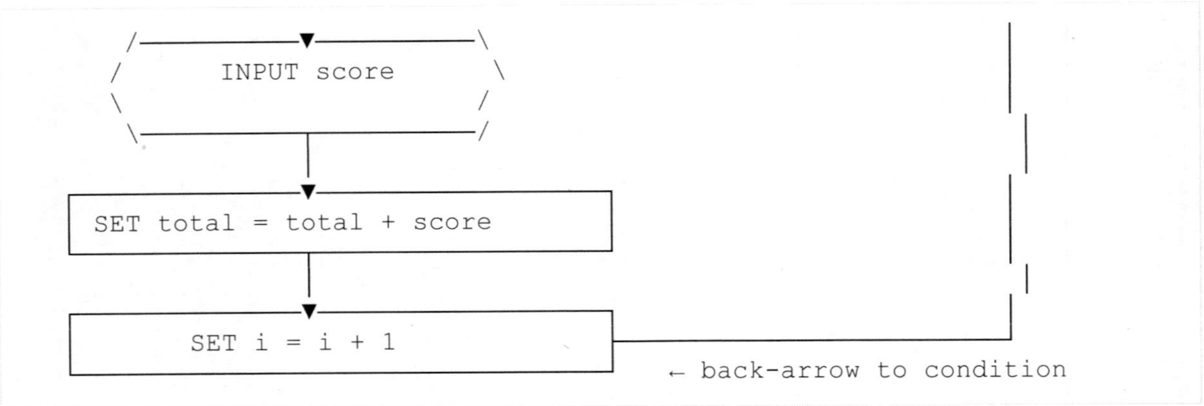

The back-arrow runs from the increment step all the way back up to the condition diamond. This creates the loop: increment, check condition, execute body if YES, increment again. The NO branch at the condition diamond exits the loop when i exceeds 5.

Example 3.15 **Real-world application — Post-Test Loop (REPEAT … UNTIL) for a Menu**

In a post-test loop, the decision diamond appears after the loop body. The loop body executes unconditionally the first time, and then the exit condition is checked. This guarantees that the menu is always displayed at least once — which is the correct behaviour for a menu-driven program.

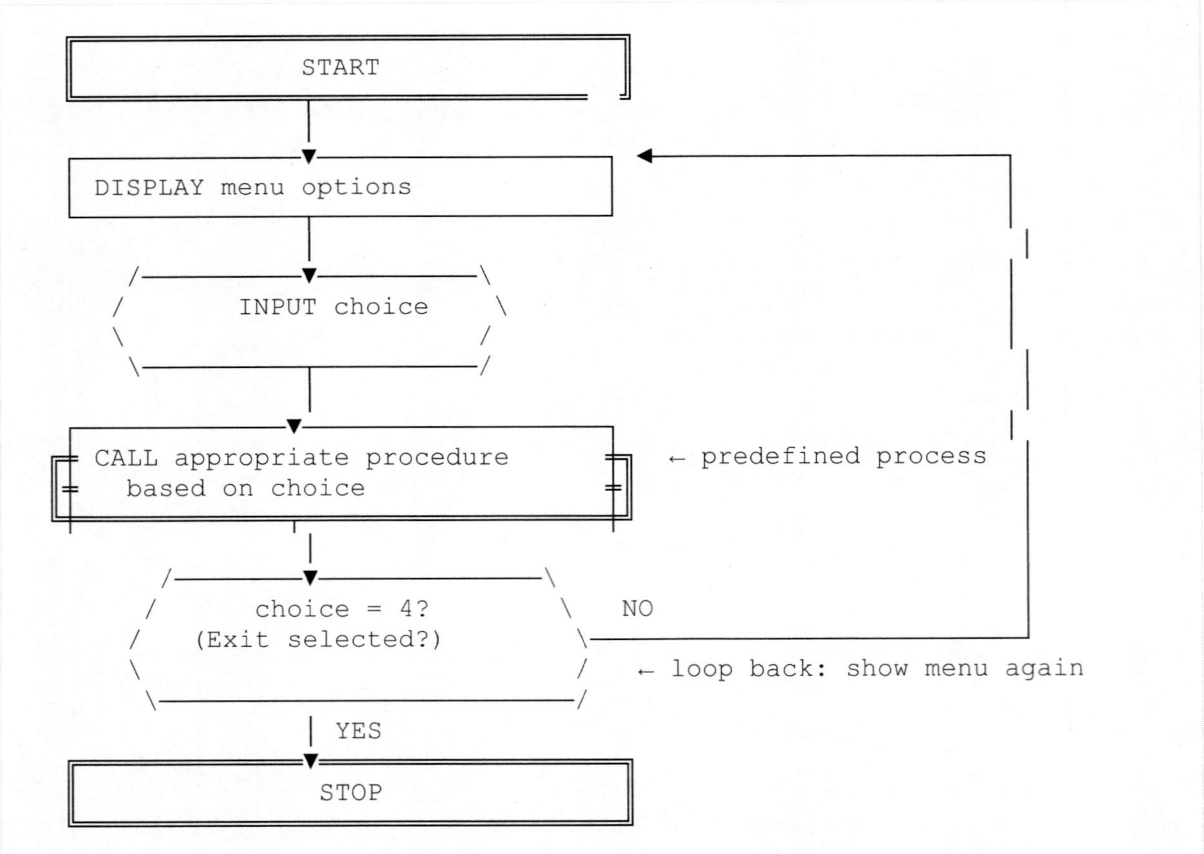

The predefined process box (shown with double vertical bars ╪) represents a call to a procedure defined elsewhere. This is the first appearance of the modular flowchart symbol in this chapter; it is explored fully in Section 6.

> ▶ **NOTE** Place the back-arrow consistently on the left side of the loop structure. Right-side arrows conventionally show the YES branch of a decision; left-side arrows conventionally show loop-back paths. Consistency in arrow direction makes complex flowcharts significantly easier to read.

You can now draw flowcharts for programs with sequences, decisions, and loops. The final structural challenge is representing programs that call named subprograms. This is the subject of the next section.

6 Flowcharts for Modular Programs

A modular program is divided into named subprograms: procedures and functions that each perform one task. In a flowchart, a call to a subprogram is represented by the predefined process symbol — a rectangle with a double vertical bar on each side. This symbol means: 'a named subprogram is invoked here; its details are defined elsewhere.'

A modular flowchart design consists of a main flowchart that shows the overall program flow using predefined process boxes for each subprogram call, plus one separate flowchart for each subprogram. The main flowchart provides the high-level view; the sub-flowcharts provide the detail. A reader can understand the overall structure from the main flowchart alone, and then drill down into any sub-flowchart for more detail.

This separation of concerns in a flowchart mirrors the separation of concerns in code. A well-structured program has a short, readable main function that calls other functions. A well-structured modular flowchart has a short, readable main diagram that references sub-diagrams. Both reflect the same design principle: keep each component focused on a single responsibility.

Example 3.16 Introduction — The Predefined Process Symbol

The predefined process symbol uses double vertical bars to visually distinguish a subprogram call from a regular processing step. The label inside the box identifies the subprogram by name, along with any parameters passed to it. The main flowchart does not show what happens inside the subprogram — that detail belongs in the sub-flowchart.

```
Main flowchart fragment:              Sub-flowchart for display_header:

╔══════════════════════════╗          ╔══════════════════════════════╗
║          START           ║          ║  START: display_header       ║
╚══════════════════════════╝          ║  (parameter: title)          ║
             │                        ╚══════════════════════════════╝
╓────────────▼─────────────╖                         │
║ CALL display_header      ║  —refers to—▶
/──────────▼───────────────\
```

```
║╪    ('Results Report') ╪║              /  OUTPUT '============='
 \
 ╙┴═══════════════════════╧╜               \                        /
              │                             \───────────────────────/
                                                        │
    ...rest of main...

/────────────▼───────────\
                                           /      OUTPUT title
\
                                           \
/
                                            \───────────────────────/
                                                        │

/────────────▼───────────\
                                           /  OUTPUT '============='
\
                                           \
/
                                            \────────────────────────/
                                                        │

╔═════════════▼════════════╗
                                           ║ STOP: display_header
║

╚══════════════════════════╝
```

The sub-flowchart for display_header begins with its own START terminal (labelled to identify the subprogram) and ends with its own STOP terminal. When the main flowchart reaches the predefined process box, execution conceptually moves to the sub-flowchart's START, runs through it, and returns to the main flowchart at the step after the predefined process box.

Example 3.17 Variation — A Main Flowchart with Multiple Subprogram Calls

A well-designed main flowchart for a student records system would consist almost entirely of predefined process boxes, each calling a specific subprogram. The main flowchart shows the sequence and conditions that govern when each subprogram is called; the sub-flowcharts show how each operation is performed.

```
MAIN FLOWCHART — Student Records System

╔══════════════════════════════╗
║            START             ║
╚══════════════════════════════╝
               │
╔╤═════════════▼═════════════╤╗
║╪   CALL load_records       ╪║   ← Defined in sub-flowchart A
╚╧═══════════════════════════╧╝
               │
┌──────────────▼──────────────┐    ◀─────────────────────────┐
│  DISPLAY menu options       │                              │
└─────────────────────────────┘                              │
               │                                              │
      /────────▼────────\                                     │
```

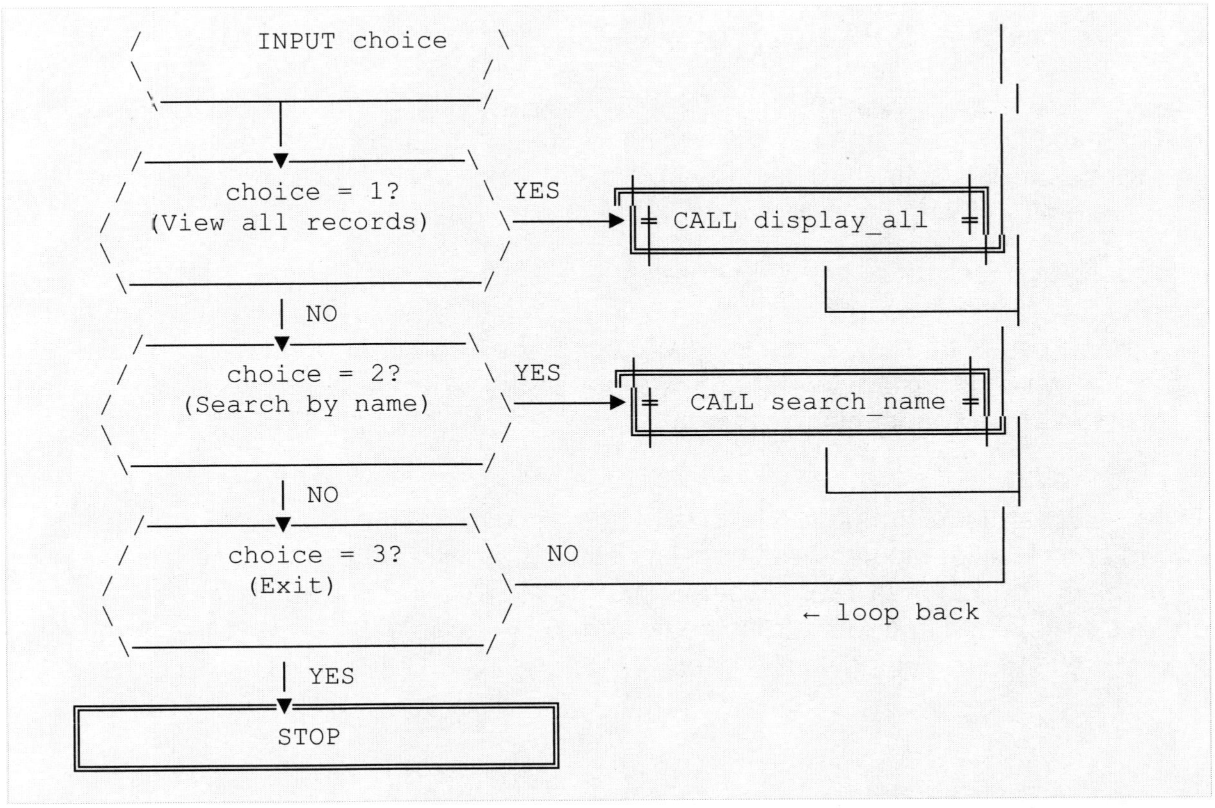

Example 3.18 **Real-world application — When Sub-Flowcharts Are Essential**

For a real-world system with ten or more operations, placing all logic in a single flowchart would produce a diagram too large to read on one page. The modular approach solves this by keeping the main flowchart to one page and assigning each major operation its own sub-flowchart page.

A school library system, for example, might have sub-flowcharts for: borrowing a book (check availability, update loan record, print slip); returning a book (find loan record, calculate fines if overdue, update inventory); and searching the catalogue (accept search term, query records, display results). The main flowchart shows only the menu and the calls to these three sub-flowcharts. A reader understands the whole system from the main flowchart; they read a sub-flowchart only when they need to understand a specific operation.

> ▶ **NOTE** Label every predefined process box with the exact name of the subprogram it calls, and include parameters if the subprogram takes them. A label like 'CALL process data' is too vague; 'CALL calculate_fine(loan_date, return_date)' is precise and self-documenting.

You now have the complete flowchart toolkit: sequential flow, decision diamonds, loop structures, and modular predefined process boxes. The final section steps back to consider when to use a flowchart versus pseudocode, and how to use both tools together.

7 Flowcharts and Pseudocode — Choosing and Combining

Flowcharts and pseudocode are complementary, not competing. Each one reveals certain aspects of a design more clearly than the other, and experienced programmers use both — choosing whichever tool best fits the current planning need, and often using them together on the same problem.

Pseudocode excels at expressing detail: the exact variables, their names, the precise structure of a conditional expression, the parameters of a function. It is fast to write and easy to translate directly into code. Flowcharts excel at expressing structure: which steps lead where, how many paths a decision produces, whether a loop's back-arrow connects to the right point. They make control flow visible at a glance.

The practical rule is straightforward: use pseudocode to plan the detail of each step and to communicate logic in writing. Use a flowchart when the control flow is complex enough that a linear reading of pseudocode is insufficient to verify its correctness. When in doubt, draw the flowchart first to verify the structure, then write the pseudocode to nail down the detail.

Example 3.19 Introduction — The Same Problem, Both Tools

This example shows the same problem — finding the highest score in a list — represented as both pseudocode and a flowchart. Read both and consider which one makes the loop structure more apparent, and which one makes the variable logic clearer.

Pseudocode — detail is clear

```
PSEUDOCODE:

  BEGIN
    INPUT scores
    SET highest = scores[0]
    FOR EACH score IN
           scores DO
      IF score > highest
            THEN
        SET highest = score
      END IF
    END FOR
    OUTPUT 'Highest:', highest
  END
```

Flowchart — loop paths are clear

```
FLOWCHART (structure):

  START
    ↓
  INPUT scores
    ↓
  SET highest = scores[0]
    ↓
←─────────────────────────────────┐
  More scores?  NO → OUTPUT       │
    ↓ YES            highest      │
  score > highest?                │
    YES ↓        NO →─────────────┤
  SET highest=score               │
    ↓                             │
└─────────────────────────────────┘
        (loop back)
```

The pseudocode makes the variable logic clear: the initial value of highest, how it is updated, and what is displayed. The flowchart makes the loop structure clear: two exit conditions (no more scores, or scores exhausted), two paths at the inner decision, both converging at the update. Use both when a design has both complex logic and complex structure.

Example 3.20 Variation — When Each Tool Has the Advantage

```
USE A FLOWCHART WHEN:
   - The program has complex branching with multiple simultaneous
paths
   - You need to count paths to verify no case has been missed
   - You are communicating a design to a non-programmer
   - The loop structure is complex (nested loops, multiple exit
points)
   - You suspect a logic error in an IF/ELSE chain and need to trace
it visually

USE PSEUDOCODE WHEN:
   - You need to plan the detail: variable names, expressions,
parameters
   - You are about to begin translating to Python
   - The algorithm is mostly sequential with minimal branching
   - You need to write the plan quickly and read it back as prose
   - You are documenting a function or procedure for another
programmer

USE BOTH WHEN:
   - The program has complex structure (flowchart) AND complex logic
(pseudocode)
   - You are working on a major assessment or project submission
   - You need to verify both the control flow AND the variable logic
   - You are unsure which is sufficient — when in doubt, draw both
```

Example 3.21 Real-world application — Combining Both Tools on a Student Project

A Year 11 student is designing a quiz program for their Digital Technologies assessment. Their planning approach uses both tools in sequence: first a flowchart, then pseudocode.

The student draws a flowchart first to map out the overall structure: a loop that shows five questions, a decision diamond for each question, convergence of YES and NO paths into a score update, and a final output after the loop. The flowchart confirms that all paths are accounted for and that the loop terminates correctly.

The student then writes pseudocode for the two most complex parts: the question-display procedure (to plan the exact output format and parameter names) and the score-calculation function (to plan how the final grade is computed from the raw score). The pseudocode confirms the variable logic and gives a direct template for the Python code.

Together, the flowchart and pseudocode constitute a complete planning document. The student submits both with their code as evidence of design thinking — which is explicitly required by the assessment criteria. The planning document also makes it easy to explain design decisions during the interview component of the assessment.

> ▶ **NOTE** When submitting a Digital Technologies assessment that includes a design component, always provide both a flowchart and pseudocode for any significant algorithm. The flowchart demonstrates structural thinking; the pseudocode demonstrates logical precision. Together they satisfy the curriculum's design documentation requirements.

This chapter has given you the complete standard flowchart toolkit: symbols, conventions, sequential diagrams, decision structures, loop structures, modular designs, and the judgement to choose between flowcharts and pseudocode or to use both. Chapter 4 introduces UML — a family of diagram types purpose-built for designing object-oriented programs.

Chapter Summary

- A flowchart uses standard symbols and connecting arrows to represent program logic visually. It excels at revealing control flow — branching, looping, and path convergence — that can be hard to verify in pseudocode alone.
- The six core symbols are: the terminal (rounded rectangle with double border, for START/STOP), the process box (rectangle, for calculations and assignments), the input/output parallelogram, the decision diamond (YES/NO only), the connector circle (for linking distant parts), and the predefined process box (rectangle with double vertical bars, for subprogram calls).
- Every flowchart must begin with a START terminal and end with at least one STOP terminal. Every symbol except terminals must have at least one incoming and one outgoing arrow. Decision diamonds must have exactly two labelled exit arrows: YES and NO.
- Sequential flowcharts contain only process boxes and input/output parallelograms in a straight vertical path from START to STOP. The order of symbols must reflect the order in which the program executes.
- Decision logic is represented by chaining decision diamonds. Each diamond produces exactly two paths. Chained NO branches implement ELSE IF logic; all paths must eventually converge or reach a STOP terminal.
- Loop structures are created by drawing a back-arrow from a later point in the flowchart to an earlier one. Pre-test loops (WHILE) place the condition diamond before the loop body; post-test loops (REPEAT … UNTIL) place it after; count-controlled loops (FOR) add initialisation and increment steps.
- Modular flowcharts use predefined process boxes (double vertical bars) to represent calls to named subprograms. Each subprogram is drawn as a separate flowchart, allowing complex systems to be described across multiple pages.
- Flowcharts and pseudocode are complementary tools. Use flowcharts when control flow is complex or needs to be verified visually. Use pseudocode when variable logic and detail need to be pinned down before coding. Use both for major designs.

Guided Exercises

Complete all five exercises before moving on to Chapter 4. For exercises that require drawing a flowchart, use paper and pencil or a free diagramming tool such as draw.io. Each exercise includes a hint to help you get started.

Exercise 1

Name the correct flowchart symbol for each of the following: (a) the beginning of the program; (b) displaying a result on screen; (c) the step that calculates total = price × quantity; (d) the check 'Is score >= 50?'; (e) a call to a procedure named print_receipt(); (f) a link between two parts of a large flowchart on the same page.

Hint: Refer to the symbol reference table in Section 2. Focus on the purpose of each symbol, not its appearance. Input/output and process are the two most commonly confused.

Exercise 2

Draw a sequential flowchart for the following program: read a student's name and three test scores, calculate the average score, and display the student's name and average. Use the correct symbol for each step.

Hint: Begin with a START terminal. Use parallelograms for all INPUT and OUTPUT steps. Use rectangles for the average calculation. Connect every symbol with a downward arrow. End with a STOP terminal.

Exercise 3

Draw a flowchart for a program that reads an integer and outputs whether it is positive, negative, or zero. Your flowchart must use decision diamonds with clearly labelled YES and NO branches, and all three paths must converge at a single STOP terminal.

Hint: Use two chained decision diamonds. The first checks whether the number is greater than zero (YES: output 'Positive'). The NO branch leads to the second diamond, which checks whether it equals zero.

Exercise 4

Draw a flowchart for a WHILE loop that reads integer values from the user one at a time and accumulates a running total, stopping when the user enters −1. After the loop, display the total. Your flowchart must clearly show the back-arrow that creates the loop.

Hint: Initialise the total to 0 before the loop. Read the first input, then enter the loop condition diamond: 'input = −1?'. The NO branch (not yet done) adds to the total and reads the next input; the YES branch exits to the output step.

Exercise 5

The pseudocode below uses a function called is_palindrome that checks whether a word reads the same forwards and backwards. Draw a main flowchart that calls this function using a predefined process symbol, and a separate sub-flowchart for the is_palindrome function itself. The function should accept a word as a parameter and return TRUE or FALSE.

Hint: The main flowchart: START → INPUT word → CALL is_palindrome(word) → decision diamond on the result → appropriate OUTPUT → STOP. The sub-flowchart reverses the word, compares it to the original, and returns TRUE or FALSE.

Challenge Tasks

These tasks have no hints. They require independent thinking and are suitable for extension or assessment. Complete the Guided Exercises before attempting these.

Challenge Task 1

Draw a complete modular flowchart set for a simple ATM system. Your design must include: a main flowchart that handles the menu (Check Balance, Withdraw, Deposit, Exit); a sub-flowchart for the Withdraw operation, which checks that the requested amount does not exceed the current balance and does not exceed a single-transaction limit of $1,000; and a sub-flowchart for the Deposit operation, which validates that the deposit amount is positive and does not exceed $10,000. All sub-flowcharts must have their own START and STOP terminals. All decision diamonds must have labelled YES and NO branches.

Challenge Task 2

A classmate has drawn a flowchart for a program that reads ten numbers and finds the largest. The flowchart has the following errors: the counter is not initialised before the loop; the decision diamond testing 'i <= 10' has three exit arrows instead of two; the back-arrow connects to the OUTPUT step instead of the condition diamond; and there is no STOP terminal. Describe each error precisely, explain what incorrect behaviour it would cause, and draw a corrected version of the flowchart.

Challenge Task 3

Design a complete planning document — both a flowchart and pseudocode — for a number guessing game. The program generates a random number between 1 and 100. The player has up to 10 guesses. After each guess, the program tells the player whether their guess was too high, too low, or correct. If the player guesses correctly within 10 attempts, the program congratulates them and shows how many guesses were used. If not, the program reveals the answer. Your flowchart must use the correct symbols for all steps, including a predefined process box for the random number generation. Your pseudocode must match the flowchart exactly.

UML Diagrams for Program Design

> This chapter introduces UML — the Unified Modelling Language — a family of diagram types used worldwide to design and document software systems. You will learn four diagram types that are directly relevant to the programs you write: Use Case diagrams to capture what a system must do; Class diagrams to design its object-oriented structure; Sequence diagrams to plan how objects interact; and Activity diagrams to model complex workflows. By the end of this chapter, you will be able to produce a complete UML design document for any object-oriented Python program.

1 What UML Is and Why It Matters

The Unified Modelling Language is a standardised visual language for describing software systems. Developed in the 1990s and adopted as an international standard (ISO/IEC 19501), UML provides a common vocabulary of diagrams that software developers, architects, and analysts use to communicate design decisions across teams, organisations, and countries.

UML is not a programming language and it is not bound to any particular language or framework. A class diagram drawn for a Python program looks identical to one drawn for a Java program — the notation is the same. This universality is UML's central value: any programmer who knows UML can read and contribute to a design document, regardless of which language the system will be implemented in.

UML defines thirteen diagram types, organised into two families: structural diagrams (which describe the static structure of a system) and behavioural diagrams (which describe how the system behaves at runtime). This chapter covers four diagram types that are most useful for student projects at Years 10 to 12: Use Case, Class, Sequence, and Activity diagrams.

Example 4.1 Introduction — The Four Diagram Types Covered in This Chapter

The table below summarises the four diagram types this chapter teaches. Each type answers a different design question, and each is most useful at a different stage of the design process.

Diagram type	What it shows	Key elements	Best used for
Use Case	What the system does from a user's perspective	Actors (users or external systems), use cases (system behaviours), system boundary	Early design; understanding requirements before writing any code

Diagram type	What it shows	Key elements	Best used for
Class	The structure of an object-oriented program	Classes, attributes, methods, visibility, and relationships between classes	Designing OOP programs; planning classes before writing Python
Sequence	How objects interact over time to achieve a goal	Objects, lifelines, synchronous messages, return messages	Planning method calls; understanding the order of interactions in a use case
Activity	The flow of behaviour through a system or process	Activities, decision nodes, start and end nodes, swim lanes for multiple actors	Modelling complex workflows; showing responsibilities across multiple actors

These four diagram types are not used in isolation. A complete design document for an OOP project would typically include a Use Case diagram (to capture requirements), one or more Class diagrams (to design the code structure), Sequence diagrams for the key interactions, and an Activity diagram for any complex workflow. Used together, they provide a thorough, consistent picture of the system before a single line of code is written.

Example 4.2 **Variation — UML in Practice vs UML in Theory**

UML is sometimes taught as a rigid, formal system where every diagram must comply with precise notation rules. In professional practice, most programmers treat UML pragmatically: they draw the diagrams that are useful for the decision at hand and skip the ones that add no value.

The practical approach — sometimes called 'just enough modelling' — means drawing a Class diagram before writing OOP code, a Sequence diagram when planning a complex method interaction, and a Use Case diagram when clarifying requirements with a stakeholder. It does not mean drawing all thirteen UML diagram types for every project. This chapter teaches UML as a practical tool, not as a formal compliance exercise.

Example 4.3 **Real-world application — UML in a Digital Technologies Assessment**

A Year 11 student is asked to design and build an object-oriented inventory management system as a major assessment task. Their design document — submitted before the code — includes: a Use Case diagram showing the two actors (Manager and Staff) and five use cases; a Class diagram showing four classes (Product, Inventory, Order, User) with attributes, methods, and relationships; a Sequence diagram showing the interaction between classes when a new order is placed; and an Activity diagram showing the order fulfilment workflow.

This design document serves three purposes: it helps the student organise their thinking before coding; it gives the teacher evidence that the student planned the system; and it provides a reference that keeps the code and the design aligned throughout development. These are exactly the purposes UML was designed to serve in professional software engineering.

> ▶ **NOTE** You do not need to memorise every UML rule before you start drawing. Learn the core notation for each diagram type, practise with simple examples, and build complexity gradually. A correct, readable UML diagram is always more valuable than a technically perfect one that nobody can understand.

The four sections that follow introduce each diagram type in turn, beginning with the one drawn earliest in the design process: the Use Case diagram.

2 Use Case Diagrams

A Use Case diagram answers the question: what can the system do, and who uses it? It is drawn at the very beginning of the design process, before any classes or code are planned, to capture requirements from the perspective of the people and systems that will interact with the software.

A Use Case diagram contains three elements. Actors are the external entities that interact with the system — usually people (Student, Librarian, Admin) but sometimes other systems (Payment Gateway, Email Server). Use cases are the specific actions the system performs for its actors — each one is a discrete piece of functionality that delivers value to at least one actor. The system boundary is a rectangle that encloses all the use cases, with its name at the top; actors are placed outside this boundary.

The key discipline in drawing a Use Case diagram is staying at the right level of abstraction. A use case should describe a complete, meaningful action — 'Borrow a Book' or 'Process a Payment' — not a low-level implementation step like 'Update the loan_count field'. Use cases capture what the system does, not how it does it.

Example 4.4 Introduction — A Library System Use Case Diagram

This Use Case diagram captures the requirements for a school library borrowing system. Two actors — Student and Librarian — each interact with a different set of use cases inside the Library System boundary.

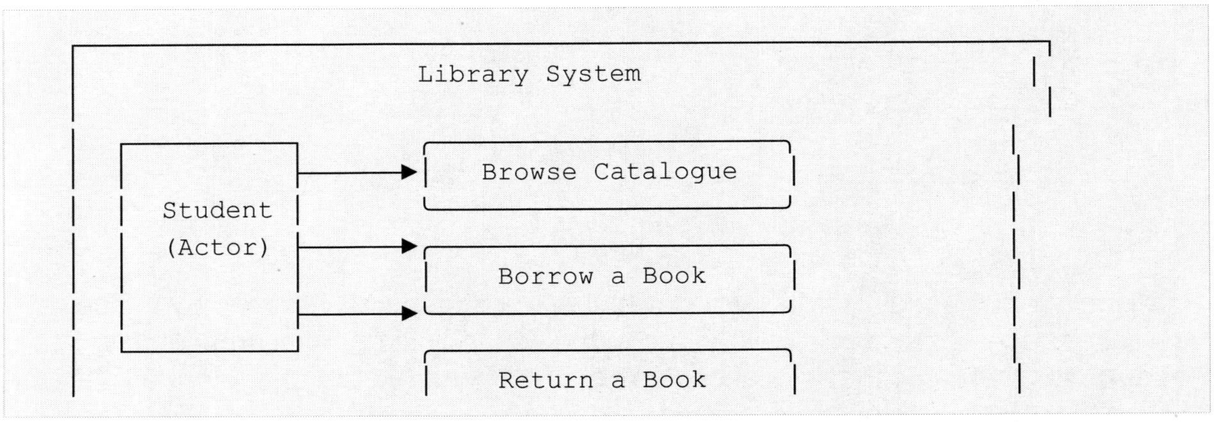

```
|                 └──────────────────────────┘          |
|                                                        |  |
|  ┌─────────────┐        ┌──────────────────────────┐  |
|  |             ├───────►| Manage Inventory         |  |
|  |Librarian    ├───────►└──────────────────────────┘  |
|  |  (Actor)    |        ┌──────────────────────────┐  |
|  |             ├───────►| Generate Report          |  |
|  └─────────────┘        └──────────────────────────┘  |
|                                                          |
└──────────────────────────────────────────────────────────┘

Actor ──────── connects to ────────► ( Use Case inside boundary )
```

Each line from an actor to a use case represents that the actor participates in that use case. A Student browses the catalogue, borrows books, and returns books. A Librarian manages inventory and generates reports. Notice that the Librarian does not interact with 'Borrow a Book' — that is a Student-only action. The diagram makes this separation of responsibilities immediately clear.

Example 4.5 **Variation — Include and Extend Relationships**

Some use cases share common behaviour. UML provides two special relationships to express this: «hinclude» and «extend». An «include» relationship means that one use case always invokes another as part of its execution. An «extend» relationship means that one use case optionally extends another under certain conditions.

```
  «include»   — The base use case ALWAYS executes the included one.
                Example: 'Borrow a Book' always includes 'Verify
Membership'.
                The line is dashed with an open arrowhead, labelled
«include».

  «extend»    — The extending use case OPTIONALLY adds to the base one.
                Example: 'Return a Book' may extend 'Calculate Fine'
                (only when the book is overdue).
                The line is dashed with an open arrowhead, labelled
«extend».

   ┌───────────────────────┐
   |    Borrow a Book      | – –«include»– ►┌───────────────────────┐
   └───────────────────────┘                | Verify Membership     |
                                            └───────────────────────┘

   ┌───────────────────────┐
   |    Return a Book      | ◄ –«extend»– – –┌──────────────────────┐
   └───────────────────────┘                 | Calculate Fine       |
                                             └──────────────────────┘
                                             (only if book is overdue)
```

Use «include» sparingly — only when a behaviour is genuinely reused by multiple use cases. Use «extend» only when the extension truly is optional and condition-dependent. Overusing these relationships creates cluttered diagrams that are harder to read than simple actor-to-use-case lines.

Example 4.6 Real-world application — School Canteen Ordering System

A school canteen system has three actors: Student (places orders), Canteen Staff (fulfils orders and manages the menu), and Admin (generates sales reports and manages staff accounts). The Use Case diagram below captures their interactions.

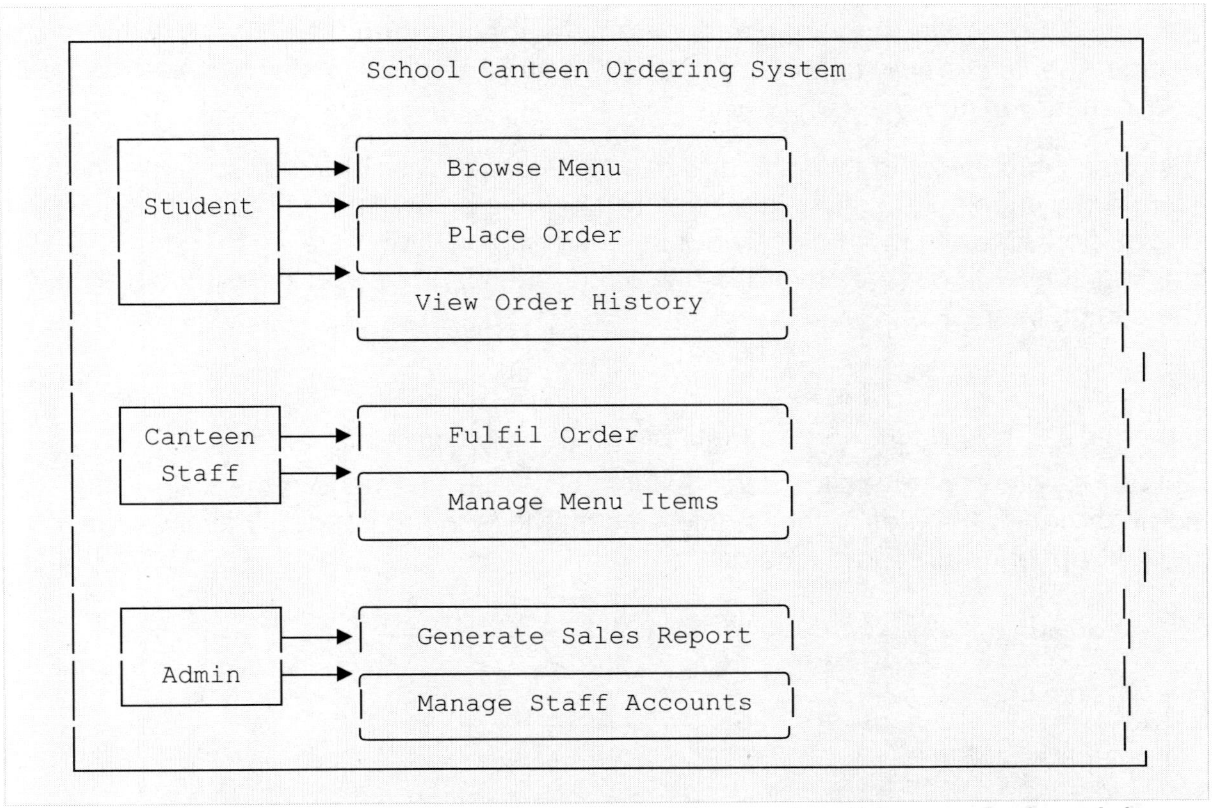

This Use Case diagram was drawn before any class or function was designed. It defines the scope of the system: what it does (eight use cases) and who uses it (three actors). Any feature not shown in this diagram is out of scope for the current version.

▶ **NOTE** Use Case diagrams define scope, not implementation. If a feature appears in a Use Case diagram, it must be implemented. If it does not appear, it is explicitly out of scope. Drawing this diagram early — and getting sign-off from the client or teacher — prevents scope creep later.

A Use Case diagram tells you what the system does. A Class diagram tells you how the system is structured to do it. The next two sections introduce Class diagrams: first for individual classes, then for the relationships between them.

3 Class Diagrams — Attributes, Methods, and Visibility

A Class diagram is the most commonly used UML diagram in object-oriented programming. It shows the structure of a program's classes: their names, the data they store (attributes), the actions they can perform (methods), and the relationships between them. A well-drawn Class diagram is the blueprint from which Python classes are written.

Each class in a Class diagram is represented as a rectangle divided into three horizontal compartments. The top compartment contains the class name, written in bold. The middle compartment lists the attributes (instance variables), each with its visibility symbol, name, and data type. The bottom compartment lists the methods, each with its visibility symbol, name, parameters, and return type. These three compartments correspond directly to the __init__ method, instance variables, and public methods of a Python class.

Visibility symbols control which parts of a class are accessible from outside. The four standard symbols are shown in the reference table below. In Python, visibility is a convention rather than an enforced rule, but mapping UML visibility to Python naming conventions (__private, _protected, public) produces code that behaves as the design intended.

Example 4.7 Introduction — A Single Class: BankAccount

This Class diagram models a bank account. The class name is in the top compartment, attributes in the middle, and methods in the bottom. Visibility symbols (+, -, #) appear before each member.

```
┌──────────────────────────────────────────────┐
│                 BankAccount                  │    ← Class name (top
compartment)
├──────────────────────────────────────────────┤
│  - __account_number : str                    │    ← private attribute
│  - __balance : float                         │    ← private attribute
│  # _owner : str                              │    ← protected
attribute
├──────────────────────────────────────────────┤
│  + __init__(number: str, owner: str)         │    ← public
constructor
│  + deposit(amount: float)                    │    ← public method (no
return)
│  + withdraw(amount: float) : bool            │    ← returns
True/False
│  + get_balance() : float                     │    ← getter (returns
float)
│  + get_owner() : str                         │    ← getter (returns
str)
│  - __validate_amount(amount: float) : bool   │    ← private helper
method
└──────────────────────────────────────────────┘

  Notation:  visibility  name  :  Type
  Method:    visibility  name(param : Type, ...)  : ReturnType
```

The double underscores on __account_number, __balance, and __validate_amount indicate Python name mangling (strong private). The single underscore on _owner indicates a protected attribute by convention. Methods with no return type listed (like deposit) return None in Python.

Example 4.8 Variation — Visibility Notation Reference

The four visibility symbols used in UML Class diagrams are standardised internationally. The table below shows each symbol, what it means, how it maps to Python naming conventions, and when to use it.

Symbol	Visibility	Meaning	Example
+	public	Accessible from any other class. Use for methods intended to be called from outside the class.	Methods: deposit(), get_balance()
-	private	Accessible only within the class itself. Use for attributes and helper methods not meant to be used externally.	Attributes: __balance, __pin
#	protected	Accessible within the class and any of its subclasses. Use for attributes intended to be inherited but not publicly exposed.	Attributes: _name, _id
~	package	Accessible to any class within the same package. Rarely used in Python; more common in Java and C#.	Uncommon in Python projects

When designing a class, a useful rule is: make attributes private by default and expose them only through methods. This is the principle of encapsulation, one of the four pillars of OOP introduced in Booklet 01. The UML visibility notation is the standard way to document and communicate encapsulation decisions.

Example 4.9 Real-world application — A Student Class for a School System

This Class diagram models a student record in a school management system. It includes validation logic (the private __validate_score method), computed properties (the public get_grade method that calculates a result from stored data), and a consistent naming convention that maps directly to Python.

```
Student
----------------------------------------------
- __student_id : str
- __name : str
- __year_level : int
- __scores : list
----------------------------------------------
+ __init__(id: str, name: str, year: int)
+ add_score(subject: str, score: float)
+ get_average() : float
+ get_grade() : str
+ get_name() : str
+ get_student_id() : str
+ display_report()
```

```
|  - __validate_score(score: float) : bool         |
|__________________________________________________|
```

Every attribute is private. Every method intended for external use is public. The single private method (__validate_score) is a helper called internally by add_score — it has no value to any caller outside the class. This design is immediately communicable to any programmer who reads the Class diagram, regardless of whether they know the Python details.

> ▶ **NOTE** Draw Class diagrams before writing the class in Python. The discipline of listing every attribute and method in advance prevents the most common OOP design error: discovering halfway through coding that you need to restructure the class because its responsibilities were not clearly defined at the start.

Individual class diagrams define what a class stores and does. Class diagrams become truly powerful when they show how classes relate to each other. The next section introduces class relationships.

4 Class Relationships — Inheritance, Association, and Multiplicity

No real object-oriented system consists of a single class in isolation. Classes are connected by relationships that express how they depend on, contain, or derive from each other. UML Class diagrams express these relationships with standardised line styles and arrowheads, each with a specific meaning.

The three relationships most relevant to student projects are: inheritance (one class derives from another), association (one class uses or knows about another), and composition (one class is made up of another). A fourth relationship — aggregation — is similar to composition but weaker, and is introduced alongside it for completeness.

Multiplicity annotations on association lines specify how many instances of one class are connected to instances of another. The notation 1 means exactly one; * means zero or more; 0..1 means zero or one; 1..* means one or more. Reading multiplicity correctly is essential to understanding the design: a Student has 0..* Enrolments, and each Enrolment belongs to exactly 1 Student and 1 Course.

Example 4.10 Introduction — Inheritance: A Bank Account Hierarchy

Inheritance in a Class diagram is shown as a solid line with an open triangle arrowhead pointing from the child class to the parent class. The open triangle means 'is a kind of': SavingsAccount is a kind of BankAccount; CheckingAccount is a kind of BankAccount.

```
                ┌──────────────────────────────────────┐
                │             BankAccount              │  ← Parent
(superclass)    │
                ├──────────────────────────────────────┤
```

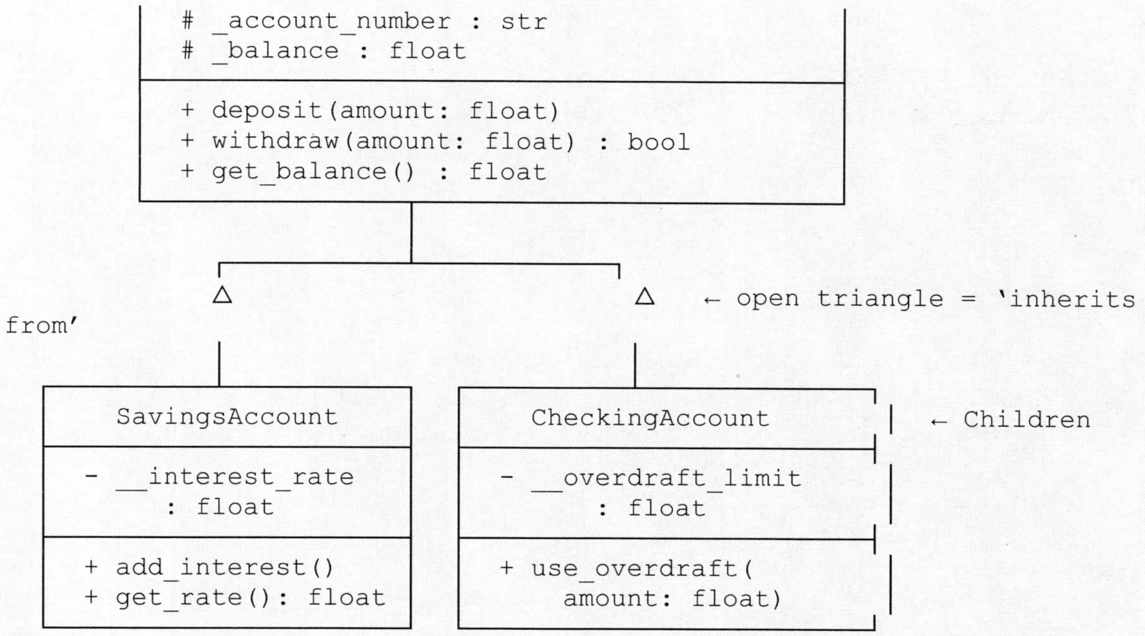

Both child classes inherit all attributes and methods from BankAccount — they do not need to redeclare them. Each child adds only what makes it unique: SavingsAccount adds an interest rate and a method to apply it; CheckingAccount adds an overdraft limit and a method to use it. This is the inheritance principle in UML and in Python.

Example 4.11 Variation — Association and Multiplicity

Association lines connect classes that use or reference each other without one being a subtype of the other. Multiplicity annotations (shown near each end of the line) specify how many instances participate in the relationship. Role labels (shown beside multiplicity) describe the meaning of the relationship.

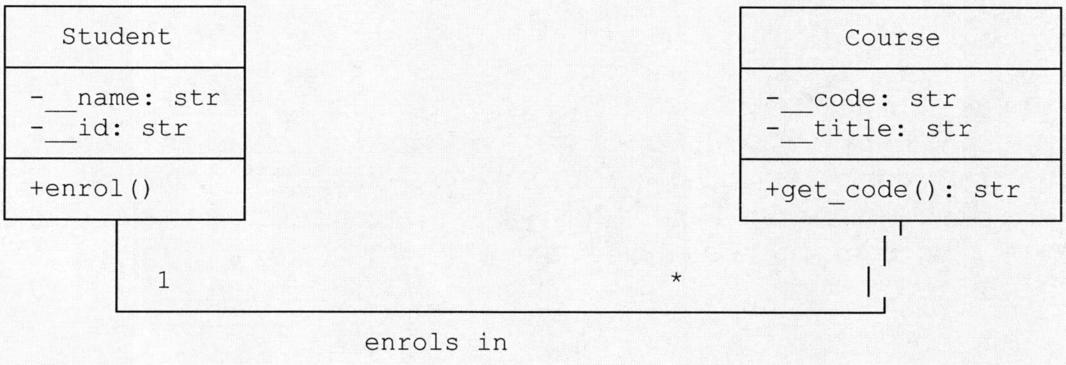


```
Read as:  One Student enrols in zero or more (*) Courses.
          One Course is taken by zero or more (*) Students.

Multiplicity quick reference:
  1      Exactly one
  *      Zero or more (also written 0..*)
  0..1   Zero or one (optional)
  1..*   One or more (at least one required)
```

```
    2..5   Between two and five (a specific range)
```

The multiplicity 1 at the Student end means each enrolment record belongs to exactly one Student. The * at the Course end means a Student can enrol in zero or more Courses. Reading both ends together gives the full relationship: one Student to many Courses.

Example 4.12 **Real-world application — A Library System Class Diagram**

This Class diagram shows four classes for a school library system, connected by inheritance and association relationships. Read each relationship line and its multiplicity carefully: they encode the system's data rules directly into the design.

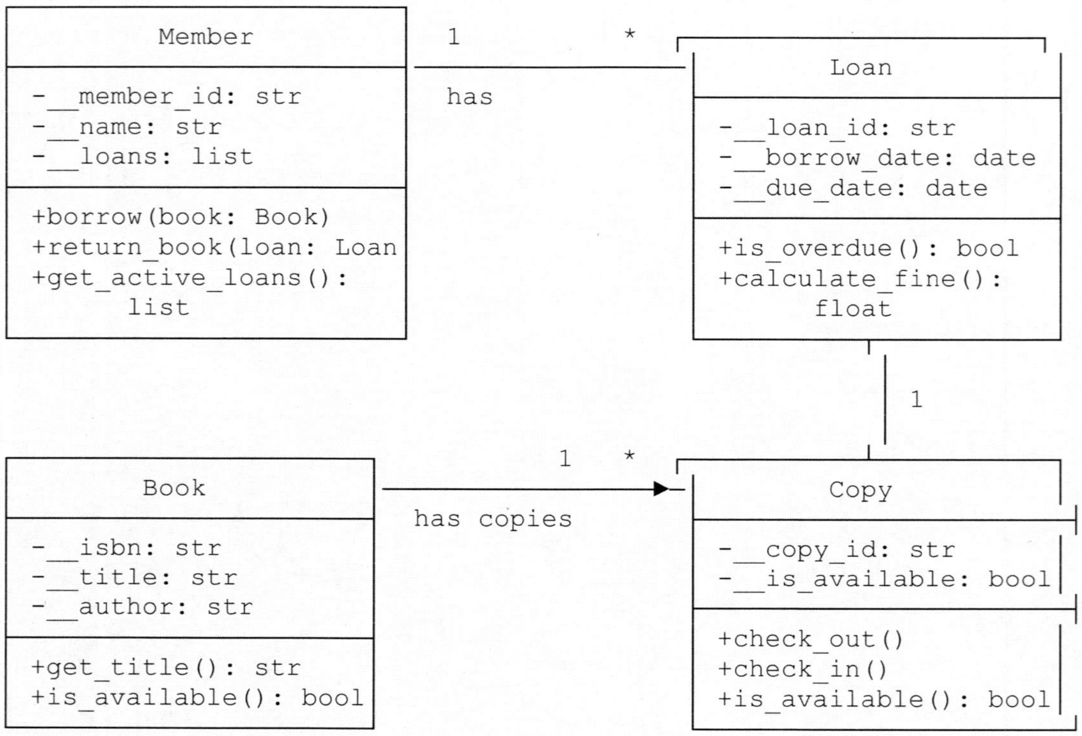

This diagram contains three associations: a Member has many Loans (1 to *); a Loan is for one Copy (1 to 1); a Book has many Copies (1 to *). Reading the diagram establishes the data rules: you cannot have a Loan without a Member and a Copy; a Copy is available only when it has no active Loan. These constraints will need to be enforced in the code — drawing the diagram first ensures they are identified before coding begins.

> ▶ **NOTE** Composition (filled diamond ◆) means the child cannot exist without the parent: a Line Item only exists as part of an Order. Aggregation (hollow diamond ◇) means the child can exist independently: a Student can exist without being enrolled in a Course. When in doubt, use a plain association line — it is always correct, even if it is less precise.

Class diagrams define structure. Sequence diagrams show how that structure is used at runtime: the order in which objects send messages to each other to accomplish a specific task. The next section introduces Sequence diagrams.

5 Sequence Diagrams

A Sequence diagram shows how a group of objects interact with each other over time to carry out a specific use case or operation. Where a Class diagram shows the static structure of a system, a Sequence diagram shows the dynamic behaviour — which object sends which message to which other object, in what order.

A Sequence diagram is read from top to bottom, in the order that events occur. Objects appear as boxes across the top of the diagram, each with a vertical dashed line called a lifeline running downward. Messages between objects are shown as horizontal arrows connecting their lifelines: a solid arrow with a filled head for a call (synchronous message), and a dashed arrow for a return. The label on each arrow is the name of the method being called, with any parameters.

Sequence diagrams are most valuable when you are designing a use case that involves several objects working together. Drawing the diagram forces you to identify which object is responsible for each action, and to determine the order of method calls before writing any code. This planning step frequently reveals missing methods, incorrect responsibilities, or circular dependencies that would be expensive to fix after the code exists.

Example 4.13 Introduction — A User Login Sequence

This Sequence diagram shows the interactions between three objects during a user login: the User (an actor), the LoginController (a Python class), and the UserDatabase (another class). Solid arrows are method calls; dashed arrows are returns.

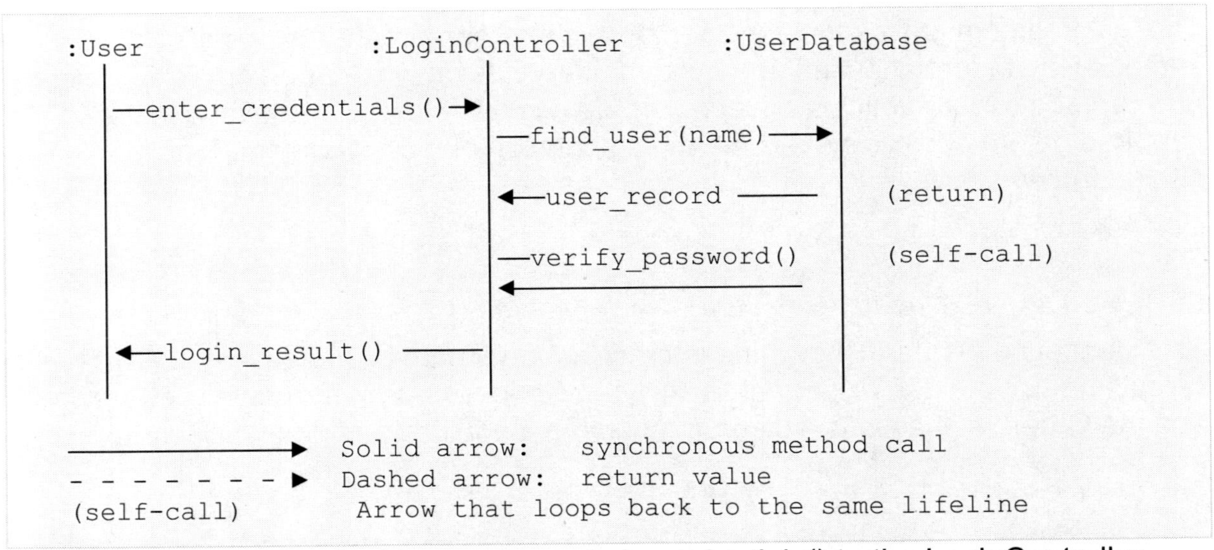

Reading this diagram: the User sends enter_credentials() to the LoginController. The controller calls find_user() on the UserDatabase and receives a user_record back. The controller then calls its own verify_password() method (a self-call). Finally, it returns login_result to the User. This sequence now defines exactly which methods each class needs: LoginController needs find_user() delegation and verify_password(); UserDatabase needs find_user().

Example 4.14 Variation — Conditional Messages and Alternative Paths

Sequence diagrams can show conditional execution using a combined fragment box labelled 'alt' (alternative) or 'opt' (optional). The alt fragment divides into sections separated by a dashed line, each guarded by a condition in square brackets. This is the Sequence diagram equivalent of an IF/ELSE structure.

```
:Student              :LibrarySystem              :Inventory
    |                         |                        |
    |—borrow(book_id)———►     |                        |
    |                         |—check_copy(book_id)►   |
    |                         |◄—copy_available ——     |
    |                         |                        |
    |              ╔══════════════════════════════╗
    |              ║ alt  [copy is available]     ║
    |              ║ ——————————————————————————   ║    |
    |              ║     |—create_loan()————————► ║    |
    |              ║     |◄—loan_record ————————  ║    |
    |◄—            ║     |                        ║    |
    |  'Loan       ║ ——————————————————————————   ║    |
    |  confirmed'  ║ [copy is NOT available]      ║    |
    |              ║ ——————————————————————————   ║    |
    |◄—            ║     |                        ║    |
    |  'No         ╚══════════════════════════════╝    |
    |  copies      |                     |
    |  available'  |                     |

  ╔═ alt ═╗  Combined fragment: one of two paths executes.
  ╔═ opt ═╗  Optional fragment: the section executes only if the
guard is true.
  ╔═ loop ═╗  Loop fragment: the section repeats while the guard is
true.
```

The 'alt' fragment makes the conditional logic explicit. A reader of this diagram immediately understands that the outcome depends on whether a copy is available, and can see exactly which messages are sent in each case. This level of detail, captured before coding, makes the implementation of LibrarySystem.borrow() straightforward.

Example 4.15 Real-world application — A Payment Processing Sequence

This Sequence diagram shows the interactions during an online payment. Four objects participate: the Customer (actor), the CheckoutForm, the PaymentGateway, and the OrderDatabase. The diagram captures the full sequence of calls, returns, and conditional outcomes.

```
:Customer     :CheckoutForm      :PaymentGateway     :OrderDatabase
    |               |                   |                  |
    |—submit_order()►|                  |                  |
    |               |—validate()———————►|                  |
```

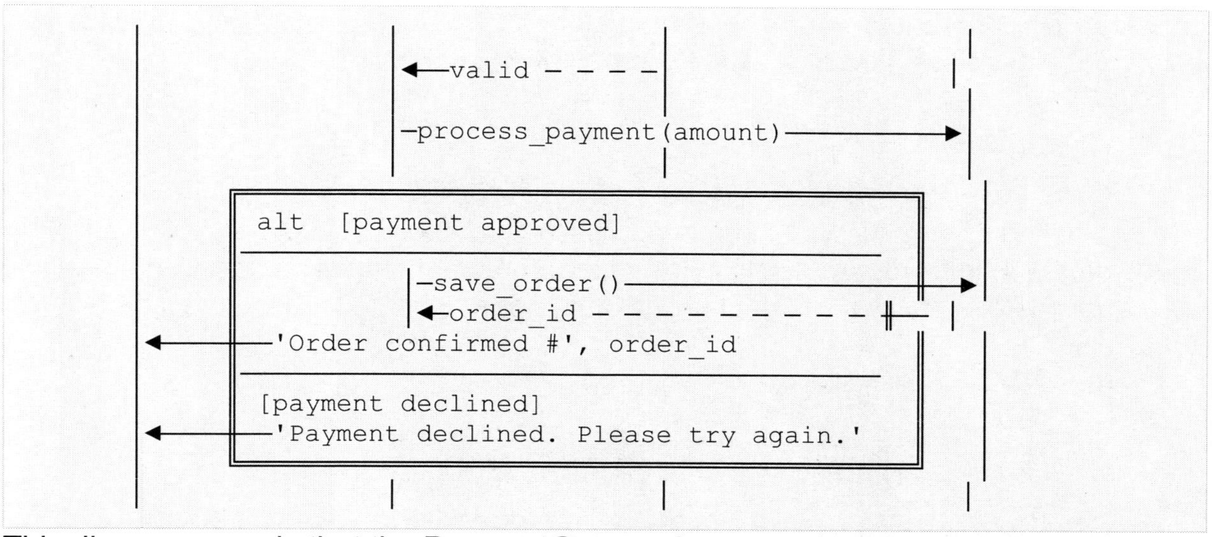

This diagram reveals that the PaymentGateway's process_payment() result determines which messages follow. If the diagram is accurate, the developer implementing CheckoutForm knows exactly which methods to call, in which order, and what to do with each return value. The sequence diagram has done the thinking before the coding begins.

> ▶ **NOTE** A Sequence diagram for a single use case should be readable in one glance — typically no more than 6 to 8 objects and 10 to 15 messages. If a diagram becomes unreadable, break the use case into smaller sub-operations and draw a separate diagram for each.

Sequence diagrams show how a single use case unfolds over time. Activity diagrams zoom out to model the workflow across an entire system or process, often involving multiple actors. The next section introduces Activity diagrams.

6 Activity Diagrams

An Activity diagram models the flow of behaviour through a system or process. It is similar to a flowchart — both use decision nodes and sequential flow — but Activity diagrams add two powerful features: swim lanes, which partition the diagram into columns showing which actor is responsible for each action, and fork/join bars, which show parallel activities that happen simultaneously.

The notation differs slightly from the flowchart symbols introduced in Chapter 3. An Activity diagram begins with a filled black circle (●) called the initial node, and ends with a filled circle inside a larger circle (◎) called the activity final node. Activities (the steps performed) are drawn as rounded rectangles rather than sharp-cornered ones. Decision nodes use the same diamond shape as flowcharts, but may have guard conditions in square brackets labelling each exit arrow.

Swim lanes are the feature that makes Activity diagrams especially valuable for multi-actor workflows. Each lane is a vertical (or horizontal) partition labelled with the name of the actor responsible for the activities inside it. Arrows that cross lane boundaries represent handoffs between actors, making it immediately clear who is responsible for each step and where the transitions occur.

Example 4.16 Introduction — A Simple Activity Diagram: User Login

This Activity diagram shows the login process without swim lanes, introducing the basic notation: initial node, activities as rounded rectangles, decisions as diamonds with guarded exit arrows, and the activity final node.

```
●    ← Initial node (filled circle)
│
╔══════════════════════════════╗
║  Display login form          ║   ← Activity (rounded rectangle)
╚══════════════════════════════╝
│
╔══════════════════════════════╗
║  Enter username & password   ║
╚══════════════════════════════╝
│
◇   ← Decision node
│  [credentials valid?]
│
├──── [YES] ────────────────────────────────┐
│                                           │
│  [NO]                                     │
▼                              ╔══════════════════════════════╗
                               ║ Grant access to dashboard    ║
╔══════════════════════════════╗╚══════════════════════════════╝
║  Display error message       ║            │
╚══════════════════════════════╝            │
│                                           │
◇   [attempts < 3?]                         │
│                                           │
├──── [YES, try again] ──────────(loop back)│
│                                           │
│  [NO, max attempts reached]               │
▼                                           │
╔══════════════════════════════╗            │
║  Lock account                ║            │
╚══════════════════════════════╝            │
│                                           │
└───────────────────────────────────────────┘
                              │
                              ◎   ← Activity final node
```

Guard conditions in square brackets ([credentials valid?], [attempts < 3?]) label the exit arrows of each decision node. This is more explicit than the YES/NO labels used in flowcharts and is particularly clear when the condition itself tells you what the branch means.

Example 4.17 Variation — Swim Lanes for a Multi-Actor Workflow

This Activity diagram uses swim lanes to show an order fulfilment process involving three actors: Customer, System, and Warehouse Staff. Arrows crossing lane boundaries represent handoffs between actors.

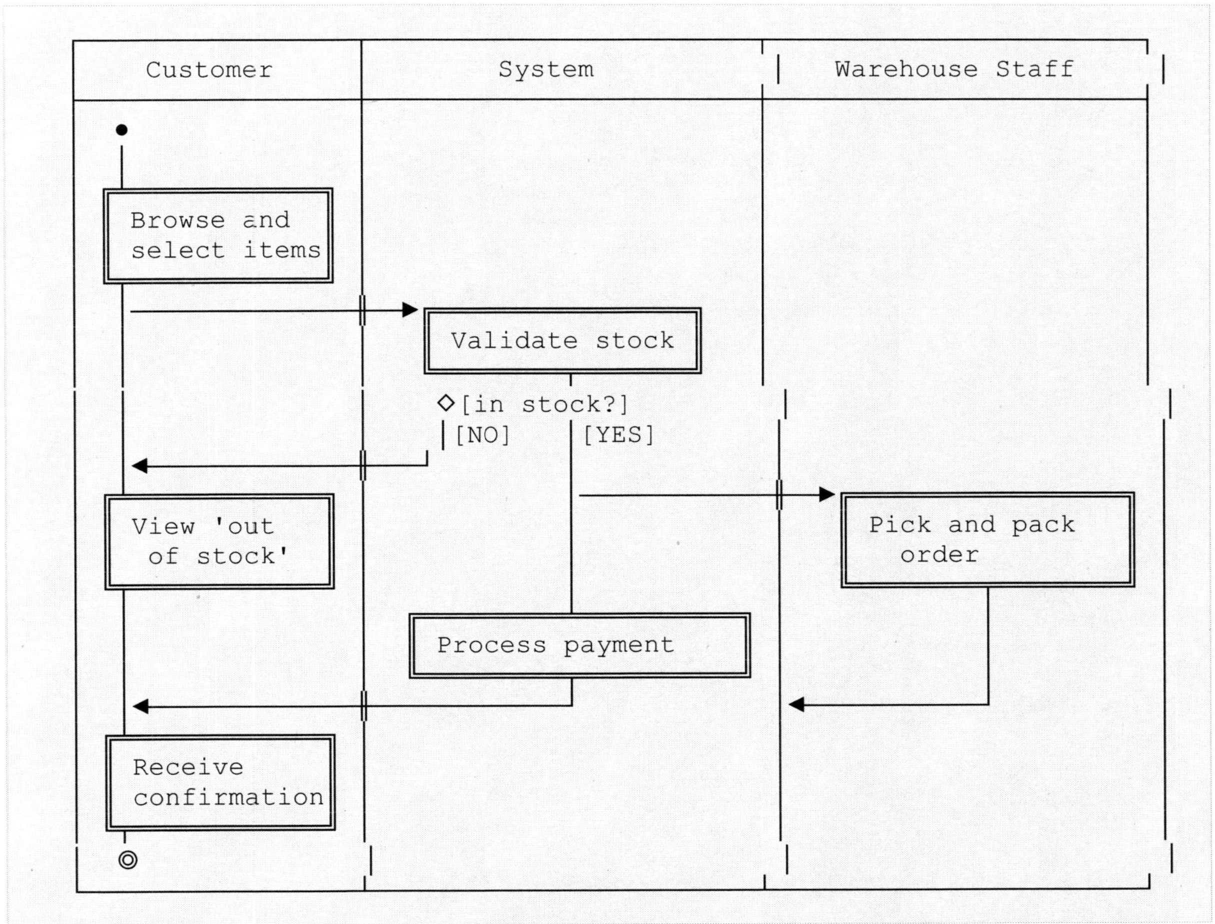

Swim lanes make actor responsibility unambiguous. The Customer browses, pays, and receives confirmation. The System validates stock and processes payment. The Warehouse Staff picks and packs. The arrows crossing lane boundaries show exactly when responsibility transfers from one actor to another.

Example 4.18 Real-world application — A School Enrolment Process

This Activity diagram models the school subject enrolment process with swim lanes for Student, Coordinator, and System. The fork bar (a thick horizontal line) at the top of the Coordinator's lane shows two activities that happen in parallel — checking prerequisites and checking class capacity — which then join before a decision is made.

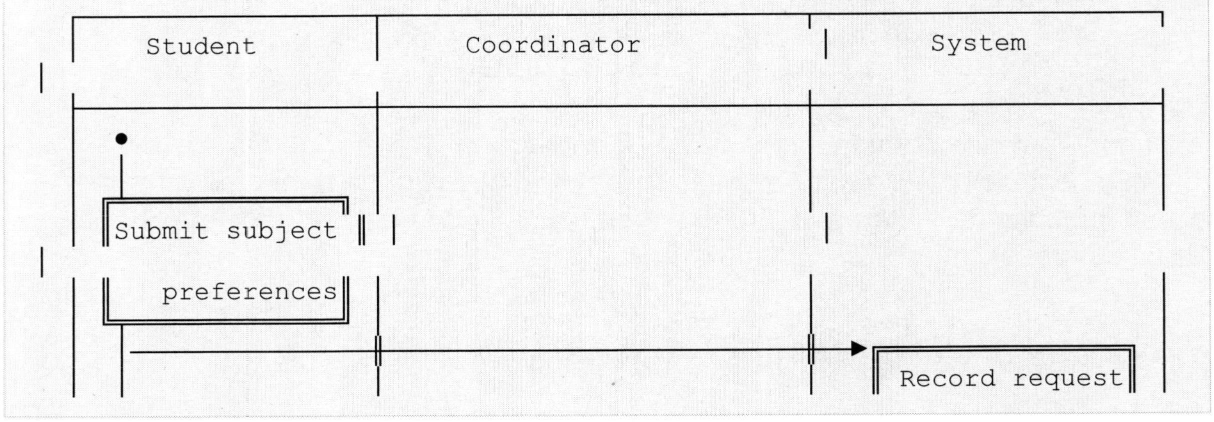

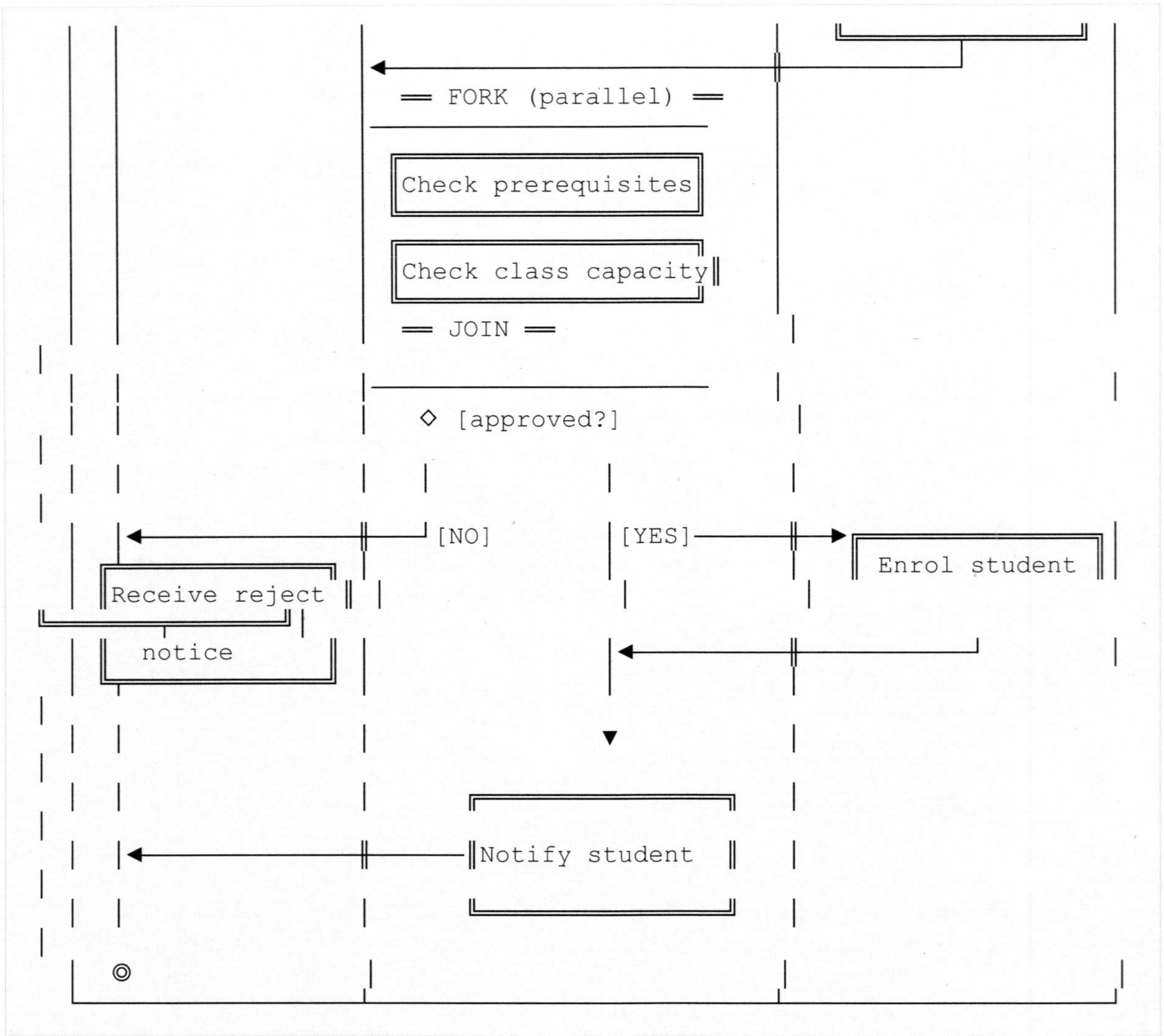

The fork bar (marked FORK) splits into two parallel activities that execute simultaneously. The join bar (marked JOIN) waits until both parallel activities have completed before the flow continues to the decision node. This notation is unique to Activity diagrams and is not available in standard flowcharts, making Activity diagrams the preferred tool for modelling concurrent workflows.

▶ **NOTE** Use swim lanes whenever more than one actor is involved in a workflow. The effort of partitioning the diagram into lanes is repaid immediately: responsibility for each activity is unambiguous, handoffs between actors are visible, and the diagram can be used to brief all stakeholders without requiring technical knowledge.

You now have the complete set of four UML diagram types. The final section steps back to consider how to use them practically — choosing the right diagrams for the right situations and integrating them into a design document that serves your project and your assessment.

7 Keeping UML Practical — Just Enough Modelling

UML has thirteen diagram types. No project requires all thirteen. No student project requires more than four. The discipline of 'just enough modelling' means drawing only the diagrams that provide genuine value for the current design decision, drawn to only the level of detail necessary to make that decision correctly.

The question to ask before drawing any UML diagram is: 'What decision does this diagram help me make, and will I make a better decision with it than without it?' If the answer is no — if the design is already clear without the diagram — skip it. If the answer is yes, draw it, but draw only what is needed. A Class diagram that shows five essential classes is more valuable than one that attempts to show fifteen classes with every attribute and method listed.

This pragmatic approach is not a shortcut. It is the approach used by experienced software designers, who know that an outdated, over-detailed diagram is worse than no diagram at all — because it creates false confidence that the design is documented when the documentation no longer matches the code.

Example 4.19 Introduction — A UML Diagram Selection Guide

```
  WHEN TO DRAW EACH DIAGRAM TYPE

  Use Case Diagram:
    ✓ At the very start of a project, before designing any classes
    ✓ When clarifying requirements with a client or teacher
    ✓ When determining the scope of the system
    ✗ Not needed for small scripts with a single user and a clear
purpose

  Class Diagram:
    ✓ Whenever you are building an OOP program with two or more classes
    ✓ Before writing a single Python class definition
    ✓ When planning which class owns which data and which methods
    ✗ Not needed for functional-style programs with no classes

  Sequence Diagram:
    ✓ When a use case involves three or more objects interacting
    ✓ When planning a complex method that delegates to other objects
    ✓ When you are unsure which class should be responsible for a step
    ✗ Not needed for simple operations that stay within one class

  Activity Diagram:
    ✓ When modelling a workflow with multiple actors or parallel
activities
    ✓ When a process has complex branching that a flowchart cannot show
clearly
    ✓ When presenting a system to a non-technical audience
    ✗ Not needed when a simpler flowchart or pseudocode is sufficient
```

Example 4.20 Variation — A Student Project Design Document

A well-structured design document for a Year 11 or 12 OOP project typically contains the following elements, in order. Each element answers a specific design question and provides evidence of planning for assessment purposes.

```
RECOMMENDED UML DESIGN DOCUMENT STRUCTURE

1. Problem Statement (plain English, 1 paragraph)
   – Restates the project requirements in your own words

2. Use Case Diagram
   – Identifies all actors and use cases
   – Defines the scope of the system

3. Class Diagram
   – Shows all classes with attributes, methods, and visibility
   – Shows relationships: inheritance, associations, multiplicity

4. Sequence Diagram(s)
   – One diagram per complex use case (not needed for trivial ones)
   – Shows which objects interact and in what order

5. Activity Diagram (if workflow is complex or multi-actor)
   – Shows the overall workflow with swim lanes if multiple actors

6. Pseudocode for Key Algorithms
   – Fills in the detail that UML diagrams leave abstract
   – Provides a direct template for the Python code

NOTE: For a simple project (1-2 classes, single actor), items 2 and 4
may be omitted. Always include items 3 and 6 for any OOP project.
```

Example 4.21 Real-world application — Translating a Class Diagram to Python

The final step in the UML design process is translating the Class diagram into Python. This translation is systematic: each element of the Class diagram maps directly to a Python construct. The diagram below shows this mapping for a simple Animal/Dog inheritance hierarchy.

UML Class Diagram

UML CLASS DIAGRAM:

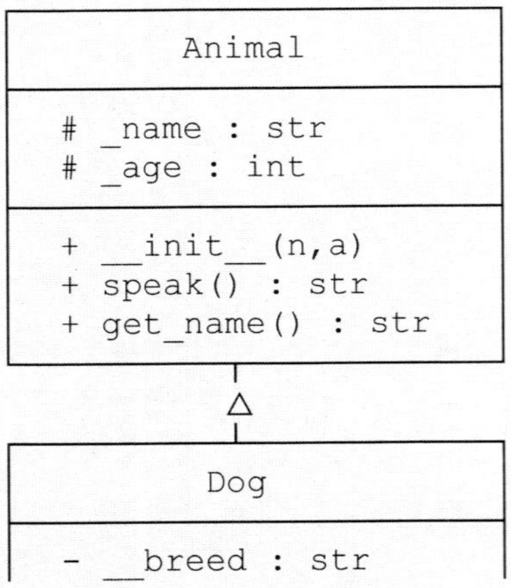

Python Translation

PYTHON CODE:

```
class Animal:
  def __init__(self,
               name, age):
    self._name = name
    self._age  = age

  def speak(self):
    return ''

  def get_name(self):
    return self._name

class Dog(Animal):  # △
  def __init__(self,
```

<pre>+ __init__(n,a,b)
+ speak() : str
+ get_breed(): str</pre>
	<pre> name, age,
	              breed):
	    super().__init__(
	          name, age)
	    self.__breed = breed
	
	  def speak(self):
	    return 'Woof!'
	
	  def get_breed(self):
	    return self.__breed</pre>

The mapping is direct and unambiguous. Protected attributes (__name, _age) become self._name and self._age in Python. Private attributes (__breed) become self.__breed. The inheritance arrow (△) maps to class Dog(Animal). The speak() method is overridden in Dog, as the Class diagram shows it defined in both classes. A programmer translating a well-drawn Class diagram into Python makes no design decisions during coding — all decisions were made when the diagram was drawn.

> ▶ **NOTE** Keep your UML diagrams and your Python code in sync. When you change the code, update the diagram. When you update the diagram, check the code. A design document that diverges from the code is worse than no document at all, because it misleads anyone who reads it about how the system actually works.

This chapter has introduced UML as a practical planning tool for object-oriented Python programs. The four diagram types — Use Case, Class, Sequence, and Activity — together describe what a system does, how it is structured, how it behaves, and who is responsible for each action. Chapter 5 addresses the structural design technique that precedes UML: decomposition and the construction of structure charts.

Chapter Summary

- UML (Unified Modelling Language) is an internationally standardised visual language for describing software systems. It is language-independent and universally readable by any programmer who knows its notation.
- Use Case diagrams capture what a system does from a user's perspective. Actors (external users or systems) connect to use cases (system behaviours) inside a system boundary rectangle. They are drawn first, before any class or code design.
- The «include» relationship indicates that one use case always executes another. The «extend» relationship indicates that one use case optionally adds behaviour to another under a specific condition.
- Class diagrams show the structure of an OOP program. Each class is drawn as a three-compartment rectangle: name, attributes (with visibility and type), and methods (with visibility, parameters, and return type).
- Visibility symbols are + (public), - (private), # (protected), and ~ (package). In Python these map to no prefix (public), double underscore (private/name-mangled), and single underscore (protected by convention).
- Class relationships include inheritance (solid line, open triangle pointing to parent), association (solid line, with multiplicity at each end), aggregation (hollow diamond at the whole end), and composition (filled diamond at the whole end).
- Sequence diagrams show how objects interact over time during a specific use case. Objects appear as boxes across the top; lifelines are vertical dashed lines; solid arrows are method calls; dashed arrows are returns. The 'alt' combined fragment models conditional message paths.
- Activity diagrams model workflows using rounded-rectangle activities, diamond decision nodes, fork/join bars for parallel activities, and swim lanes to partition responsibilities across multiple actors.

Guided Exercises

Complete all five exercises before moving on to Chapter 5. Use pencil and paper or a free UML tool such as draw.io for exercises requiring diagrams. Each exercise includes a hint to help you get started.

Exercise 1

Identify the correct UML diagram type for each of the following design questions: (a) 'Which classes does this program need, and how do they relate to each other?'; (b) 'What can a Student do with this system?'; (c) 'In what order do objects send messages during a login?'; (d) 'Who is responsible for each step in the order fulfilment process, and does anything happen in parallel?'

Hint: Refer to the UML diagram types table in Section 1. Match each question to the diagram type that explicitly answers it: structure, requirements, interaction, or workflow.

Exercise 2

Draw a Use Case diagram for a simple ATM system. The system has two actors: Customer and Bank Technician. Customers can check their balance, withdraw cash, deposit cash, and change their PIN. Bank Technicians can restock cash and view system logs. Include a system boundary labelled 'ATM System'.

Hint: Draw the system boundary rectangle first. Place Customer and Bank Technician as actor boxes outside the boundary. Add each use case as an oval inside the boundary. Connect each actor to the use cases they participate in.

Exercise 3

Draw a Class diagram for a Rectangle class. It must have two private attributes (width: float and height: float), a public constructor that takes width and height as parameters, and three public methods: area() returning float, perimeter() returning float, and is_square() returning bool. Show all visibility symbols, attribute types, and method return types.

Hint: Use the three-compartment box. In the middle compartment, write each attribute as: - attribute_name : Type. In the bottom compartment, write each method as: + method_name(params) : ReturnType. The constructor has no return type.

Exercise 4

Draw a Class diagram showing an inheritance relationship between a Vehicle parent class and two child classes: Car and Motorcycle. Vehicle should have protected attributes for make, model, and year, and a public method start_engine(). Car adds a private doors attribute and a public open_boot() method. Motorcycle adds a private sidecar attribute and a public pop_wheelie() method. Show the inheritance relationship correctly.

Hint: Draw Vehicle first. Then draw Car and Motorcycle below it. Connect each child to the parent with a solid line and an open triangle arrowhead (△) pointing toward Vehicle. Children inherit all parent members — do not repeat them in the child boxes.

Exercise 5

Draw a Sequence diagram for the following scenario: A Customer calls place_order() on a ShoppingCart object. The ShoppingCart calls check_stock(item_id) on an Inventory object. Inventory returns True if the item is in stock. If in stock, ShoppingCart calls process_payment(amount) on a PaymentService. PaymentService returns a transaction_id. ShoppingCart then returns an order_confirmation to the Customer. Use an 'alt' combined fragment to show what happens if the item is not in stock (output an 'Out of stock' message to the Customer).

Hint: List the four objects (:Customer, :ShoppingCart, :Inventory, :PaymentService) as boxes across the top with vertical lifelines. Draw solid arrows for calls and dashed arrows for returns, left to right in time order. Wrap the conditional section in an 'alt' fragment box.

Challenge Tasks

These tasks have no hints. They require independent thinking and are suitable for extension or assessment. Complete the Guided Exercises before attempting these.

Challenge Task 1

Produce a complete UML design document for a simple hotel booking system. Your document must include: (a) a Use Case diagram with at least two actors (Guest and Receptionist) and at least six use cases; (b) a Class diagram with at least four classes (such as Guest, Room, Booking, and Payment) showing all attributes with visibility and type, all methods with visibility and return type, and at least one inheritance relationship and two associations with multiplicity; (c) a Sequence diagram for the 'Make a Booking' use case, showing interactions between at least three objects.

Challenge Task 2

A fellow student has submitted a Class diagram with the following errors: a class named 'do_stuff' (no capitalisation, vague name); attributes listed without visibility symbols or types; a method named 'function1' with no parameters or return type listed; an inheritance arrow drawn with a filled triangle instead of an open one; and the multiplicity on an association reading 'many' instead of using UML notation. Identify and explain each error precisely, state what rule it violates, and produce a corrected version of the Class diagram for a realistic class that the student might have intended to model.

Challenge Task 3

Design a complete Activity diagram with swim lanes for the process of publishing a student assignment through an online learning management system (LMS). The process involves four actors: Student (drafts and submits the assignment), Teacher (reviews and marks), System (automatically checks for plagiarism and records grades), and Admin (resolves any disputes and manages the gradebook). Include at least one parallel activity using fork/join notation, at least two decision nodes with guarded exit arrows, and correct use of initial and activity final nodes. Annotate the diagram to explain any design decisions that are not self-evident from the notation.

Decomposition and Structured Design

> This chapter introduces decomposition: the discipline of breaking a large problem into smaller, independently solvable pieces. You will learn how to apply top-down design and stepwise refinement, how to document a decomposed design using structure charts, and how to translate those charts directly into Python function hierarchies. The chapter also introduces two fundamental software design principles — cohesion and coupling — that determine whether a decomposition produces clean, maintainable code or a tangled collection of functions that are hard to test, understand, and modify.

1 What Decomposition Is and Why It Matters

Decomposition is the process of breaking a complex problem into a set of smaller, simpler sub-problems, each of which can be understood, designed, and solved independently. It is the single most important structural skill in programming — the discipline that separates a wall of inscrutable code from a program that any competent programmer can read, maintain, and extend.

A function that does one thing can be read in isolation. Its name tells you what it does; its parameters tell you what it needs; its return value tells you what it produces. A function that does ten things requires you to understand all ten things simultaneously before you can understand any of them. Decomposition makes each piece understandable on its own.

The benefits of decomposition extend beyond readability. A function that does one thing can be tested independently, with known inputs and expected outputs, without having to set up the entire program. It can be reused in different contexts without modification. When a bug is found, it can be isolated to one function rather than searched for across hundreds of lines of mixed logic. Every benefit of good software design flows, directly or indirectly, from decomposition.

Example 5.1 Introduction — A Wall of Code vs a Decomposed Design

The contrast below shows the same program written as one monolithic function on the left, and decomposed into focused functions on the right. Both programs do the same thing. Only one of them is maintainable.

✗ Everything in one function

✗ Monolithic (hard to maintain):

```
def run_program():
  records = []
  try:
    f = open('students.csv')
```

✓ Each function does one thing

✓ Decomposed (easy to maintain):

```
def main():
  records = load_records(
              'students.csv')
  display_all(records)
```

```
    for line in f:
      parts = line.strip()
                 .split(',')
      if len(parts) == 3:
        records.append({
         'name': parts[0],
         'score': float(
                   parts[1]),
         'grade': parts[2]
        })
    f.close()
  except FileNotFoundError:
    print('File not found')
    return
  # ... 80 more lines of
  # display, search, save ...
```

```
  name = input('Search: ')
  result = search(
              records, name)
  save_records(records,
               'students.csv')

def load_records(filename):
  ... # one job only

def display_all(records):
  ... # one job only

def search(records, name):
  ... # one job only

def save_records(r, fname):
  ... # one job only
```

The decomposed version on the right has a main() function that reads like a plain-English description of the program: load the records, display them, search, save. Each detail is hidden inside a named function. To understand how searching works, you read search(). You do not have to read the entire program.

Example 5.2 **Variation — The Assembly Line Analogy**

A car assembly line is a physical decomposition. Each station does one task — fit the engine, paint the body, install the glass — and passes the partially complete car to the next station. No station does everything; every station does its one task well. The result is consistent, testable, and efficient: if the paint station produces defective cars, you fix the paint station without touching any other station.

A well-decomposed program works the same way. Each function is a station: it receives its inputs, does its one job, and passes results to the next function. If the load_records() function produces incorrect data, you fix load_records() without touching display_all() or search(). Decomposition is the assembly-line principle applied to code.

Example 5.3 **Real-world application — How Professional Software Is Structured**

Every major software system in professional use is decomposed across multiple levels. A web application decomposes into layers (presentation, business logic, data access). Each layer decomposes into modules. Each module decomposes into classes. Each class decomposes into methods. At every level, the same principle applies: each component has a single, clear responsibility.

Python's own standard library demonstrates this at scale. The csv module handles only CSV reading and writing. The os module handles only operating system interactions. The json module handles only JSON serialisation. Each module is named for exactly what it does, and does exactly what it is named for. When you write Python programs, you are building on a library that embodies decomposition at every level.

> ▶ **NOTE** The simplest test for decomposition quality is the function name test: if you can describe what a function does in one short sentence without using the word 'and', it is probably well decomposed. If you find yourself writing 'loads the data and validates it and displays the header', that function does three jobs and should become three functions.

Knowing that decomposition is valuable is the first step. Knowing how to do it — where to draw the lines, how fine-grained to go, in what order to think about the pieces — is the skill. The next section introduces the systematic approach: top-down design with stepwise refinement.

2 Top-Down Design and Stepwise Refinement

Top-down design is the practice of starting with the whole problem and progressively dividing it into parts. You begin with a single statement of what the program must do — the highest level of abstraction — and then identify the major steps that, taken together, accomplish that goal. Each step is then refined into its own sub-steps, and so on, until every step is simple enough to be directly implemented as a short Python function.

Stepwise refinement is the technique of adding detail one level at a time. At the first refinement pass, you identify the three to seven major tasks that make up the program. At the second pass, you refine each of those tasks into its own sub-tasks. At the third pass, you refine any sub-tasks that are still too complex to code directly. You stop refining when every task is simple enough that a competent programmer could implement it from the description alone in ten to twenty lines of code.

The key discipline is to refine one level at a time. Resist the urge to jump straight from a high-level task ('display all records') to implementation details ('iterate through the list using enumerate and format each field with f-strings'). That jump skips the design level that produces reusable, testable code. Work level by level, and the structure emerges naturally.

Example 5.4 **Introduction — Three Passes of Stepwise Refinement**

This example shows three passes of refinement for a grade report program. Each pass adds one level of detail without worrying about the levels below.

```
PASS 1 — The whole program in one sentence:
  Produce a grade report for a class of students.

PASS 2 — The major tasks (first refinement):
  1. Load student data from a file
  2. Calculate each student's grade from their scores
  3. Display the grade report
  4. Save the report to a file

PASS 3 — Refine each task (second refinement):
```

```
1. Load student data from a file
   1a. Open the file and handle file-not-found errors
   1b. Read each line and parse it into name and scores
   1c. Return the list of student records

2. Calculate each student's grade from their scores
   2a. Calculate the average of the student's scores
   2b. Determine the grade band from the average
   2c. Return the grade string

3. Display the grade report
   3a. Print a formatted header
   3b. For each student: print name, average, grade
   3c. Print a summary (class average, highest, lowest)

4. Save the report to a file
   4a. Open the output file for writing
   4b. Write the report lines to the file
   4c. Close the file
```

Each item in Pass 3 is now simple enough to implement as a short function. The refinement has produced a clear, hierarchical design with no ambiguity about what each part must do.

Example 5.5 **Variation — Knowing When to Stop Refining**

Stepwise refinement stops when every item in the current pass meets two criteria: it can be described in one clear sentence without using 'and'; and a competent programmer could implement it directly without further planning. These are the 'leaf' tasks of the decomposition — the tasks that map directly to functions.

```
STOP REFINING when a task is:
  ✓ Described by a single clear verb phrase
  ✓ Small enough for 10-20 lines of Python code
  ✓ Independent enough to test with known inputs and outputs

KEEP REFINING when a task:
  ✗ Requires 'and' to describe ('read the file AND validate each
line')
  ✗ Would need more than 30 lines to implement cleanly
  ✗ Mixes concerns (e.g., input, calculation, and output in one step)

EXAMPLES:
  ✓ 'Open the file and return its contents as a list of lines.'
    → Clear, small, testable. Stop here.

  ✗ 'Load the file, validate each record, compute averages,
     and write a summary report.'
    → Four jobs in one. Refine into four separate tasks.
```

Example 5.6 **Real-world application — Decomposing a Canteen Ordering System**

A school canteen ordering system is decomposed top-down in three passes. The first pass identifies the four major operations. The second pass reveals that order processing has enough internal complexity to warrant further subdivision. The third pass produces leaf tasks that map directly to Python functions.

```
LEVEL 0:  Canteen Ordering System

LEVEL 1:  1. Manage menu items
          2. Process a customer order
          3. Generate daily sales report
          4. Handle end-of-day close

LEVEL 2 (refining Level 1.2 only — most complex):
          2. Process a customer order
             2a. Display available menu items
             2b. Accept item selections from customer
             2c. Apply any applicable discounts
             2d. Calculate the order total (including GST)
             2e. Record the order in the day's transaction log
             2f. Display the receipt

Each of 2a–2f is now a leaf task:
  display_menu(items)              ← one job: display only
  accept_order(items)              ← one job: input only
  apply_discount(order)            ← one job: calculation only
  calculate_total(order)           ← one job: calculation only
  record_transaction(order, log)   ← one job: data storage only
  print_receipt(order)             ← one job: output only
```

Notice that display_menu(), accept_order(), and print_receipt() are all separated even though they all involve output or interaction. Each does a different thing for a different reason: separating them makes each independently testable and independently modifiable.

> ▶ **NOTE** When you first attempt top-down design, it is common to produce only two levels before running out of ideas. Push for a third level. The most common decomposition error is stopping too early — producing tasks that are still too large to implement cleanly. If a task would take more than 20 lines of Python, refine it further.

Top-down design with stepwise refinement produces a hierarchy of tasks. A structure chart is the standard diagram for documenting and communicating that hierarchy. The next section introduces structure charts.

3 Structure Charts and Hierarchy Diagrams

A structure chart is a diagram that shows the hierarchical decomposition of a program into modules. Each box represents one module (function or procedure); lines connect parent modules to the child modules they call; and small annotations on the connecting lines show what data passes between modules. A structure chart makes the architecture of a program visible at a glance, in a way that neither pseudocode nor flowcharts can achieve.

Structure charts were formalised as part of structured systems analysis and design in the 1970s and remain in use today, particularly as a teaching tool and as a way to communicate system architecture to team members who do not write code. The notation is simple enough to sketch on paper in minutes, yet precise enough to serve as a specification for implementation.

The relationship shown by a connecting line in a structure chart is always the same: the module above calls the module below. The top module is called by the runtime environment (it is the main function). Modules at the same level are siblings — they do not call each other; they are each called by their shared parent. Data passes between modules through parameters (downward on the line) and return values (upward on the line).

Example 5.7 **Introduction — Structure Chart Notation**

The notation used in structure charts is small but precise. The reference below defines every symbol used in the structure charts throughout this chapter.

```
  STRUCTURE CHART NOTATION

   ┌───────────────────────┐
   │     module_name       │     MODULE (FUNCTION)
   └───────────────────────┘     A rectangle represents one function or
procedure.
                                 The name should describe exactly what it does.

                 │               CONNECTION LINE
                 │               A vertical line from parent to child means
                 │               'the parent module calls the child module.'
                 │               Arrows are not used — the hierarchy implies
direction.

         name ⇓                  DATA COUPLE — parameter passed DOWN
                 │               A label beside the line with a down-arrow
shows
                 │               data passed from parent to child as a
parameter.

         name ⇑                  DATA COUPLE — return value passed UP
                 │               A label beside the line with an up-arrow shows
                 │               data returned from child to parent.

         o — — —                 LOOP MARKER
                 │               A small open circle on the connection line
indicates
                 │               the child module is called repeatedly (in a
loop).

         ◇ — — —                 CONDITIONAL MARKER
                                 A small diamond on the connection line
indicates
                                 the child module is called only under certain
conditions.
```

Example 5.8 Variation — A Three-Level Structure Chart for a Grade Calculator

This structure chart documents the grade calculator decomposition from Section 2. Each box corresponds to one function; the lines show the call hierarchy; the annotations show what data flows between them. Read from the top down to understand which module calls which.

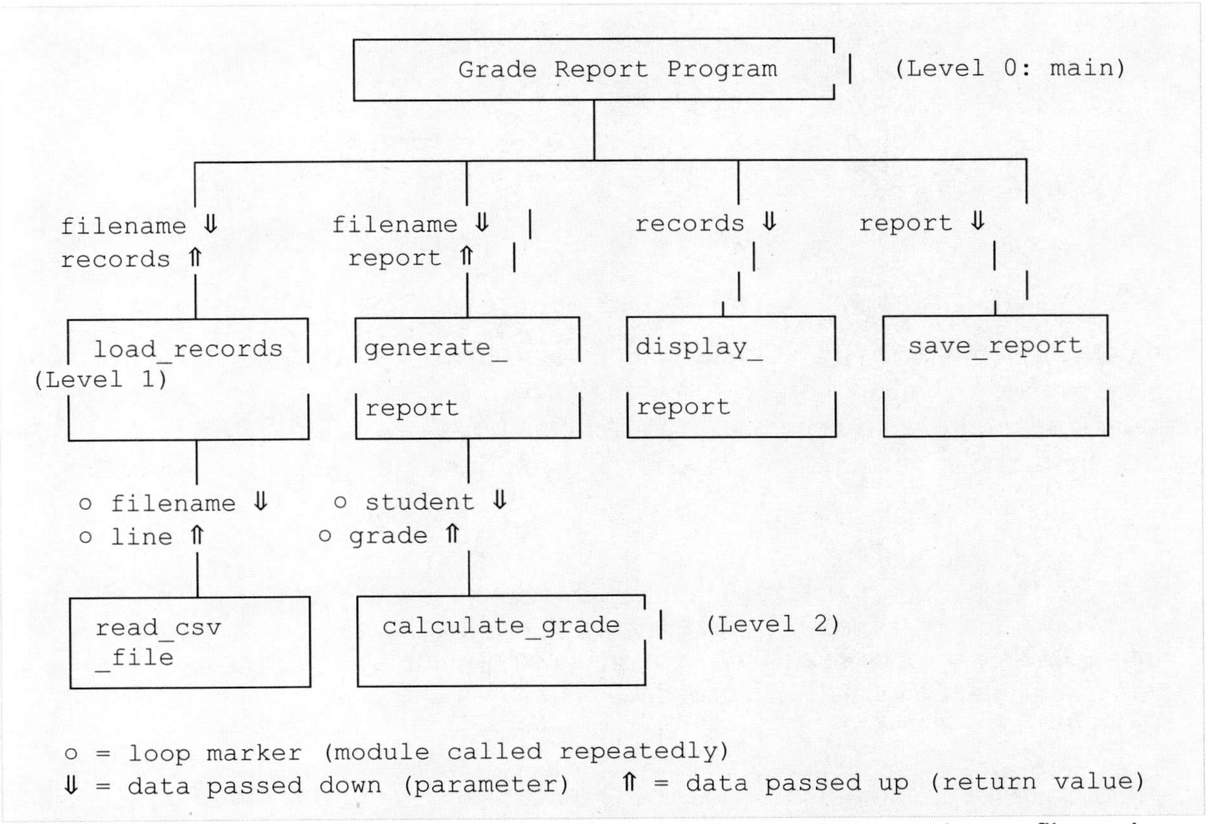

The loop markers (○) on the connections from load_records to read_csv_file and from generate_report to calculate_grade indicate that these calls happen inside a loop — once for each line in the file, and once for each student, respectively.

Example 5.9 Real-world application — Library Borrowing System Structure Chart

This structure chart documents a library borrowing system. Notice that the structure chart shows WHAT each module does and WHAT data flows between them, but says nothing about HOW each module does its job. The 'how' belongs in pseudocode and in the Python implementation.

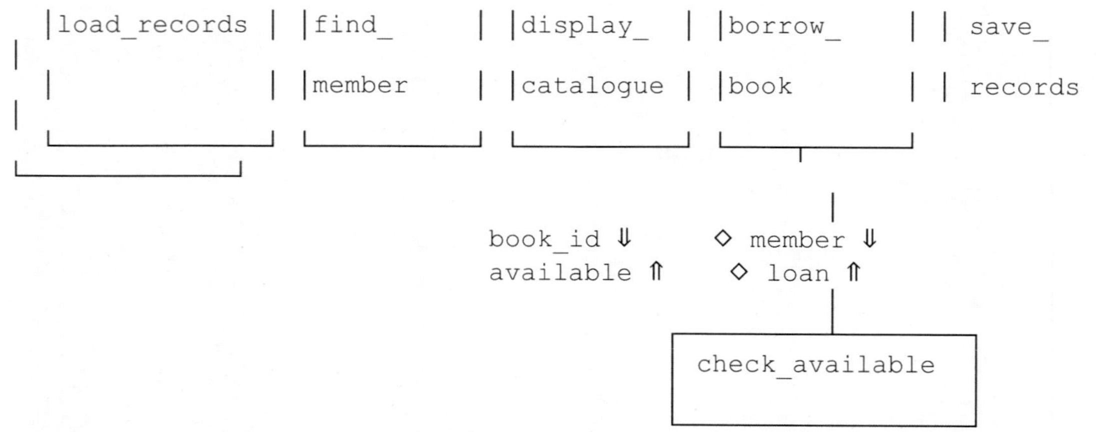

◇ = conditional marker (module called only if copy is available)

The conditional marker (◇) on the connections from borrow_book to check_available and the implicit conditional on the loan creation (only if available = True) reflects the business rule: a book can only be borrowed if a copy is available. The structure chart makes this conditionality visible without specifying how the check is implemented.

> ▶ **NOTE** A structure chart is read from top to bottom (hierarchy) and left to right at each level (order of operations, where relevant). It is normal for some modules to appear on only one side of a chart — structure charts are trees, not balanced diagrams. Let the structure follow the problem, not the page.

A structure chart documents the design. The next section shows how to translate it directly into Python function definitions and calls.

4 From Structure Chart to Python Functions

The translation from a structure chart to Python is one of the most direct mappings in program design. Each box in the structure chart becomes one Python function. Each connecting line becomes a function call inside the parent module. Each data couple with a downward arrow becomes a parameter in the function signature. Each data couple with an upward arrow becomes a return value.

This directness is not a coincidence — structure charts were designed with this mapping in mind. If a structure chart is drawn correctly, a programmer can write the function signatures (names, parameters, return types) for the entire program without writing a single line of logic. The signatures come from the chart; the logic comes from the pseudocode; the structure chart and pseudocode together fully specify the implementation.

One common mistake is to add function calls inside a module that are not shown in the structure chart. If function A calls function B, that call should appear as a line in the structure chart between A and B. A structure chart that does not match the code is no longer a useful design document. Keep them synchronised.

Example 5.10 Introduction — Direct Mapping: Box to Function

The table below shows how each element of a structure chart maps to Python. This mapping is systematic and applies consistently to any structure chart drawn following the notation in Section 3.

```
  STRUCTURE CHART ELEMENT → PYTHON EQUIVALENT

  Box:           module_name              def module_name(...):
                                              ...

  Downward    filename ⇓                    def load_records(filename):
  data couple                                   ...  # filename is a parameter

  Upward      records ⇑                     def load_records(filename):
  data couple                                   ...  # records is the return
value
                                                return records

  Connection                                def main():
  line:             main                        records =
load_records('f.csv')

                                            def load_records(filename):
             load_records                       ...

  Loop        o filename ⇓                  for line in lines:
  marker:                                       record = parse_line(line)
             parse_line

  Conditional ◇ member ⇓                    if is_member_valid(member_id):
  marker:                                      loan = create_loan(member)
             create_loan
```

Example 5.11 Variation — Writing Function Signatures from Data Couple Annotations

Given a structure chart, you can write all function signatures before writing any logic. The signatures define the interface between modules — what each function promises to accept and what it promises to deliver.

```
  From the Grade Report structure chart (Section 3, Example 5.8):

  Module          Parameters          Returns        Python signature
  ______________  __________________  _____________  _____________________

  main            (none)              (none)         def main():
  load_records    filename            records        def
load_records(filename):
```

```
  read_csv_file   filename           line(s)       def
read_csv_file(filename):
  generate_report records            report        def
generate_report(records):
  calculate_grade student            grade         def
calculate_grade(student):
  display_report  report             (none)        def
display_report(report):
  save_report     report, filename   (none)        def
save_report(report, fname):

  These seven signatures fully specify the program's interface.
  Each function's logic can be written (and tested) independently.
```

With function signatures defined, a team of programmers could divide the implementation: one person writes and tests load_records() while another writes calculate_grade(), and both can work simultaneously because the interface between them is already agreed in the structure chart.

Example 5.12 Real-world application — A Complete Grade Calculator in Python Structure

The structure below shows the complete Python function skeleton derived from the structure chart in Section 3. Each function has its signature, a docstring describing its single responsibility, and a placeholder for the implementation. The structure itself — which functions exist, what they accept, and what they return — comes entirely from the structure chart.

```
  def main():
      """Entry point. Orchestrates the grade report workflow."""
      records = load_records('students.csv')
      report  = generate_report(records)
      display_report(report)
      save_report(report, 'report.txt')

  def load_records(filename):
      """Read student data from CSV. Returns a list of record dicts."""
      lines = read_csv_file(filename)
      return [parse_line(line) for line in lines]

  def read_csv_file(filename):
      """Open filename and return its non-empty lines as a list."""
      ...

  def generate_report(records):
      """Calculate grade for each student. Returns a list of report
lines."""
      return [calculate_grade(s) for s in records]

  def calculate_grade(student):
      """Return a formatted grade string for one student dict."""
      ...

  def display_report(report):
```

```
        """Print all report lines to the screen with a formatted
header."""
        ...

    def save_report(report, filename):
        """Write all report lines to filename."""
        ...
```

Every function has exactly one job. main() orchestrates but does not implement. load_records() coordinates reading and parsing but delegates each step. The skeleton is ready for implementation — and ready for testing, because every function has a defined interface.

> ▶ **NOTE** Write function signatures and docstrings before writing the function bodies. This forces you to commit to the interface before the implementation. If you cannot write a clear, one-sentence docstring, the function's purpose is not yet clear enough. Clarify the design before writing the logic.

Decomposition produces a hierarchy of functions. The quality of that hierarchy depends on two principles: cohesion (how focused each function is) and coupling (how dependent functions are on each other). The next two sections introduce these principles in detail.

5 Cohesion — Designing Modules That Do One Thing Well

Cohesion measures how well the internal elements of a module belong together — how focused and unified its purpose is. A highly cohesive module does one thing and does it completely. A weakly cohesive module does several unrelated things, or several related things that would be better separated. High cohesion is always the goal.

The classic test for cohesion is the 'and' test: try to describe what a function does in one sentence without using the word 'and'. A function that 'calculates the average of a list of scores' passes. A function that 'reads the input file and validates the data and calculates the average and writes the report' fails three times. Each 'and' represents a missed decomposition opportunity.

Seven levels of cohesion have been formally identified, ranging from coincidental cohesion (the worst, where a module's contents have no logical relationship) to functional cohesion (the best, where a module does exactly one thing). The table below summarises all seven. In practice, aim for functional or sequential cohesion and avoid logical and coincidental cohesion entirely.

Example 5.13 Introduction — The Seven Levels of Cohesion

Cohesion Level	Quality	Description and example
✓✓ Functional	Best	The module does exactly one well-defined task and does it completely. Every line of code contributes directly to that single purpose. Example: calculate_average(scores) — computes and returns an average, nothing else.
✓ Sequential	Good	The output of one part of the module is the input to the next part. The steps are tightly related in sequence. Example: read_and_parse_file(filename) — reads the file and immediately parses it; parsing cannot happen without reading.
✓ Communicational	Good	All parts of the module operate on the same data. Example: display_student_report(student) — all output operations use data from the same student object.
✓ Procedural	Fair	Parts are grouped because they follow a specific procedural order (initialise, then check, then process), but are not otherwise related. The grouping is sequential in time, not in data flow.
✗ Temporal	Weak	Parts are grouped because they execute at the same time (e.g., all startup tasks in one function, all shutdown tasks in another). The tasks are unrelated except by timing.
✗ Logical	Weak	Parts perform similar types of operations (e.g., a function that handles all input operations), selected by a parameter. The module does different things depending on a flag passed to it.
✗✗ Coincidental	Worst	Parts are grouped arbitrarily with no logical relationship. Example: utilities() — prints the header, validates a score, and saves the file. These tasks have nothing to do with each other.

In everyday programming, you will encounter three of these levels most often: functional cohesion (the goal), communicational cohesion (acceptable), and coincidental or logical cohesion (the most common problems to fix). The examples that follow focus on recognising and eliminating the two worst levels.

Example 5.14 **Variation — Recognising and Fixing Low Cohesion**

The function on the left suffers from coincidental cohesion: it does three completely unrelated things. The functions on the right replace it with three highly cohesive functions, each doing exactly one thing.

✗ One function, three unrelated jobs

✗ Low cohesion (coincidental):

```
def utilities(data, mode):
  if mode == 'header':
    print('==========',
          'REPORT',
          '==========')
  elif mode == 'average':
    total = sum(data)
    return total / len(data)
  elif mode == 'save':
    with open('out.txt','w')
         as f:
      f.write(str(data))

# Three jobs, one function.
# Caller must know 'mode'.
# Cannot test average
# without the rest.
```

✓ Three functions, one job each

✓ High cohesion (functional):

```
def print_header():
  """Print report header."""
  print('==========',
        'REPORT',
        '==========')

def calculate_average(data):
  """Return mean of data."""
  return sum(data)/len(data)

def save_data(data, fname):
  """Write data to file."""
  with open(fname, 'w') as f:
    f.write(str(data))

# Three jobs, three functions.
# Each is testable alone.
# No 'mode' flag needed.
```

The right-hand version is simpler to test, simpler to read, and simpler to modify. If the report format changes, only print_header() needs updating. If the calculation changes, only calculate_average() changes. The functions are independent because they are cohesive.

Example 5.15 Real-world application — Refactoring a Data Processing Function

A data processing function written without decomposition often accumulates responsibilities over time as new features are added: first it just read the file, then it also validated, then it also filtered, then it also calculated. The result is a function that does five things. Refactoring it into five focused functions restores cohesion.

```
BEFORE REFACTORING — low cohesion:

def process_student_data(filename):
    # Read the file
    records = []
    with open(filename) as f:
        for line in f:
            records.append(line.strip().split(','))
    # Validate records
    records = [r for r in records if len(r) == 3]
    # Filter to passing students
    records = [r for r in records if float(r[1]) >= 50]
    # Calculate average
    scores = [float(r[1]) for r in records]
    avg = sum(scores) / len(scores) if scores else 0
    # Display results
    for r in records:
        print(f'{r[0]:20} {r[1]:6} {r[2]}')
    print(f'Class average (passing): {avg:.1f}')
```

```
AFTER REFACTORING — high cohesion:

def load_raw_records(filename): ...
def validate_records(records):  ...
def filter_passing(records):    ...
def calculate_average(records): ...
def display_results(records, avg): ...

def process_student_data(filename):
    records = load_raw_records(filename)
    records = validate_records(records)
    records = filter_passing(records)
    avg     = calculate_average(records)
    display_results(records, avg)
```

After refactoring, process_student_data() is itself cohesive: it orchestrates the workflow without implementing any step. Each sub-function is cohesive: it does exactly one thing. The total number of lines of code is similar; the testability and maintainability are vastly improved.

> ▶ **NOTE** Every time you add a new feature to an existing function, ask: does this feature belong here? If the function already does one thing, adding a second thing reduces cohesion. Add a new function instead, and call it from the orchestrator. The orchestrator grows by one line; the system's cohesion is preserved.

Cohesion is internal to a module: how well its parts belong together. Coupling is external: how dependent a module is on other modules. High cohesion and low coupling work together — you cannot achieve one without the other. The next section introduces coupling.

6 Coupling — Designing Modules That Depend on Each Other as Little as Possible

Coupling measures the degree of dependency between two modules. Tightly coupled modules cannot be understood, tested, or modified independently — a change to one ripples through the other. Loosely coupled modules interact only through well-defined interfaces (parameters and return values), so each can be changed without affecting the other, as long as the interface is preserved.

The goal is always the lowest practical level of coupling. Two modules that share only the data they need, passed explicitly as parameters, have data coupling — the loosest and best form. Two modules that both read and write the same global variable have common coupling — a much tighter and problematic form. One module that reaches inside another and modifies its internal data has content coupling — the tightest and worst form, which Python's encapsulation conventions make very difficult to achieve accidentally.

Coupling and cohesion are related: a module with low cohesion — one that does many things — tends to be tightly coupled with many other modules, because it depends on many different pieces of external data. Increasing cohesion naturally decreases coupling. The two principles reinforce each other, and together they define the primary quality criterion for a decomposed design.

Example 5.16 Introduction — The Six Levels of Coupling

Coupling Level	Quality	Description and example
✓✓ Data	Loosest / Best	Modules share data only through parameters and return values. Each parameter carries exactly the data needed. Example: calculate_gst(price) — receives one value, returns one value. No hidden dependencies.
✓ Stamp	Loose	One module passes an entire data structure to another, even though only part of it is needed. Example: print_name(student) where only student.name is used. Slightly better to pass the name directly.
✓ Control	Moderate	One module passes a flag that controls what the other module does. Example: process(data, mode='summarise') where mode changes the behaviour. Suggests the module may be doing two different jobs.
✗ External	Tight	Modules share a dependency on an external format, protocol, or device. A change to that external element forces changes in all connected modules. Example: two modules that both know the exact format of a CSV file.
✗ Common	Tight	Modules communicate through shared global variables. Any module can read or change the global state, making it impossible to understand one module without understanding all others. Example: using a global records list across all functions.
✗✗ Content	Tightest / Worst	One module directly accesses or modifies the internal data of another — bypassing its public interface entirely. Example: function A reads function B's local variable. This is impossible in Python if encapsulation is used correctly.

In Python programs written by students, the two most common coupling problems are common coupling (using global variables) and stamp coupling (passing an entire object when only one attribute is needed). Both are easy to fix once identified.

Example 5.17 Variation — Global Variables vs Parameters

Global variables are the most common source of unwanted coupling in student programs. When a function reads or writes a global variable, it is coupled to any other function that uses the same variable. The two functions cannot be tested independently, because each depends on the global state that the other may have changed.

✗ Global variables = hidden coupling

```
✗  Common coupling (global var):

  records = []    # global
  total   = 0     # global

  def load_data(filename):
    global records
    # reads file, fills records
    ...

  def compute_total():
    global total, records
    # reads records, sets total
    for r in records:
      total += r['score']

  # Cannot test compute_total()
  # without first calling
  # load_data(). Globals create
  # hidden dependencies.
```

✓ Parameters = explicit, testable

```
✓  Data coupling (parameters):

  # No globals

  def load_data(filename):
    # reads file, returns records
    ...
    return records

  def compute_total(records):
    # receives records, returns
total
    return sum(r['score']
               for r in records)

  # Can test compute_total() with
  # any list — no setup needed.
  # Functions are independent.
```

The right-hand version can be tested immediately: compute_total([{'score': 80}, {'score': 60}]) returns 140, with no setup, no file, and no global state. The test is fast, reliable, and independent of all other functions.

Example 5.18 **Real-world application — Reducing Coupling Through Interface Design**

Stamp coupling occurs when a function receives a whole object or structure but only uses one part of it. This creates an unnecessary dependency on the object's full structure. The fix is to pass only the data the function actually needs.

✗ Passing the whole object

```
✗  Stamp coupling:

  def send_welcome_email(
        student):   # whole object
    # Uses only student.email
    # and student.name
    subject = 'Welcome!'
    body = f'Hi {student.name}'
    send(student.email,
         subject, body)

  # This function knows about
  # the Student class structure.
  # Change Student and this
  # function may break.
```

✓ Passing only what is needed

```
✓  Data coupling:

  def send_welcome_email(
        name, email):  # just data
    subject = 'Welcome!'
    body = f'Hi {name}'
    send(email, subject, body)

  # This function knows nothing
  # about Student. It works with
  # any name/email pair.
  # Reusable; easily tested.
```

The rule is simple: pass only the data a function needs, never more. If a function receives five fields of an object but uses only one, the coupling is higher than necessary. Pass the one field. The function becomes more general, more testable, and more reusable.

> ▶ **NOTE** Aim for data coupling in every function you write: parameters going in, return values coming out, no global state read or modified. If a function needs more than four or five parameters, consider whether it is doing too much (low cohesion) or whether the parameters should be bundled into a purpose-built data structure.

Cohesion and coupling are the quality criteria for decomposition. The final section brings all the tools from this chapter together in a complete, worked example: decomposing a Student Records application from a blank problem statement all the way to a function skeleton ready for implementation.

7 A Complete Worked Example — The Student Records Application

This section applies every technique from the chapter to a single, realistic problem. The starting point is a plain-English problem description; the end point is a complete function skeleton with documented interfaces, ready for pseudocode and implementation. Every step is shown explicitly.

The process follows the design-first workflow: understand the problem, apply top-down design to identify tasks, draw a structure chart to document the hierarchy and data flow, derive function signatures from the chart, and evaluate the result against the cohesion and coupling principles. This is the complete structured design process.

Example 5.19 Introduction — Problem Statement and First-Level Decomposition

Problem: Build a command-line student records application. The program loads student records from a CSV file (name, score, year level). It presents a menu that allows the user to view all records, search for a student by name, add a new student record, and quit. Changes are saved back to the file when the user quits.

```
UNDERSTAND STAGE

Inputs:     CSV file (name, score, year_level per row)
            Menu choice (integer 1-4)
            Search name (string)
            New student data (name, score, year_level)
Outputs:    Formatted display of all records
            Search result (found or not found message)
            Confirmation of new record added
            Updated CSV file on exit
Constraints: Validate score (0-100), year_level (7-12)
             Handle missing file gracefully

LEVEL 1 DECOMPOSITION (major tasks identified from Understand stage)
```

```
     1.  load_records(filename)         → read and return all records
from file
     2.  run_menu(records)              → display menu, dispatch to
operations
     3.  display_all(records)           → show all records formatted
     4.  search_by_name(records, name) → find and show matching student
     5.  add_record(records)            → collect, validate, append new
student
     6.  save_records(records, filename)→ write all records back to CSV
```

Example 5.20 Variation — Full Structure Chart with Data Couples

The structure chart below documents the complete decomposition. Each box is one function; connecting lines show calls; annotations show data passed in each direction. Two tasks require sub-functions: load_records delegates to parse_csv_line; add_record delegates to validate_input.

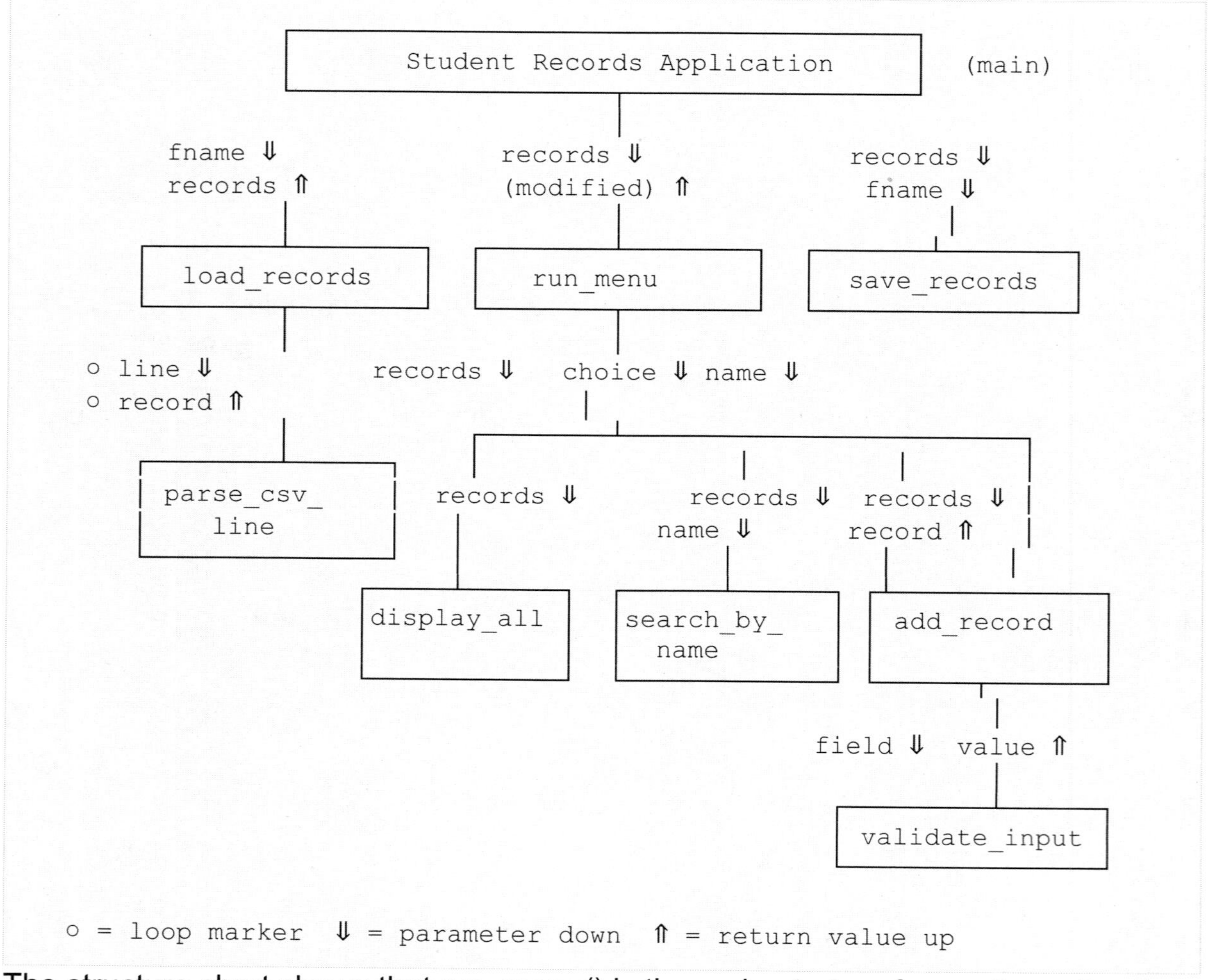

The structure chart shows that run_menu() is the orchestrator of operations: it calls display_all(), search_by_name(), and add_record() based on the user's menu choice. main() orchestrates the session: it loads records, runs the menu, and saves when done. These two functions are orchestrators; they contain no business logic of their own.

Example 5.21 Real-world application — Function Skeleton and Design Evaluation

The function skeleton below is derived directly from the structure chart. Each function has a signature consistent with its data couple annotations and a docstring that confirms its single responsibility. The design is then evaluated against the cohesion and coupling principles.

```
def main():
    """Load records, run the session, save on exit."""
    records = load_records('students.csv')
    run_menu(records)
    save_records(records, 'students.csv')

def load_records(filename):
    """Read filename and return a list of student record dicts."""
    ...
    # calls parse_csv_line() in a loop

def parse_csv_line(line):
    """Parse one CSV line string and return a student dict."""
    ...

def run_menu(records):
    """Show menu, accept choice, dispatch to appropriate
operation."""
    ...
    # calls display_all, search_by_name, or add_record

def display_all(records):
    """Print all student records in a formatted table."""
    ...

def search_by_name(records, name):
    """Print the record matching name, or a not-found message."""
    ...

def add_record(records):
    """Collect a new student's data, validate, and append to
records."""
    ...
    # calls validate_input()

def validate_input(field, value):
    """Return True if value is valid for the named field; False
otherwise."""
    ...

def save_records(records, filename):
    """Write all records from records back to filename as CSV."""
    ...

DESIGN EVALUATION:
  Cohesion:  Every function does exactly one thing (functional
cohesion). ✓
  Coupling:  All data passed as parameters or return values.
✓
```

```
                No global variables.
✓
                Validate_input receives individual values, not whole
records. ✓
    Testable:   Each function can be tested with known inputs
independently.  ✓
```

This skeleton is the output of the structured design process: a set of function definitions that fully specify the program's architecture before a single line of business logic is written. Each function can now be filled in with pseudocode (Chapter 2) and translated to Python. The design is done; the implementation follows the design.

> ▶ **NOTE** A complete structured design — structure chart, function signatures, and docstrings — is the most valuable planning document you can produce before writing code. It answers every structural question in advance. When you sit down to implement each function, you know what it receives, what it must do, and what it must return. Implementation becomes translation.

This chapter has introduced decomposition as the foundation of structured program design, top-down design and stepwise refinement as the process for performing it, structure charts as the tool for documenting it, and cohesion and coupling as the principles for evaluating the quality of the result. Chapter 6 addresses the errors that remain even after good decomposition — the common logic mistakes that careful planning can prevent.

Chapter Summary

- Decomposition is the process of breaking a complex problem into smaller, independently solvable sub-problems. Every benefit of good software design — readability, testability, reusability, maintainability — flows from effective decomposition.
- The function name test: if you can describe what a function does in one sentence without using 'and', it is probably well decomposed. Each 'and' in a description is a missed decomposition opportunity.
- Top-down design starts with the whole problem and progressively divides it into parts. Stepwise refinement adds one level of detail per pass. Stop refining when every task can be described by a single verb phrase and implemented in ten to twenty lines of Python.
- Structure charts document a decomposed design: each box is one module; connecting lines represent calls from parent to child; data couple annotations (with ⇓ down-arrows and ⇑ up-arrows) show parameters and return values; loop (○) and conditional (◇) markers indicate how child modules are called.

- Each box in a structure chart maps directly to one Python function. Data couples map to parameters and return values. The structure chart and function signatures fully define the program's architecture before any logic is written.
- Cohesion measures how well a module's internal elements belong together. Functional cohesion (one module, one job, completely done) is the ideal. Coincidental cohesion (unrelated elements grouped arbitrarily) is the worst case and should always be refactored.
- Coupling measures the dependency between modules. Data coupling (modules share data only through parameters and return values) is the goal. Common coupling (shared global variables) and content coupling (direct access to another module's internals) are the most harmful and should be eliminated.
- High cohesion and low coupling are complementary and mutually reinforcing. A module that does one thing (high cohesion) needs little external data (low coupling). Together they define the standard of quality for any structured design.

Guided Exercises

Complete all five exercises before moving on to Chapter 6. Each exercise includes a hint to help you get started.

Exercise 1

Apply the 'and' test to each of the following function descriptions. State whether each is acceptably cohesive or needs further decomposition, and if decomposition is needed, list the separate functions it should be split into: (a) 'Calculate the average of a list of numbers'; (b) 'Read the input file and validate each record and calculate the total'; (c) 'Display a formatted student report'; (d) 'Log the error and retry the connection and update the status flag'.

Hint: Apply the rule strictly: any description requiring 'and' indicates multiple responsibilities. For (b) and (d), identify how many separate functions are implied and name each one clearly.

Exercise 2

Perform two passes of stepwise refinement on the following problem: 'Build a program that reads a list of grocery items and prices from a file, allows the user to add items, and saves the updated list.' Pass 1 should identify three to five major tasks. Pass 2 should refine each major task into its sub-tasks. Every leaf task in Pass 2 should be describable without using 'and'.

Hint: Start Pass 1 by identifying the major operations: loading, interacting, and saving are typically the top-level tasks for any data management program. Refine each task in Pass 2 by asking: 'What separate steps are inside this task?'

Exercise 3

Draw a structure chart for the following program: A temperature converter that asks the user to choose a conversion direction (Celsius to Fahrenheit, or Fahrenheit to

Celsius), reads a temperature, performs the conversion, displays the result, and asks whether to convert another. Your chart must include at least three levels, loop and conditional markers where appropriate, and data couple annotations on every connecting line.

Hint: The main function orchestrates. Level 1 functions include: get_menu_choice, read_temperature, convert_temperature, display_result. Convert_temperature is conditional (direction determines which sub-function is called). Use loop markers on any module called repeatedly.

Exercise 4

Identify the coupling level in each of the following situations, and for each one that is not data coupling, explain how to reduce the coupling: (a) function A passes a score as a float to function B, which returns a grade string; (b) functions A, B, and C all read and update a global dictionary called student_data; (c) function A passes an entire Student object to function B, which only uses the student's name attribute; (d) function A directly modifies a list that is a local variable inside function B by importing function B's module and accessing its internal namespace.

Hint: Use the coupling types table in Section 6 as a reference. For (b), the fix is to pass student_data as a parameter and return the modified version. For (c), consider passing only the name string. (d) is the extreme case of content coupling.

Exercise 5

Using the structure chart you drew in Exercise 3 (or the student records structure chart from Section 7 if you did not complete Exercise 3), write the complete Python function skeleton: all function signatures, all docstrings, and all function calls in the correct place. Do not write any logic — use pass or ... as placeholders. Ensure every function's parameters match the data couple annotations in the structure chart.

Hint: Work top-down from the chart. Write main() first, calling the Level 1 functions. Then write each Level 1 function, calling the Level 2 functions where the chart shows connections. Write docstrings before signatures if that helps clarify the purpose.

Challenge Tasks

These tasks have no hints. They require independent thinking and are suitable for extension or assessment. Complete the Guided Exercises before attempting these.

Challenge Task 1

A student has submitted a Python program for a quiz application. The program consists of three functions: run_quiz() which reads questions from a file, presents them to the user, accepts answers, checks each answer, tracks the score, and prints the final result; display_score(correct, total) which prints the score; and a main() that calls run_quiz(). Analyse run_quiz() for cohesion and coupling problems. Produce a complete restructured design: a structure chart showing the correct decomposition (at least three levels), a list of all function signatures with docstrings, and an explanation of how each identified problem was resolved.

Challenge Task 2

Design a complete structured decomposition for a personal budget tracking program. The program allows a user to: record income and expense transactions with a category and description; view a summary of income and expenses by category; set a monthly budget limit per category and receive a warning when 80% of the limit is reached; and export a monthly report to a text file. Produce: a two-pass stepwise refinement showing the progression from problem statement to leaf tasks; a full structure chart with data couple annotations, loop markers, and conditional markers; and a complete Python function skeleton. Evaluate the final design explicitly against the cohesion and coupling principles.

Challenge Task 3

Cohesion and coupling are principles, not rules with a single correct answer. Find a Python program you have previously written (from this book, from the Think, Code, Create foundation text, or from your own projects). Evaluate it systematically: for each function, state its cohesion level using the terminology from the cohesion table; for each pair of functions that interact, state the coupling level; identify the two or three most significant design problems in terms of cohesion or coupling; and produce a redesigned version with a structure chart showing how the program should be restructured. Compare the original and redesigned versions and explain, for each change, why the redesign is an improvement.

Common Logic Errors and How to Prevent Them

> This chapter catalogues the most common logic errors encountered in student programs and shows, for each one, why it occurs and how planning prevents it. Logic errors are the hardest category of error to find because they produce no error message — the program runs, but produces wrong results. You will study off-by-one errors in loops, boundary condition mistakes in decisions, the dangers of unvalidated input, infinite loops and missing termination conditions, and scope and initialisation errors. Each section shows the error in pseudocode, demonstrates how a desk check catches it, and gives the corrected version.

1 Why Logic Errors Are Different from Other Errors

Every program error belongs to one of three categories. A syntax error is a violation of the language's grammar rules — a missing colon, an unmatched bracket, a misspelled keyword. The interpreter catches syntax errors before the program runs and reports them with a line number and an error type. They are easy to find and easy to fix.

A runtime error occurs while the program is executing. It happens when the program attempts something impossible: dividing by zero, accessing an index that does not exist, calling a method on None. The interpreter raises an exception, prints a traceback, and halts execution. Runtime errors are harder to find than syntax errors but still produce a clear signal — an exception message and a stack trace that points directly to the problem.

A logic error produces none of these signals. The program runs to completion without raising an exception. It simply produces the wrong answer. The program might calculate 73.5 when the correct answer is 75.0, process 99 items instead of 100, or apply a discount to the wrong customers. Nothing in Python's output tells you anything is wrong — you must know what the correct answer should be and compare it to what the program actually produces. This is why logic errors are the hardest to find and the most important to prevent.

Example 1.1 Introduction — The Three Error Categories

```
CATEGORY 1 — SYNTAX ERROR (caught before running):
  def calculate average(scores)     ← Missing underscore in name
    return sum(scores) / len(scores    ← Missing closing bracket
  Error: SyntaxError: invalid syntax
  Signal: Clear. Line number provided. Easy to fix.

CATEGORY 2 — RUNTIME ERROR (caught while running):
```

```
    def calculate_average(scores):
      return sum(scores) / len(scores)   ← What if scores is empty?
    Error: ZeroDivisionError: division by zero
    Signal: Clear. Traceback identifies the exact line.

  CATEGORY 3 — LOGIC ERROR (no signal at all):
    def calculate_average(scores):
      return sum(scores) / (len(scores) + 1)   ← Off-by-one in divisor
    Error: None. Program runs. Result is silently wrong.
    Signal: None. You must know the expected answer to detect this.

  With scores = [80, 70, 90, 60, 75]:
    Correct answer:  375 / 5 = 75.0
    Buggy answer:    375 / 6 = 62.5    ← no error raised
```

The logic error in the example above divides by len(scores) + 1 instead of len(scores). Python happily performs that division. The result is wrong, and nothing in the program's output says so. Only knowing that the average of [80, 70, 90, 60, 75] should be 75.0, and comparing it to the returned 62.5, reveals the problem.

Example 1.2 Variation — Logic Errors Survive Testing

Logic errors are particularly dangerous because they often survive basic testing. A program tested only with 'happy path' inputs — inputs that work correctly — may appear to function perfectly. The error only manifests with specific inputs: boundary values, edge cases, or combinations that the programmer did not test.

```
  BUGGY PSEUDOCODE — grade classification:

    IF score > 85 THEN             ← should be >= 85
      SET grade = 'High Distinction'
    ELSE IF score > 75 THEN        ← should be >= 75
      SET grade = 'Distinction'
    ...

  Testing with score = 90:  grade = 'High Distinction'  ✓ (appears
correct)
  Testing with score = 80:  grade = 'Distinction'       ✓ (appears
correct)
  Testing with score = 70:  grade = 'Credit'            ✓ (appears
correct)

  But:
  Testing with score = 85:  grade = 'Distinction'       ✗ (should be
'HD')
  Testing with score = 75:  grade = 'Credit'            ✗ (should be
'D')

  The error is invisible unless a test uses exactly a boundary value.
  A desk check with test value = 85 would have caught this immediately.
```

Example 1.3 Real-world application — The Cost of Logic Errors

Logic errors in production software have caused significant real-world harm. Calculation errors in billing systems have overcharged customers. Off-by-one errors in medical device software have delivered incorrect dosages. Boundary condition failures in navigation systems have produced wrong coordinates. In every case, the program ran without error — it simply produced wrong results that were believed to be correct.

The earlier a logic error is caught, the cheaper it is to fix. A logic error caught during planning — in the pseudocode stage, by asking 'what happens at the boundary?' — costs nothing but a correction to the pseudocode. The same error caught in a desk check costs minutes. Caught in testing it costs hours. Caught in production it costs far more, and may also cost reputation and trust. Planning-stage detection is always the goal.

> ▶ **NOTE** Logic errors are silent. No error message identifies them; no traceback points to their location. The only way to detect them is to know what the correct output should be and compare it to what the program produces. Desk checking — tracing pseudocode manually with known inputs and comparing each step to expected values — is the most reliable planning-stage technique for catching them.

With an understanding of what logic errors are and why they are difficult to detect, the next five sections address the specific types that occur most frequently in student programs. Each section introduces the error, shows how planning catches it, and gives the corrected version.

2 Off-by-One Errors in Loops

An off-by-one error (OBOE) is the most common logic error in programming. It occurs when a loop iterates one too many or one too few times, when an index is one position off from its intended value, or when a range boundary is inclusive where it should be exclusive (or vice versa). The error is called 'off by one' because the result is always exactly one step away from correct.

Off-by-one errors arise from a recurring ambiguity: when we count things in everyday language, we use inclusive boundaries ('from 1 to 5 means 1, 2, 3, 4, and 5'). When Python's range() function is used, the upper boundary is exclusive: range(1, 5) produces 1, 2, 3, 4 — not 5. Pseudocode uses inclusive boundaries by convention (FOR i FROM 1 TO 5 means five iterations). The translation from pseudocode to Python requires careful attention to this difference.

The most reliable way to catch an off-by-one error before coding is a targeted desk check. Trace the loop for its very first iteration (what is i at the start?) and its very last iteration (what is i when the loop exits?). If either answer is not what the problem requires, the loop boundaries are wrong. Do this for every loop before translating pseudocode to Python.

Example 2.1 Introduction — The Loop That Stops One Step Too Early

A student writes pseudocode to print the five-times multiplication table from 1 × 5 to 10 × 5. They write the loop as FOR i FROM 1 TO 9 instead of FOR i FROM 1 TO 10. The desk check immediately shows the problem.

✗ **Off by one: TO 9 stops early**	✓ **Correct: TO 10 runs all rows**
✗ Buggy pseudocode:	✓ Corrected pseudocode:

✗ Buggy pseudocode:

```
BEGIN
  FOR i FROM 1 TO 9 DO
    OUTPUT i, '× 5 =', i * 5
  END FOR
END

Desk check (last 2 rows):
i  | Output
8  | 8 × 5 = 40
9  | 9 × 5 = 45
(loop ends here)

Missing: 10 × 5 = 50  ✗
The loop runs 9 times
instead of 10.
```

✓ Corrected pseudocode:

```
BEGIN
  FOR i FROM 1 TO 10 DO
    OUTPUT i, '× 5 =', i * 5
  END FOR
END

Desk check (last 2 rows):
i   | Output
9   | 9 × 5 = 45
10  | 10 × 5 = 50
(loop ends here)

All 10 rows printed.  ✓
The desk check confirms
the correct range.
```

The fix is a single digit: 9 becomes 10. The desk check cost two minutes and found the error before a single line of Python was written. This is the typical off-by-one fix — minimal in effort once identified, expensive to track down if discovered only after the code exists.

Example 2.2 **Variation — The Fence-Post Problem**

The fence-post problem describes a classic source of off-by-one confusion: if you build a fence 10 metres long with posts every 1 metre, how many posts do you need? The intuitive answer is 10, but the correct answer is 11 — one at each end, and one between each pair of adjacent sections. The confusion between counting sections and counting boundaries produces off-by-one errors in loops that process separators, gaps, or transitions.

```
FENCE-POST SCENARIO: Print separating lines between N items,
not after the last one.

✗  Buggy version (N lines printed, N separators – one too many):
  FOR i FROM 1 TO N DO
    OUTPUT items[i]
    OUTPUT '----------'     ← separator printed after EVERY item
  END FOR
  Output for N=3: item1 / --- / item2 / --- / item3 / ---
  Problem: trailing separator after the last item.

✓  Corrected version (N items, N-1 separators):
  FOR i FROM 1 TO N DO
    OUTPUT items[i]
    IF i < N THEN
```

```
        OUTPUT '----------'  ← separator only between items, not after
last
      END IF
    END FOR
    Output for N=3: item1 / --- / item2 / --- / item3
    Correct: separator between items only.

  RULE: N items require N-1 separators between them.
        N fence sections require N+1 posts to hold them up.
```

Example 2.3 Real-world application — The Index Off-by-One

When processing a list by index, off-by-one errors often arise from confusion between 0-based indexing (Python's convention) and 1-based counting (how humans naturally count). A loop intended to process all five elements of a list may start at index 1, skipping the first element, or end at index 5, causing an IndexError. The desk check below catches the skipped element before any Python is written.

```
PROBLEM: Sum the scores in a list of five results.
scores = [85, 72, 91, 68, 79]   (indices 0 to 4)

✗  Buggy pseudocode (starts at 1, skips index 0):
  SET total = 0
  FOR i FROM 1 TO 4 DO         ← starts at 1, not 0
    SET total = total + scores[i]
  END FOR
  OUTPUT total / 5

Desk check:
i  | scores[i]  | total
1  |    72      |  72        ← scores[0] = 85 was never added!
2  |    91      | 163
3  |    68      | 231
4  |    79      | 310
Output: 310 / 5 = 62.0   Expected: 395 / 5 = 79.0   ✗

✓  Corrected pseudocode (starts at 0, processes all 5 elements):
  SET total = 0
  FOR i FROM 0 TO 4 DO         ← correct: 0-based indexing
    SET total = total + scores[i]
  END FOR
  OUTPUT total / 5
Desk check: total = 395, output = 79.0  ✓
```

⚠ **COMMON ERROR** When translating pseudocode to Python, FOR i FROM 1 TO N becomes range(1, N+1) because Python's range() excludes its upper bound. FOR i FROM 0 TO N-1 becomes range(N). Always verify the translation with a desk check of the first and last iteration.

Off-by-one errors live at the boundaries of loops. Boundary condition errors live at the edges of decisions. These two error types often appear together in programs that combine loops with conditional logic, making the next section a natural companion to this one.

3 Boundary Condition Errors in Decisions

A boundary condition error occurs when a decision uses the wrong comparison operator at a critical threshold, causing incorrect behaviour for inputs that sit exactly on the boundary. The program behaves correctly for inputs well above or well below the threshold, so the error is only revealed by testing with the exact boundary value — which many programmers forget to do.

The distinction between > and >=, and between < and <=, is the source of nearly all boundary condition errors. In natural language, we often blur this distinction: 'scores above 50 are a Pass' could mean > 50 or >= 50 depending on interpretation. In code, the difference is absolute: a score of exactly 50 either passes or fails, with no ambiguity. Getting this wrong by one comparison operator produces a program that is correct for 999 out of 1000 possible inputs and wrong for exactly the one input that sits on the boundary.

The planning technique for catching boundary conditions is the three-point desk check: test with the value one below the boundary, the value exactly at the boundary, and the value one above the boundary. If the program produces the correct output for all three, the boundary is correct. If any of the three produces a wrong output, the comparison operator needs adjustment.

Example 3.1 Introduction — The Grade Boundary Error

A student implements grade classification with the boundaries shown below. All tests with typical values pass. Only a test at the exact boundary (score = 75) reveals the error.

✗ Using > excludes the boundary

```
✗  Buggy pseudocode:

  IF score > 85 THEN
    SET grade = 'High Distinction'
  ELSE IF score > 75 THEN
    SET grade = 'Distinction'
  ELSE IF score > 65 THEN
    SET grade = 'Credit'
  ELSE IF score > 50 THEN
    SET grade = 'Pass'
  ELSE
    SET grade = 'Fail'
  END IF

  Three-point test (score = 75):
  74 → 'Credit'            ✓
  75 → 'Credit'            ✗ (should
be 'D')
  76 → 'Distinction'       ✓
```

✓ Using >= includes the boundary

```
✓  Corrected pseudocode:

  IF score >= 85 THEN
    SET grade = 'High Distinction'
  ELSE IF score >= 75 THEN
    SET grade = 'Distinction'
  ELSE IF score >= 65 THEN
    SET grade = 'Credit'
  ELSE IF score >= 50 THEN
    SET grade = 'Pass'
  ELSE
    SET grade = 'Fail'
  END IF

  Three-point test (score = 75):
  74 → 'Credit'            ✓
  75 → 'Distinction'       ✓
  76 → 'Distinction'       ✓
```

The difference is four characters: four instances of > changed to >=. A three-point desk check at each boundary value (74/75/76, 64/65/66, 49/50/51, 84/85/86) would have caught all four errors simultaneously during the planning stage.

Example 3.2 **Variation — Overlapping and Gapped Boundaries**

Two related boundary errors are overlapping conditions (where the same value satisfies two branches) and gapped conditions (where some values satisfy no branch and fall through to an incorrect ELSE). Both are detected by tracing boundary values through the decision chain.

```
  ✗  OVERLAPPING CONDITIONS — score = 75 satisfies TWO branches:

    IF score >= 75 THEN      ← score=75 enters here ...
      SET grade = 'Distinction'
    ELSE IF score >= 65 THEN
      SET grade = 'Credit'  ← ... never reached for score=75, but
    END IF                     IF/ELSE IF prevents double-entry anyway.
    (This specific example is actually fine in IF/ELSE IF chains
because
    the first matching branch is taken. BUT see the danger in CASE
below.)

  ✗  GAPPED CONDITIONS — score = 65 satisfies NO branch:

    IF score >= 66 THEN         ← score=65: 65 >= 66 is FALSE
      SET grade = 'Credit'
    ELSE IF score >= 50 THEN    ← score=65: 65 >= 50 is TRUE
      SET grade = 'Pass'        ← score=65 gets 'Pass' — should be
'Credit'
    END IF
    Gap: scores 65 are misclassified as 'Pass' instead of 'Credit'.

  THREE-POINT TEST CATCHES BOTH:
    Test 65 → gap/overlap revealed    Test 66 → boundary confirmed
```

Example 3.3 **Real-world application — Inclusive vs Exclusive in a Validation Range**

A school canteen system accepts orders for between 1 and 10 items. A student writes the validation check using incorrect operators, causing orders of exactly 1 or exactly 10 to be rejected as invalid.

```
  PROBLEM: Validate that quantity is between 1 and 10 items
(inclusive).

  ✗  Buggy validation (excludes the boundary values 1 and 10):
    IF quantity > 1 AND quantity < 10 THEN
      OUTPUT 'Order accepted'
    ELSE
      OUTPUT 'Invalid: enter between 1 and 10 items'
    END IF

  Three-point desk check:
```

```
    quantity = 0  → 'Invalid'                ✓ (correct, 0 is below range)
    quantity = 1  → 'Invalid'                ✗ (wrong! 1 is valid)
    quantity = 5  → 'Order accepted'         ✓ (correct)
    quantity = 10 → 'Invalid'                ✗ (wrong! 10 is valid)
    quantity = 11 → 'Invalid'                ✓ (correct, 11 is above range)

  ✓ Corrected validation (includes boundary values 1 and 10):
    IF quantity >= 1 AND quantity <= 10 THEN
      OUTPUT 'Order accepted'
    ELSE
      OUTPUT 'Invalid: enter between 1 and 10 items'
    END IF

  Corrected three-point desk check:
    quantity = 1  → 'Order accepted'   ✓
    quantity = 10 → 'Order accepted'   ✓
```

> ⚠ **COMMON ERROR** Always perform a three-point desk check at every boundary in a decision: one value below, the exact boundary, and one value above. If the specification says ‘between 1 and 10’, test 0, 1, 10, and 11. The boundary values are the inputs most likely to expose errors, yet they are the inputs most often omitted from testing.

Boundary errors arise at the edges of conditions. The next category of error arises when no condition is checked at all: when a program assumes its input will always be reasonable and does not defend against the cases where it is not.

4 Assuming Input Is Always Valid — Defensive Design

Defensive design is the practice of writing programs that handle invalid, unexpected, and malicious input gracefully rather than crashing or producing wrong results. The fundamental assumption of defensive design is that user input cannot be trusted: it may be the wrong type, outside the expected range, empty, None, negative when positive is required, or deliberately crafted to break the program.

The most common manifestation of this error in student programs is the unguarded conversion: int(input()) without checking that the input is actually a valid integer. If the user types ‘hello’, Python raises a ValueError and the program crashes. If the user types nothing, an empty string causes the same crash. If the user types a float like ‘3.7’, int() truncates it silently, producing an unexpected result. All three cases can be addressed during the pseudocode stage by adding validation before the conversion.

Defensive design is not about expecting the worst from users. It is about recognising that mistakes happen — typographical errors, misunderstandings of the input format, accidental key presses — and writing programs that guide users toward valid input rather than punishing them with crashes. A well-validated program is more useful, more professional, and far more robust than one that works only when given perfect input.

Example 4.1 Introduction — The Unguarded Conversion

Every program that accepts numeric input from the user must validate that input before converting it. The three-step validation pattern — read, check, convert — should appear in the pseudocode before any line that uses the numeric value.

✗ Crashes on bad input

```
✗  No validation:

  BEGIN
    INPUT age_string
    SET age = INT(age_string)
    ← Crashes if user enters
    ← 'hello', '', or '3.5'
    IF age >= 18 THEN
      OUTPUT 'Adult'
    ELSE
      OUTPUT 'Minor'
    END IF
  END

  Input 'hello' → ValueError ✗
  Input ''      → ValueError ✗
  Input '-5'    → -5 accepted ✗
```

✓ Re-prompts until valid

```
✓  With validation:

  BEGIN
    INPUT age_string
    WHILE age_string is not a
          valid positive integer DO
      OUTPUT 'Please enter a
                whole number > 0'
      INPUT age_string
    END WHILE
    SET age = INT(age_string)
    IF age >= 18 THEN
      OUTPUT 'Adult'
    ELSE
      OUTPUT 'Minor'
    END IF
  END

  Any bad input → re-prompt ✓
  Only proceeds with valid age.
```

The validation WHILE loop in the corrected version keeps asking until the input is a valid positive integer. The program cannot proceed to the conversion or the calculation until valid input has been received. This guarantees that INT(age_string) will succeed.

Example 4.2 Variation — Layered Validation: Type, Range, and Logic

Complex inputs require layered validation: first check the type, then the range, then any logical constraints. Each layer builds on the previous one. Pseudocode makes this layering explicit before any code is written.

```
  PROBLEM: Accept a student's test score (must be a number from 0 to
100).

  LAYER 1 — Type validation (is it a number at all?):
    WHILE score_input is not a valid number DO
      OUTPUT 'Error: please enter a numeric value.'
      INPUT score_input
    END WHILE
    SET score = FLOAT(score_input)

  LAYER 2 — Range validation (is the number in the valid range?):
    WHILE score < 0 OR score > 100 DO
      OUTPUT 'Error: score must be between 0 and 100.'
```

```
      INPUT score_input
      IF score_input is a valid number THEN
        SET score = FLOAT(score_input)
      END IF
    END WHILE

  LAYER 3 — Logic validation (does the value make sense in context?):
    ← For this problem, any value 0-100 is logically valid.
    ← For other problems: is quantity > stock on hand? Is date in the
future?

  AFTER ALL LAYERS PASS: score is a valid float between 0 and 100.
  Only now should any calculation using score be performed.
```

Example 4.3 Real-world application — Defensive Design in a Withdrawal Function

A bank account withdrawal function must validate three conditions before processing: the amount must be a positive number; it must not exceed the current balance; and it must not exceed the single-transaction limit. Each failed condition should produce a specific, helpful error message — not a crash and not a silent failure.

```
  FUNCTION withdraw(balance, amount, single_limit):

    ✓ Validation before any processing:

    IF amount <= 0 THEN
      RETURN 'Error: withdrawal amount must be positive.'
    END IF

    IF amount > single_limit THEN
      RETURN 'Error: amount exceeds single-transaction limit of $',
             single_limit
    END IF

    IF amount > balance THEN
      RETURN 'Error: insufficient funds. Balance: $', balance
    END IF

    ← Only reaches here if ALL validations pass:
    SET balance = balance - amount
    RETURN 'Withdrawal successful. New balance: $', balance

  END FUNCTION

  NOTE: Return early for each error. Never reach the calculation
  unless all inputs are known to be valid. This pattern is called
  'guard clauses' and is a professional defensive design technique.
```

> ⚠ **COMMON ERROR** Never assume that a function will be called with valid arguments. Validate all parameters at the start of any function that accepts user-supplied or externally-sourced data. A function that crashes because a caller passed it

invalid data has a bug — even if the caller is at fault. Defensive validation is not optional.

Unvalidated input causes programs to crash or produce wrong results because they encounter data they cannot handle. The next error type — infinite loops — causes programs to run forever because they encounter a condition they can never escape.

5 Infinite Loops and Missing Termination Conditions

An infinite loop is a loop whose exit condition never becomes true. The program enters the loop and never leaves it. In Python, this causes the program to run indefinitely — consuming processor time, producing no further output, and requiring the user to terminate it manually. Infinite loops are one of the most immediately obvious errors (the program freezes) but one of the hardest to diagnose (the cause is not always evident from the symptom).

Infinite loops arise from three common mistakes. The first is a counter that is never incremented (or is incremented in the wrong direction). The second is a condition that references one variable while the loop body updates a different variable. The third is a WHILE condition that can never become false given the data in the program — for example, WHILE x != 0 when x starts at 3 and is decremented by 2 each iteration, passing from positive to negative without ever equalling zero.

The flowchart is the best planning tool for catching potential infinite loops. Draw the loop structure and trace every path from inside the loop back to the condition diamond. Ask: is there always a path that eventually makes the condition false? If the back-arrow in the flowchart has no effect on any variable that the condition checks, the loop will run forever. Identifying this visually during planning is far faster than discovering it at runtime.

Example 5.1 **Introduction — The Counter That Never Changes**

The most common infinite loop: a WHILE loop with a counter that should be incremented inside the loop but is not. The condition checks the counter; the loop body never updates it; the condition remains true forever.

✗ No increment: runs forever

```
✗  Infinite loop:

  BEGIN
    SET i = 1
    SET total = 0
    WHILE i <= 5 DO
      INPUT score
      SET total = total + score
      ← i is NEVER incremented!
    END WHILE
    OUTPUT total / 5
  END
```

✓ Increment added: exits after 5

```
✓  Correct version:

  BEGIN
    SET i = 1
    SET total = 0
    WHILE i <= 5 DO
      INPUT score
      SET total = total + score
      SET i = i + 1  ← added
    END WHILE
    OUTPUT total / 5
  END
```

i stays at 1 forever. Condition (i <= 5) is always TRUE. Loop never exits. ✗	i goes 1, 2, 3, 4, 5, 6. When i = 6, condition (i <= 5) is FALSE. Loop exits correctly. ✓

A desk check of the buggy version reveals the problem immediately: the column for i never changes. At every iteration, i = 1. The condition i <= 5 is always true. The loop body executes forever. The missing SET i = i + 1 is obvious from the trace table, even though the pseudocode might be read quickly without noticing its absence.

Example 5.2 Variation — Updating the Wrong Variable

A subtler infinite loop occurs when the loop body updates a variable but the exit condition checks a different variable. The updated variable changes correctly; the condition variable never changes. This error is easy to introduce when two similarly-named variables exist in the same scope.

```
✗  Wrong variable updated — an infinite loop:

SET count = 0              ← condition variable
SET counter = 0            ← differently-named variable
WHILE count < 10 DO
  INPUT value
  SET total = total + value
  SET counter = counter + 1    ← updates 'counter', not 'count'!
END WHILE

Desk check after 3 iterations:
  count   = 0    ← never changes — condition always TRUE
  counter = 3    ← changes, but is not in the condition
Result: infinite loop.

✓  Corrected (update the variable named in the condition):

SET count = 0
WHILE count < 10 DO
  INPUT value
  SET total = total + value
  SET count = count + 1      ← now updates the condition variable
END WHILE

Prevention: use clear, distinct variable names.
In a desk check, always verify that the condition variable changes.
```

Example 5.3 Real-world application — Missing Recursion Base Case

Infinite loops are not limited to WHILE and FOR structures. Recursive functions without a base case produce infinite recursion: the function calls itself indefinitely until Python raises a RecursionError (stack overflow). The base case — the condition under which the function returns immediately without a recursive call — must appear in the pseudocode before the recursive case.

```
✗  Infinite recursion (no base case):

FUNCTION countdown(n)
  OUTPUT n
  CALL countdown(n - 1)     ← always recurses, never stops
END FUNCTION

countdown(3): outputs 3, 2, 1, 0, -1, -2, ... forever
Python: RecursionError: maximum recursion depth exceeded

✓  Corrected (base case added first):

FUNCTION countdown(n)
  IF n < 0 THEN             ← BASE CASE: stop condition checked first
    RETURN                   ← return without recursing
  END IF
  OUTPUT n
  CALL countdown(n - 1)     ← recursive case: only reached if n >= 0
END FUNCTION

countdown(3): outputs 3, 2, 1, 0, then stops.

RULE: Always write the base case FIRST in recursive pseudocode.
Ask: 'What is the simplest input to this function?'
'Does the function return immediately for that input?'
```

> ⚠ **COMMON ERROR** Before writing any loop in pseudocode, ask: 'What makes the exit condition eventually become false?' Identify the specific variable that the condition checks, and confirm that the loop body always moves that variable toward the exit condition. If no such movement exists, the loop is infinite.

Infinite loops are visible immediately when the program runs. The next category of error — scope and variable errors — is subtler: the program runs and produces a result, but it is a result calculated with the wrong data, from the wrong scope, or with an uninitialised starting value.

6 Scope and Uninitialised Variable Errors

A scope error occurs when a variable is read or written in the wrong context — either from outside the scope where it was defined, or when a local variable with the same name as an outer variable shadows the outer one, producing unexpected results. An uninitialised variable error occurs when a variable is used before it has been given a starting value, either crashing the program (NameError in Python) or producing garbage results (if the variable was accidentally used with an old value from a previous iteration).

The most common uninitialised variable error in student programs is the accumulator that never receives an initial value. An accumulator — a variable that collects a running total, a maximum, a minimum, or a count across iterations — must be set to a known starting value before the loop begins. Without this initialisation, the accumulator may carry a value from a previous function call, or Python will raise a NameError when the first iteration tries to add to a variable that does not yet exist.

Scope errors are best caught by pseudocode: the discipline of writing every variable's initial value as an explicit SET statement forces the programmer to declare where every variable lives and what its starting value is. A desk check then catches uninitialised accumulators because the variable column cannot be populated if no SET statement precedes the loop.

Example 6.1 Introduction — The Uninitialised Accumulator

An accumulator variable must be explicitly set to its starting value before the loop that updates it. The starting value is determined by the operation: totals start at 0; products start at 1; maximum trackers start at the smallest possible value (or the first element); minimum trackers start at the largest possible value (or the first element).

✗ No initialisation: error or garbage

```
✗  Accumulator not initialised:

BEGIN
  FOR i FROM 1 TO 5 DO
    INPUT score
    SET total = total + score
    ← 'total' used before
    ← it was ever set!
  END FOR
  OUTPUT total / 5
END

Desk check: first iteration
  i=1, score=80
  total = total + 80
  ← What is 'total' here?
  → NameError or wrong value
```

✓ SET total = 0 before the loop

```
✓  Initialised before loop:

BEGIN
  SET total = 0    ← added
  FOR i FROM 1 TO 5 DO
    INPUT score
    SET total = total + score
  END FOR
  OUTPUT total / 5
END

Desk check: first iteration
  total=0, i=1, score=80
  total = 0 + 80 = 80
  ↔ value is correct  ✓
  Proceeds cleanly.
```

The desk check makes the missing initialisation unmistakable: the column for total has no starting value, so its first entry cannot be computed. Adding SET total = 0 before the loop fills the column, and the desk check proceeds correctly.

Example 6.2 Variation — Variable Shadowing

Variable shadowing occurs when a variable inside an inner scope (such as a loop or a function) has the same name as a variable in an outer scope. The inner variable 'shadows' the outer one, causing reads and writes inside the inner scope to affect only the inner variable, while the outer variable remains unchanged — or vice versa, depending on the language's scoping rules.

```
✗  Shadowing: outer 'total' not updated by the loop:

SET total = 100    ← outer total: starts at 100
```

```
PROCEDURE add_scores(scores):
  SET total = 0     ← inner total: shadows the outer one!
  FOR EACH score IN scores DO
    SET total = total + score  ← updates INNER total only
  END FOR
  OUTPUT 'Sum inside procedure: ', total
END PROCEDURE

CALL add_scores([10, 20, 30])
OUTPUT 'Outer total: ', total     ← still 100! Inner changes not
visible

✓  Prevention: use distinct variable names across scopes:

SET grand_total = 100     ← outer: named distinctly

PROCEDURE add_scores(scores):
  SET scores_total = 0    ← inner: named distinctly
  FOR EACH score IN scores DO
    SET scores_total = scores_total + score
  END FOR
  RETURN scores_total     ← return the result rather than relying
END PROCEDURE              ← on shared state

SET grand_total = grand_total + CALL add_scores([10, 20, 30])
```

Example 6.3 **Real-world application — Updating the Wrong Variable in a Loop**

A particularly insidious variable error occurs when two variables have similar roles and the programmer updates one in a step that should update the other. The program runs without error; the wrong variable accumulates the data; the output is plausible but incorrect. Only a desk check reveals which variable received the updates.

```
PROBLEM: Track the highest score and the student who achieved it.

✗  Wrong variable updated (highest_score vs best_score):

SET highest_score = 0
SET best_student  = ''

FOR EACH student IN students DO
  IF student.score > highest_score THEN
    SET best_score     = student.score     ← sets 'best_score'
(undefined!)
    SET best_student   = student.name      ← this one is correct
  END IF
END FOR

OUTPUT 'Top student: ', best_student, 'Score: ', highest_score
                                             ← still 0! Never
updated.

Desk check reveals:
```

```
    highest_score = 0 throughout  ← condition never triggers after
first pass
    best_score    = ... (undefined outside IF) → NameError or wrong
value

  ✓  Corrected (update 'highest_score' as the condition checks):

    IF student.score > highest_score THEN
      SET highest_score = student.score   ← updates the variable in the
condition
      SET best_student  = student.name
    END IF
```

> ⚠ **COMMON ERROR** Initialise every accumulator, maximum tracker, minimum tracker, and counter before the loop that updates it. Write the SET statement explicitly in your pseudocode. In a desk check, the column for every variable must have a value in its first row before any loop iteration can be traced. If a column is empty in row one, a SET statement is missing.

The six error types in this chapter — off-by-one, boundary conditions, unvalidated input, infinite loops, and scope and variable errors — are all preventable through planning. The final section provides a comprehensive reference: which planning tool catches which error, and a checklist to apply to every program before coding begins.

7 A Planning Checklist for Logic Error Prevention

The six error types covered in this chapter are not random. They are predictable — they arise from the same design oversights in program after program. This predictability means they are preventable: with the right planning habits applied consistently, most logic errors are caught before a single line of Python is written.

Each planning tool in this book addresses a different aspect of logic error prevention. Pseudocode forces explicit statement of variable initialisations and validation checks. Flowcharts reveal loop exit paths and make infinite-loop risks visible. Desk checks trace the exact values of every variable at every step, catching off-by-one errors, boundary mismatches, wrong variable updates, and uninitialised accumulators. Structure charts ensure that validation belongs in the right module and is not accidentally omitted when functions are split across a decomposed design.

No single planning tool catches all error types. A complete plan uses them together: pseudocode for detail and structure, flowchart for control-flow verification, desk check for value-level correctness. The checklist that follows consolidates the questions that each tool answers, producing a single planning habit that addresses all six error types systematically.

Example 7.1 Introduction — Which Planning Tool Catches Which Error

The reference table below maps each error type to the planning tool best suited to prevent it and the specific question that tool answers about that error.

Error type	Best prevention tool	Key question to ask before coding
Off-by-one in loops	Desk check — trace first and last iteration	Does the loop variable hold the expected value on the first and last iteration? Run the desk check explicitly for i = start and i = end.
Boundary condition errors	Desk check — test the exact boundary value	What output does the program produce when the input equals exactly the boundary? Test with boundary − 1, boundary, and boundary + 1 as separate desk check cases.
Missing input validation	Pseudocode — write the validation check first	What happens if the user enters a letter, a negative number, zero, or nothing? Add the IF/WHILE validation check before any processing step in the pseudocode.
Infinite loops	Flowchart — trace every path to the exit	Is there a guaranteed path from the current state to the loop exit condition? Can the condition ever become false? Draw the flowchart and trace all paths.
Uninitialised variables	Pseudocode — SET every variable before use	Does every variable have an explicit starting value before the first step that reads or uses it? Add SET statements at the top of the pseudocode block.
Wrong variable updated	Desk check — one column per variable	After each step in the desk check, is the value in each variable column what was expected? A mismatch at any step identifies the incorrect update.
Missing recursion base case	Pseudocode — write the base case first	What is the simplest possible input to this function? Does the function return a value immediately for that case, without making a recursive call?

The desk check appears in four of the seven rows because it is the most comprehensive tool for value-level logic errors. The flowchart is most powerful for structural errors (infinite loops, missing exit paths). Pseudocode prevents errors that arise from missing design elements (validation, initialisation, base cases).

Example 7.2 **Variation — The Logic Error Prevention Checklist**

Apply this checklist to every pseudocode design before translating it to Python. Each item corresponds to one of the error types in this chapter. A design that passes all items is ready to be coded.

```
  LOGIC ERROR PREVENTION CHECKLIST

  LOOPS:
    ☐ Is the loop counter/condition variable initialised before the
loop?
```

```
    □ Does the loop start at the correct value? (first iteration desk
check)
    □ Does the loop end at the correct value? (last iteration desk
check)
    □ Is the condition variable updated inside the loop body?
    □ Can the exit condition always eventually become true?
    □ Are all accumulators initialised to a correct starting value?

  DECISIONS:
    □ Are boundary operators correct? (>= vs > and <= vs <)
    □ Is there a three-point desk check at every boundary value?
    □ Is there an ELSE or OTHERWISE branch for unexpected inputs?
    □ Are all cases covered with no gaps and no overlaps?

  INPUT VALIDATION:
    □ Is the input type validated before conversion or arithmetic?
    □ Is the input range validated after type conversion?
    □ Is missing, empty, or None input explicitly handled?
    □ Does each error message describe what valid input looks like?

  VARIABLES:
    □ Does every variable have an explicit SET before its first use?
    □ Are all variable names distinct across nested scopes?
    □ Is the correct variable updated at each step? (desk check
columns)

  RECURSION:
    □ Is the base case written first, before the recursive case?
    □ Does the recursive call always move toward the base case?
    □ Is there a value that will eventually satisfy the base case?
```

Example 7.3 Real-world application — A Desk Check That Catches Two Errors

This example shows a single desk check that catches two separate logic errors in the same pseudocode: an off-by-one in the loop range, and a divisor error in the average calculation. Both are caught before any Python is written.

```
PROBLEM: Read 5 student scores and calculate their average.
Test data: scores = [80, 72, 91, 68, 79]
Expected: total = 390, average = 78.0

✗ BUGGY PSEUDOCODE:
  SET total = 0
  FOR i FROM 1 TO 4 DO          ← Bug 1: TO 4, should be TO 5
    INPUT score
    SET total = total + score
  END FOR
  SET average = total / 4       ← Bug 2: / 4, should be / 5
  OUTPUT average

DESK CHECK WITH TEST DATA:
Step           | i  | score | total | average
────────────── | ── | ───── | ───── | ───────
SET total=0    | -  |  -    |   0   | -
i=1, score     | 1  |  80   |  80   |
i=2, score     | 2  |  72   | 152   |
```

```
  i=3, score     | 3  |  91    | 243    |
  i=4, score     | 4  |  68    | 311    |
  (loop ends)    |    |        |        |  ← sccre 79 never read! Bug 1
visible.
  average=311/4|     |        |        | 77.75 ← Bug 2: wrong total AND
divisor.

  ERRORS IDENTIFIED:
    Bug 1: Loop ran 4 times (scores 80,72,91,68). Score 79 was skipped.
           Fix: FOR i FROM 1 TO 5 DO
    Bug 2: Average divided by 4. Should divide by 5.
           Fix: SET average = total / 5

  ✓  CORRECTED DESK CHECK:
  After fix: total = 80+72+91+68+79 = 390, average = 390/5 = 78.0  ✓
```

Both errors were found in a single desk check that took approximately five minutes. Without planning, these errors would have been discovered during testing after the code was written — at significantly greater cost in time and effort. The desk check is the most direct path from 'plan' to 'correct'.

> ▶ **NOTE** Apply the logic error prevention checklist to every significant pseudocode design before coding begins. Use the three-point desk check at every boundary value. Trace the first and last iteration of every loop. Check that every column in the desk check has a valid value before the loop starts. These habits, practised consistently, will eliminate the vast majority of logic errors before they ever appear in Python.

This chapter has catalogued the six most common logic error types and shown how the planning tools from earlier chapters — pseudocode, flowcharts, and desk checks — prevent each one. Chapter 7 focuses exclusively on desk checking as a discipline: how to construct trace tables, choose test data, and trace complex pseudocode to verify correctness before implementation.

Chapter Summary

- Logic errors are the most dangerous category of program error because they produce no error message. The program runs to completion and returns a wrong result silently. The only way to detect them is to know the expected output and compare it to the actual output.
- Off-by-one errors occur when a loop iterates one too many or one too few times, or when an index is one position off from its intended value. They are caught by a targeted desk check of the first and last iterations. When translating FOR loops to Python, remember that range() excludes its upper bound.
- Boundary condition errors occur when a comparison operator (> vs >=, < vs <=) is wrong at a critical threshold. They are caught by a three-point desk check: test with the value one below the boundary, the exact boundary, and

the value one above. A correct boundary produces the right output for all three.

- Defensive design validates all input before using it. The three validation layers are: type (is it the right kind of data?), range (is it in the valid range?), and logic (does it make sense in context?). Validation checks should appear in pseudocode before any step that uses the input value.
- Infinite loops occur when the exit condition never becomes true. The three common causes are: the loop counter is never incremented; the loop body updates the wrong variable; or the condition can never become false given the program's data. Flowcharts reveal infinite-loop risks by making every path from the loop body to the condition diamond visible.
- Missing recursion base cases cause infinite recursion. Always write the base case first in recursive pseudocode and verify that the recursive call always moves toward that base case.
- Uninitialised variable errors occur when a variable is used before it has been given a starting value. Accumulators, counters, maximum trackers, and minimum trackers must all be explicitly SET before the loop that updates them. Variable shadowing occurs when inner and outer scope variables share a name; use distinct names to prevent it.
- The logic error prevention checklist provides a systematic pre-coding review: check loop boundaries and counter updates, apply three-point desk checks at boundaries, verify all input validation, and confirm every variable is initialised. A design that passes the checklist is ready to be coded.

Guided Exercises

Complete all five exercises before moving on to Chapter 7. Each exercise includes a hint to help you get started.

Exercise 1

Each pseudocode fragment below contains an off-by-one error. Identify the error in each case and write the corrected version: (a) FOR i FROM 0 TO N DO (intended to process N items in a 0-based list); (b) FOR i FROM 1 TO COUNT(items) − 1 DO (intended to process all items); (c) WHILE count < 5 DO ... SET count = count + 1 (intended to execute exactly 5 times, starting with count = 1).

Hint: For each fragment, perform a desk check of the first and last iteration using a small concrete value for N or COUNT. Trace what the loop variable equals at entry and at exit, and compare to what was intended.

Exercise 2

A student has written the following validation condition for accepting a password of between 8 and 20 characters: IF LENGTH(password) > 8 AND LENGTH(password) < 20. Apply a three-point desk check to this condition using passwords of length 7, 8, 20, and 21. Identify what is wrong with the condition and write the corrected version.

Hint: The three-point test uses values just outside, exactly at, and just inside each boundary. There are two boundaries here (8 and 20), so test all four edge values: 7, 8, 20, and 21. For each, determine what the current condition returns and what it should return.

Exercise 3

Add input validation to the following pseudocode so that it correctly handles: (a) non-numeric input for the score; (b) a score below 0 or above 100; (c) an empty response (no input given). Write the validation using WHILE loops, and include a helpful error message for each invalid case. BEGIN INPUT score OUTPUT 'Grade:', calculate_grade(score) END

Hint: Use a WHILE loop for type validation (keep asking until a valid number is entered). After type validation and conversion, use a second WHILE loop for range validation (keep asking until the number is between 0 and 100). Empty input can be treated as a special case of non-numeric input.

Exercise 4

Identify the error in the following pseudocode and explain what type of logic error it is (off-by-one, boundary condition, infinite loop, scope/uninitialised, or wrong variable): SET maximum = 0 FOR EACH value IN data DO IF value > maximum THEN SET highest = value END IF END FOR OUTPUT 'Maximum:', maximum Then write the corrected version and perform a desk check with data = [5, 3, 8, 1, 6] to verify it.

Hint: Trace through the pseudocode with data = [5, 3, 8, 1, 6] using a desk check table with columns: value, maximum, highest. Look at what gets updated when each condition is true, and what gets output at the end. The error type will become clear from the trace.

Exercise 5

Apply the complete Logic Error Prevention Checklist from Section 7 to the following pseudocode, noting which checklist items pass and which fail. Then write the corrected version of the pseudocode. SET i = 0 WHILE i <= COUNT(scores) DO SET running_total = running_total + scores[i] SET i = i + 1 END WHILE OUTPUT running_total / COUNT(scores)

Hint: Work through the checklist systematically. Check: is i initialised correctly (0-based, so first valid index is 0, last is COUNT−1)? Is the WHILE condition correct (should it be < or <=)? Is running_total initialised? Would a desk check with scores = [10, 20, 30] reveal any errors?

Challenge Tasks

These tasks have no hints. They require independent thinking and are suitable for extension or assessment. Complete the Guided Exercises before attempting these.

Challenge Task 1

The following pseudocode is intended to find both the maximum and minimum values in a list of temperatures recorded over a month (31 values, stored in a list called temps). It contains at least four separate logic errors spanning multiple categories from this chapter. Identify every error, state which error category it belongs to (off-by-one, boundary condition, missing validation, infinite loop, scope/uninitialised, wrong variable), explain what the consequence of each error would be at runtime, and write the fully corrected pseudocode. SET max_temp = 0 SET min_temp = 0 FOR i FROM 1 TO 31 DO IF temps[i] > max_temp THEN SET max_temperature = temps[i] END IF IF temps[i] < min_temp THEN SET min_temp = temps[i] END IF END FOR OUTPUT 'Maximum: ', max_temp OUTPUT 'Minimum: ', min_temp

Challenge Task 2

Design and write a complete, defensively designed pseudocode function called safe_divide(numerator, denominator) that performs division with full input validation. The function must handle: non-numeric numerator or denominator; a denominator of zero; numerators and denominators that are valid numbers but result in a value outside a specified acceptable range (given as parameters min_result and max_result). For each invalid case, the function should return a meaningful error message as a string rather than raising an exception. Write a desk check for at least five test cases covering the normal case, each validation failure case, and a result that falls outside the acceptable range.

Challenge Task 3

This challenge asks you to deliberately introduce, then find and fix, logic errors. Write pseudocode for a function that reads a list of 10 student names and scores from the user, computes the class average, identifies the student with the highest score, and lists all students who scored below the class average. Once your pseudocode is complete and you believe it is correct, deliberately introduce one error of each of the following types: off-by-one, boundary condition, uninitialised variable, and wrong variable updated. Exchange your deliberately-broken pseudocode with a classmate (or re-read it yourself after a break). Apply the logic error prevention checklist and a full desk check to identify and fix all four introduced errors. Document each error found: its type, its location, its consequence, and the fix.

Desk Checking and Algorithm Tracing

This chapter teaches desk checking as a systematic discipline: the skill of tracing pseudocode manually, step by step, to verify that it produces the correct result for every category of input before a single line of Python is written. You will learn how to set up a trace table, how to record each step of sequential, conditional, and iterative pseudocode, how to trace complex algorithms including nested loops, and how to choose test data that exposes errors rather than concealing them. The chapter concludes with a complete worked example showing how a desk check identifies a bug, and how updating the pseudocode resolves it.

1 What a Desk Check Is and Why It Works

A desk check is a manual, step-by-step trace of a pseudocode algorithm using specific test data. The programmer reads each statement of the pseudocode in execution order, computes the effect of that statement by hand, and records the result in a structured table — one column per variable, one row per step. The completed table shows the exact state of every variable at every point in the algorithm's execution.

A desk check works because it forces the programmer to think precisely about what each statement does, rather than what they intend it to do. When we write pseudocode, it is easy to read what we expect to see rather than what is actually written. A desk check removes this ambiguity: each step is evaluated using the current values in the table, not the values we wish were there. Errors surface immediately, because the computed values in the table disagree with the expected output.

The desk check originated in the era before interactive computers, when programmers had to verify their programs entirely by hand before submitting them for batch processing. Today, it remains the most reliable planning-stage technique for catching logic errors — more reliable than reading pseudocode, more revealing than informal mental simulation, and vastly cheaper than discovering errors after the code is written.

Example 1.1 Introduction — The Desk Check vs Mental Simulation

A student writes pseudocode to calculate the average of three test scores. They read it through mentally and are satisfied it is correct. A desk check with test data immediately reveals the error: the divisor is 4 instead of 3.

```
  PSEUDOCODE:                         MENTAL READ:
  SET total = s1 + s2 + s3           'Adds the three scores — looks
right'
```

```
  SET average = total / 4          'Divides by... um, three scores...
looks right'
  OUTPUT average

  Mentally, we see what we expect. The desk check sees what is written.
```

Trace table — Test data: s1 = 80, s2 = 70, s3 = 90 (expected average = 80.0)

Step	total	average	Output
SET total = s1 + s2 + s3	240	—	—
SET average = total / 4	—	60.0	—
OUTPUT average	—	—	60.0 ✗ expected 80.0

The desk check reveals the error at the second row: 240 / 4 = 60.0, not the expected 80.0. The fix is immediate: the divisor should be 3, not 4. Two minutes of desk checking saved an unknown amount of debugging time.

Example 1.2 Variation — Four Things a Desk Check Confirms

```
A complete desk check confirms four things simultaneously:

1. CORRECTNESS: Does the algorithm produce the expected output
                for the given test data?

2. COMPLETENESS: Are all variables initialised before they are
                 first used? (Empty cells in the first row flag
                 missing SET statements.)

3. TERMINATION: In a loop, does each iteration move closer to
                the exit condition? (A variable that never changes
                in its column signals an infinite loop.)

4. BOUNDARY ACCURACY: Does the algorithm produce the correct
                      output for edge-case inputs, not just
                      typical ones?

A mental read of pseudocode checks none of these reliably.
A desk check checks all four simultaneously.
```

Example 1.3 Real-world application — Desk Checks in Professional Practice

In safety-critical software domains — medical devices, aviation control systems, financial trading platforms — formal verification of algorithm correctness is mandated before implementation. The desk check is the accessible, practical version of formal verification that every programmer can apply to any algorithm.

Professional developers performing code reviews frequently trace through a submitted algorithm with a specific test case before approving it. This is a desk check performed at the review stage. Performing the same desk check at the planning stage — before any code is written — produces the same value at a fraction of the cost, because the pseudocode can be corrected with an eraser rather than a code rewrite.

> ▶ **NOTE** Always perform a desk check on pseudocode before translating it to Python. The desk check is the single most effective technique for catching logic errors before they become bugs. For short algorithms (under 10 steps), a desk check takes two to five minutes. For complex algorithms, it takes ten to twenty. Both are faster than the debugging time saved.

2 Setting Up a Trace Table

The trace table is the record of a desk check. Setting it up correctly before tracing begins determines whether the check is systematic and complete, or incomplete and likely to miss errors. A well-constructed trace table has one column for the step description, one column for every variable in the pseudocode, and one column for any outputs the algorithm produces. Each row represents one step that changes at least one variable's value.

To identify the columns, read through the entire pseudocode before drawing anything. List every variable name that appears in a SET statement. These are the variable columns. Add a step column on the left and an output column on the right. The step column contains a brief description of the pseudocode line being executed — not the full line, but enough to identify it unambiguously: 'SET total = 0' or 'i = 3, check condition'.

The convention for unchanged variables is to leave the cell blank — or to write a dash (—) to signal explicitly that no change occurred. Either convention is acceptable; the important thing is to be consistent throughout a single trace table. A blank or dash in a column means 'this variable has the same value it had in the most recent non-blank row of this column'.

Example 2.1 **Introduction — Identifying Columns from Pseudocode**

Before drawing the trace table, read the pseudocode and list every variable. The variables become the column headers. The example below shows the process for a short pseudocode block.

```
PSEUDOCODE to analyse:

SET price    = 49.95        ← variable: price
SET quantity = 3             ← variable: quantity
SET subtotal = price × quantity ← variable: subtotal
SET gst      = subtotal × 0.10  ← variable: gst
SET total    = subtotal + gst   ← variable: total
OUTPUT 'Total: $', total
```

```
Variables identified: price, quantity, subtotal, gst, total
Output column needed: yes (one OUTPUT statement)

Trace table columns:
| Step | price | quantity | subtotal | gst | total | Output |

NOTE: Constants (0.10) do not get their own column.
NOTE: Input values (price=49.95) appear in the first data row.
```

Example 2.2 Variation — What Counts as a Step

Each row in the trace table corresponds to one step that changes the state of at least one variable, or that produces output. Pseudocode lines that purely define structure (BEGIN, END, END IF, END FOR) do not need their own rows — they are not executable in the sense of changing values. The step column describes what happened, not just which line was reached.

```
  PSEUDOCODE LINE                 TRACE TABLE STEP DESCRIPTION
  ________________________    _____________________________
  BEGIN                        (not a row — no state change)
  SET total = 0               'SET total = 0'
  INPUT score                 'INPUT score' (shows value in column)
  IF score >= 50 THEN         'score >= 50? [TRUE/FALSE]'
  SET grade = 'Pass'          'SET grade = Pass'
  ELSE                        (not a row — structural only)
  SET grade = 'Fail'          'SET grade = Fail'  (if FALSE branch
taken)
  END IF                      (not a row — structural only)
  FOR i FROM 1 TO 5 DO       'i = 1, condition 1 <= 5? [TRUE]'
  SET total = total + val    'SET total = total + val'
  SET i = i + 1              'SET i = i + 1' (or show as part of FOR
row)
  END FOR                    'i = 6, condition 6 <= 5? [FALSE] → exit'
  OUTPUT result              'OUTPUT result'
  END                        (not a row)
```

Example 2.3 Real-world application — Setting Up Before Tracing

A complete trace table setup for the grade classification pseudocode below is shown. Notice that the table is drawn — with all columns and the header row — before a single data row is filled in. Drawing the structure first, then filling in values step by step, is the correct procedure.

```
  PSEUDOCODE:                          TRACE TABLE STRUCTURE (before tracing):

  INPUT score                          | Step          | score | grade |
Output |
  IF score >= 85 THEN
|———————————————|————————|————————|————————|
    SET grade='High Distinction'  | INPUT score    |        |        |
|
  ELSE IF score >= 75 THEN         | score >= 85?  |        |        |
|
```

```
    SET grade='Distinction'       | SET grade = ? |        |       |
|
  ELSE IF score >= 65 THEN       | OUTPUT grade  |        |       |
|
    SET grade='Credit'
  ELSE IF score >= 50 THEN       Numbers are filled in during the trace.
    SET grade='Pass'             The structure is decided first.
  ELSE
    SET grade='Fail'
  END IF
  OUTPUT grade
```

▶ **NOTE** Set up the entire trace table structure — all column headers, and one row label per step — before filling in any values. Writing the structure first gives you an overview of the whole algorithm and prevents the common mistake of forgetting a step halfway through the trace.

3 Tracing Sequential Pseudocode

Tracing a sequential algorithm is the simplest form of desk check: every statement executes in order, no branch is taken, no step is repeated. Each row of the trace table shows one assignment or output statement, with the new value recorded in the appropriate column and all other columns left blank (unchanged). The trace reads from top to bottom exactly as the pseudocode does.

Sequential traces are useful for verifying ordering correctness — ensuring that every variable is assigned a value before it is first used, and that calculations are performed in the correct sequence. They also provide a reference for expected intermediate values, which becomes important when a longer algorithm contains bugs: you can compare the trace to the program's actual output at each step to pinpoint exactly where the divergence occurs.

When tracing a sequential algorithm, pay particular attention to the first row: if any column other than the step column is blank in the first data row, a variable is being used before it is initialised. That blank cell identifies a missing SET statement. This is the uninitialised variable error discussed in Chapter 6, and a desk check catches it immediately.

Example 3.1 Introduction — A GST Receipt Calculation

This sequential algorithm calculates the GST-inclusive total for a purchase. The trace uses concrete test values: price = $49.95, quantity = 3. Every variable is set before it is used; the trace confirms the ordering is correct.

Trace table — Test data: price = 49.95, quantity = 3

Step	price	quantity	subtotal	gst	total
SET price = 49.95	49.95	—	—	—	—
SET quantity = 3	—	3	—	—	—

Step	price	quantity	subtotal	gst	total
SET subtotal = price × qty	—	—	149.85	—	—
SET gst = subtotal × 0.10	—	—	—	14.985	—
SET total = subtotal + gst	—	—	—	—	164.835

Reading down the trace: price and quantity are set first; subtotal uses both (both exist); gst uses subtotal (it exists); total uses subtotal and gst (both exist). No variable is used before it is set. The final value of total is 164.835 — confirmed before any Python is written. A separate OUTPUT row would show the formatted value displayed to the user.

Example 3.2 **Variation — Weighted Assessment Mark**

This trace checks a weighted mark calculation in which three assessment components contribute different percentages. The trace makes the intermediate weighting values visible, allowing each component's contribution to be verified independently.

Trace table — Test data: task1 = 78, task2 = 85, exam = 72

Step	task1	task2	exam	wt1	wt2	wexm	final
Inputs	78	85	72	—	—	—	—
SET wt1 = task1 × 0.30	—	—	—	23.4	—	—	—
SET wt2 = task2 × 0.30	—	—	—	—	25.5	—	—
SET wexm = exam × 0.40	—	—	—	—	—	28.8	—
SET final = wt1 + wt2 + wexm	—	—	—	—	—	—	77.7

The expected final mark is 78×0.30 + 85×0.30 + 72×0.40 = 23.4 + 25.5 + 28.8 = 77.7. The trace confirms this before any code is written. Each weighting can be checked independently by reading the relevant row.

Example 3.3 **Real-world application — Payroll with Overtime**

This payroll calculation includes a branching rule (overtime at 1.5× for hours above 38), but the branching is simple enough that the sequential trace with a test case of 42 hours clearly shows the standard and overtime components.

Trace table — Test data: rate = 25.00, hours = 42

Step	std_h	ot_h	std_pay	ot_pay	gross
Inputs: rate=25.00, hours=42	—	—	—	—	—
SET std_h = MIN(42, 38) = 38	38	—	—	—	—
SET ot_h = MAX(0, 42−38) = 4	—	4	—	—	—
SET std_pay = 38 × 25.00	—	—	950.00	—	—
SET ot_pay = 4 × 25.00 × 1.5	—	—	—	150.00	—

Step	std_h	ot_h	std_pay	ot_pay	gross
SET gross = std_pay + ot_pay	—	—	—	—	1100.00

> ▶ **NOTE** In a sequential trace, if any column other than 'Step' is blank in the very first data row, the algorithm uses a variable before setting it. Add the missing SET statement and restart the trace. Never proceed past an uninitialised variable.

4 Tracing Conditional Logic

Tracing conditional logic requires at least one test case per branch. A single test case that follows the 'happy path' may pass every row of its trace correctly while leaving other branches completely unchecked. A complete desk check of conditional pseudocode runs the trace once for each distinct path the algorithm can take, including the boundary values discussed in Chapter 6.

In the trace table, the decision step is recorded as a question with its result: 'score >= 75? [TRUE]' or 'score >= 75? [FALSE]'. When the condition is TRUE, only the steps inside that branch are recorded in subsequent rows — the steps in all other branches are skipped. When the condition is FALSE, those steps are skipped and the trace continues from the next ELSE IF or ELSE.

The minimum number of test cases for a complete conditional trace is: one test case per branch, plus one test case at each boundary value. For a five-band IF/ELSE IF chain (HD/D/C/P/Fail), a complete trace requires at least five test cases (one per band), plus boundary tests at the four thresholds. The desk check confirms both that each band produces the correct grade and that each boundary is correctly placed.

Example 4.1 Introduction — Two Test Cases for an IF/ELSE

This pseudocode classifies a temperature as 'Hot' (>= 35) or 'Comfortable' (< 35). Two test cases are needed to trace both branches. Note how the FALSE branch step is simply omitted from the second trace — it is not executed.

Test case 1: temp = 38 → expected output: Hot

Step	temp	status	Output
INPUT temp	38	—	—
temp >= 35? TRUE	—	—	—
SET status = 'Hot'	—	'Hot'	—
OUTPUT status	—	—	Hot

Test case 2: temp = 22 → expected output: Comfortable

Step	temp	status	Output
INPUT temp	22	—	—

Step	temp	status	Output
temp >= 35? FALSE → ELSE	—	—	—
SET status = 'Comfortable'	—	`'Comfortable'`	—
OUTPUT status	—	—	`Comfortable`

Two separate trace tables, one per branch, confirm both outcomes. Adding a third trace with temp = 35 (the boundary) would verify the >= operator is correct for that threshold.

Example 4.2 Variation — ELSE IF Chain with Boundary Testing

For a grade classification with four ELSE IF branches, the table below shows three test cases in a single condensed table, separated by shaded dividers. Each test case is traced only through the steps that execute for that input.

Grade classifier — Three test cases: score = 91 (HD), 75 (D boundary), 49 (Fail)

Step / Test case	score	grade	Output
TEST CASE 1: score = 91	—	—	—
INPUT score	91	—	—
score >= 85? TRUE → HD branch	—	—	—
SET grade = 'High Distinction'	—	`'High Distinction'`	—
OUTPUT grade	—	—	`High Distinction`
TEST CASE 2: score = 75 (boundary)	—	—	—
INPUT score	75	—	—
score >= 85? FALSE	—	—	—
score >= 75? TRUE → D branch	—	—	—
SET grade = 'Distinction'	—	`'Distinction'`	—
OUTPUT grade	—	—	`Distinction`
TEST CASE 3: score = 49	—	—	—
INPUT score	49	—	—
score >= 85? FALSE	—	—	—
score >= 75? FALSE	—	—	—
score >= 65? FALSE	—	—	—
score >= 50? FALSE	—	—	—
ELSE → SET grade = 'Fail'	—	`'Fail'`	—
OUTPUT grade	—	—	`Fail`

Test case 2 (score = 75) is the boundary test. It confirms that score = 75 correctly enters the Distinction branch (‘score >= 75’ is TRUE). A bug using > instead of >= would produce ‘Credit’ for this input — the boundary trace would catch it.

Example 4.3 **Real-world application — Tracing Nested Decisions**

Nested IF structures require tracing the outer condition first, then the inner condition only if the outer was TRUE. Each level of nesting adds one more condition step in the trace. This example shows a two-level nested decision for a library borrowing check.

Nested decision trace — Test data: is_member = TRUE, copies_available = 0

Step	is_member	copies_avail	Output
Inputs	TRUE	0	—
is_member? TRUE → enter outer branch	—	—	—
copies_avail > 0? FALSE → inner ELSE	—	—	—
OUTPUT 'No copies available'	—	—	No copies available

> ▶ **NOTE** Always trace one test case per branch, and include at least one boundary test at every threshold. A conditional desk check that uses only ‘comfortable’ mid-range values will pass even when the boundary operators are wrong. The boundary test is the one that matters most.

5 Tracing Loops and Iterative Algorithms

Tracing a loop requires one row (or one group of rows) per iteration, showing how each variable changes as the loop executes. For short loops with few iterations (say, five or fewer), trace every iteration explicitly. For longer loops, trace the first two, the third, and the last — the first two establish the pattern, the third confirms it, and the last verifies the termination condition.

The most important rows in a loop trace are the first iteration (verifying initialisation and that the loop enters correctly), the last iteration (verifying the final state of accumulators and that the exit condition fires at the right point), and any iteration where a conditional inside the loop changes state. All other iterations can be condensed to a single row showing only the variables that change.

WHILE loop traces must show the condition check at the start of each iteration. If the condition is checked and found FALSE at any point, the trace exits the loop and continues with the statement after END WHILE. FOR loop traces show the current value of the loop variable at each iteration and the condition check at the end or beginning (depending on the loop type). The loop variable’s final value — just beyond the exit condition — is often informative: it confirms that the loop ran exactly the right number of times.

Example 5.1 Introduction — WHILE Loop with a Sentinel Value

This algorithm reads integer values until the user enters −1 (the sentinel), accumulates their total, and counts how many were entered. The trace uses input values 8, 5, 12, 3, −1.

Trace table — Input sequence: 8, 5, 12, 3, −1 (expected: total=28, count=4, average=7.0)

Step / Iteration	value	total	count	Output
Initialise: SET total=0, count=0	—	0	0	—
Iter 1: input 8; 8 ≠ −1 TRUE	8	8	1	—
Iter 2: input 5; 5 ≠ −1 TRUE	5	13	2	—
Iter 3: input 12; 12 ≠ −1 TRUE	12	25	3	—
Iter 4: input 3; 3 ≠ −1 TRUE	3	28	4	—
Input −1; −1=−1 FALSE → exit	-1	—	—	—
OUTPUT 28 / 4	—	—	—	7.0 ✓

The trace confirms: the loop ran exactly 4 times (count = 4); total accumulated correctly to 28; the sentinel (−1) caused a FALSE condition and the loop exited; the output of 7.0 matches the expected average of 28/4 = 7.0.

Example 5.2 Variation — FOR Loop Finding Maximum and Total

This condensed trace shows one row per iteration for a FOR loop that accumulates a running total and tracks the maximum value. Each row shows all variables that change in that iteration. The condensed style is appropriate when the pattern is clear after two or three iterations.

Condensed trace — data = [14, 8, 22, 11, 17] (expected: total=72, maximum=22)

Iteration	value	total	maximum	Note
Initialise	—	0	0	SET total=0, maximum=0
i = 1	14	14	14	14 > 0: update maximum
i = 2	8	22	—	8 > 14? No: no update
i = 3	22	44	22	22 > 14: update maximum
i = 4	11	55	—	11 > 22? No: no update
i = 5	17	72	—	17 > 22? No: no update
Final	—	—	—	total=72, maximum=22 ✓

The 'Note' column provides a brief explanation of why maximum did or did not change in each iteration. This optional annotation makes the trace self-documenting and easier to review. For iterations 2, 4, and 5 where maximum does not change, the dash (—) signals no update without requiring a full explanation.

Example 5.3 Real-world application — Nested Loop Trace

Nested loops require a complete iteration of the inner loop for each iteration of the outer loop. The trace below shows every combination of outer (row) and inner (col) variables for a 3 × 3 multiplication table. Because the pattern is repetitive and clear, the trace is shown in condensed form.

Nested loop trace — 3×3 multiplication table (row FROM 1 TO 3, col FROM 1 TO 3)

Outer (row)	Inner (col)	row × col	Output
row = 1	1	1	1
row = 1	2	2	2
row = 1	3	3	3 ← inner loop exits (col=4 > 3)
row = 2	1	2	2
row = 2	2	4	4
row = 2	3	6	6 ← inner loop exits
row = 3	1	3	3
row = 3	2	6	6
row = 3	3	9	9 ← both loops exit

> ▶ **NOTE** In a nested loop trace, the inner loop variable resets to its starting value at the beginning of each outer loop iteration. Show this reset explicitly in the trace by starting the inner loop rows from 1 (or whatever the starting value is) at the beginning of each outer iteration. A nested loop trace has outer×inner rows, not outer+inner.

6 Choosing Meaningful Test Data

The quality of a desk check depends entirely on the test data used. Test data that only exercises the 'happy path' — typical, in-range, well-behaved inputs — may pass the trace even when the algorithm contains errors that will surface with boundary or erroneous inputs. A complete desk check uses test data from three distinct categories: normal, boundary, and erroneous.

Normal test data represents the typical inputs the program will receive: mid-range values, the most common use case, inputs that should produce straightforward outputs. These tests confirm that the algorithm works correctly under ordinary conditions. Boundary test data tests the exact edges of acceptable ranges: the smallest valid value, the largest valid value, and the values just outside those limits.

These tests reveal off-by-one errors, incorrect operators, and gaps or overlaps in conditional chains. Erroneous test data represents inputs that should be rejected: values outside the valid range, wrong data types, empty inputs. These tests confirm that the defensive design from Chapter 6 is functioning correctly.

Equivalence partitioning is a technique for choosing test data efficiently: rather than testing every possible value (impossible for most real inputs), identify groups of inputs that the algorithm treats identically, and test one value from each group. For a grade classification, scores 60, 61, 62, …, 74 all produce ‘Credit’ — they are equivalent. Testing one value from the Credit band is sufficient, plus boundary tests at the Credit thresholds.

Example 6.1 **Introduction — The Three Test Data Categories**

The table below shows a complete test data set for a grade classification algorithm that accepts scores from 0 to 100. Every category is represented, including both sides of each boundary.

Category	`Test value`	Expected output	What it tests
Normal	`72`	`Credit`	`Typical mid-range value in Credit band`
Normal	`88`	`High Distinction`	`Typical high value in HD band`
Normal	`45`	`Fail`	`Typical low value, clearly below Pass threshold`
Boundary	`85`	`High Distinction`	`Exact lower boundary of HD band`
Boundary	`84`	`Distinction`	`One below HD boundary — should NOT be HD`
Boundary	`75`	`Distinction`	`Exact lower boundary of Distinction band`
Boundary	`50`	`Pass`	`Exact lower boundary of Pass band`
Boundary	`49`	`Fail`	`One below Pass boundary — should be Fail`
Boundary	`0`	`Fail`	`Minimum valid score`
Boundary	`100`	`High Distinction`	`Maximum valid score`
Erroneous	`'hello'`	`Error message`	`Non-numeric input — tests type validation`
Erroneous	`''`	`Error message`	`Empty input — tests empty input handling`
Erroneous	`-15`	`Error message`	`Below valid range — tests range validation`
Erroneous	`105`	`Error message`	`Above valid range — tests range validation`

Example 6.2 Variation — Equivalence Partitioning

Equivalence partitioning reduces a large input space to a manageable set of test cases without sacrificing coverage. For the grade classifier, there are five equivalence classes of valid scores (one per grade band), plus the boundary values between them, plus the erroneous inputs. Testing one value from each class — rather than all possible values — is both efficient and sufficient.

```
  EQUIVALENCE CLASSES for grade classifier (score range 0-100):

  Valid inputs — five classes:
    Class 1: score >= 85              (High Distinction) → test with 91
    Class 2: 75 <= score < 85         (Distinction)      → test with 80
    Class 3: 65 <= score < 75         (Credit)           → test with 70
    Class 4: 50 <= score < 65         (Pass)             → test with 57
    Class 5: score < 50               (Fail)             → test with 35

  Boundary values — one test above and one at each class boundary:
    84, 85    (HD lower boundary)
    74, 75    (Distinction lower boundary)
    64, 65    (Credit lower boundary)
    49, 50    (Pass lower boundary)
     0, 100   (absolute limits of valid range)

  Erroneous inputs — one per error type:
    -1        (negative: below range)
    101       (positive: above range)
    'hello'   (wrong type: not numeric)
    ''        (empty: no input given)

  Total: 5 class tests + 10 boundary tests + 4 erroneous = 19 test
cases.
  Covers the entire input space without testing every integer from 0 to
100.
```

Example 6.3 Real-world application — Erroneous Data Reveals Missing Validation

Running an erroneous test case through a desk check often reveals missing validation — the algorithm has no step that handles the invalid input, so the trace proceeds through the algorithm with unexpected data and produces a wrong or crashed result. The desk check of the erroneous case answers: 'What does the algorithm actually do with this input?' If the answer is wrong, a validation step is missing from the pseudocode.

Trace with erroneous input: score = 'hello' (expected: error message)

Step	score	grade	Output
INPUT score	`'hello'`	—	—
IF score >= 85? → CRASH	—	—	`TypeError: cannot compare str to int` ✗

The erroneous desk check reveals that the pseudocode has no validation step before the IF condition. The fix is to add a validation WHILE loop (as shown in

Chapter 6) before the comparison. The desk check with erroneous data made the missing validation visible at the planning stage.

> ▶ **NOTE** Always include at least one erroneous test case in your desk check. If the trace reaches a calculation step with erroneous data, the algorithm is missing a validation check. Add the check to the pseudocode and re-trace with the erroneous input to confirm it is now correctly rejected.

7 Desk Checking a Complete Algorithm — Finding and Fixing a Bug

This section applies every technique from this chapter to a complete algorithm: setting up the trace table, choosing test data from all three categories, tracing the algorithm step by step, identifying a bug in the trace, correcting the pseudocode, and verifying the fix with a second trace. This is the full desk checking workflow as it is applied in practice.

The algorithm in this section finds the student with the highest score in a class list. It contains a single bug that is invisible when tested with normal data — the algorithm gives correct results for the normal test case — but is revealed by an erroneous test case that the desk check exposes. This is exactly the scenario that makes desk checking indispensable: the normal test passes; the real-world edge case fails.

The bug-finding workflow is: run the normal test case first (it passes, but confirms the trace is set up correctly); then run a boundary or erroneous test case that is likely to expose errors; identify the row where the trace diverges from the expected output; trace back from that row to identify the source of the error; correct the pseudocode; and re-run the trace to confirm the fix.

Example 7.1 Introduction — The Algorithm and Normal Test Case

The pseudocode below finds the name and score of the student with the highest score in a list. It contains a bug that affects only specific inputs. The first desk check uses normal test data — it passes, which is why the bug is easy to miss.

```
PSEUDOCODE — Find the top-scoring student:

SET highest   = 0              ← initialised to 0
SET top_name = ''
FOR EACH student IN class DO
  IF student.score > highest THEN
    SET highest   = student.score
    SET top_name = student.name
  END IF
END FOR
OUTPUT top_name, 'scored', highest
```

Normal test — class = [Ana:85, Ben:72, Cat:91, Dan:68, Eli:79] (expected: Cat scored 91)

Iteration	student	Condition	highest	top_name
Initialise	—	—	0	''
i=1 (Ana: 85)	Ana:85	85 > 0? TRUE	85	Ana
i=2 (Ben: 72)	Ben:72	72 > 85? FALSE	—	—
i=3 (Cat: 91)	Cat:91	91 > 85? TRUE	91	Cat
i=4 (Dan: 68)	Dan:68	68 > 91? FALSE	—	—
i=5 (Eli: 79)	Eli:79	79 > 91? FALSE	—	—
OUTPUT	—	—	—	Cat scored 91 ✓

The normal test passes perfectly: Cat scored 91, which is correct. The bug is not visible here. This is why normal-only testing is insufficient — a bug that only affects specific edge cases will never be caught by a normal test alone.

Example 7.2 Variation — The Erroneous Test Case That Reveals the Bug

Now run the desk check with an erroneous test case: all scores are negative (a perfectly valid scenario if scores represent a penalty system or a deviation from a baseline). Expected output: Dan scored −1 (the least negative, i.e. highest score). Actual output from the buggy pseudocode: '' scored 0.

Erroneous test — class = [Ana:−5, Ben:−3, Cat:−8, Dan:−1, Eli:−4] (expected: Dan scored −1)

Iteration	student	Condition	highest	top_name
Initialise	—	—	0	''
i=1 (Ana: −5)	Ana:-5	(-5) > 0? FALSE	—	—
i=2 (Ben: −3)	Ben:-3	(-3) > 0? FALSE	—	—
i=3 (Cat: −8)	Cat:-8	(-8) > 0? FALSE	—	—
i=4 (Dan: −1)	Dan:-1	(-1) > 0? FALSE	—	—
i=5 (Eli: −4)	Eli:-4	(-4) > 0? FALSE	—	—
OUTPUT	—	—	—	'' scored 0 ✗ BUG!

The bug is now visible. Because highest is initialised to 0, and all scores are negative (therefore all less than 0), the condition 'student.score > highest' is never true. The algorithm never updates highest or top_name, and the output is the uninitialised values: empty string and 0. Neither is correct.

The source of the bug: SET highest = 0. The fix: initialise highest to the first student's score, not to 0. This ensures that highest is a real score from the start, and all subsequent scores are compared against a real score rather than an arbitrary constant.

Example 7.3 Real-world application — The Corrected Pseudocode and Confirming Trace

The corrected pseudocode initialises highest and top_name to the first student's values, then compares the remaining students against that starting value. The desk check with the previously-failing test data now produces the correct output.

```
  CORRECTED PSEUDOCODE:

  SET highest  = class[1].score     ← initialise to FIRST student's
score
  SET top_name = class[1].name       ← initialise to FIRST student's
name
  FOR EACH student IN class[2..] DO  ← compare remaining students only
    IF student.score > highest THEN
      SET highest  = student.score
      SET top_name = student.name
    END IF
  END FOR
  OUTPUT top_name, 'scored', highest
```

Confirming trace — same erroneous data: [−5, −3, −8, −1, −4] (expected: Dan scored −1)

Iteration	student	Condition	highest	top_name
Initialise to first	—	—	-5	Ana
i=2 (Ben: −3)	Ben:-3	(-3) > (-5)? **TRUE**	-3	Ben
i=3 (Cat: −8)	Cat:-8	(-8) > (-3)? **FALSE**	—	—
i=4 (Dan: −1)	Dan:-1	(-1) > (-3)? **TRUE**	-1	Dan
i=5 (Eli: −4)	Eli:-4	(-4) > (-1)? **FALSE**	—	—
OUTPUT	—	—	—	Dan scored -1 ✓

The confirming trace produces the correct output: Dan scored −1. Re-running the normal test case (Ana:85 etc.) with the corrected pseudocode also produces the correct output Cat:91, confirming that the fix works for both test cases. The desk check caught the bug, the pseudocode was corrected, and both test cases were re-verified — all before any Python was written.

> ▶ **NOTE** When a desk check reveals a bug: stop the trace at the row where the error first appears; trace back from that row to identify its source; correct the pseudocode; re-run the complete trace from the beginning with the original test data. Do not simply patch the output row — always correct the source and re-verify the whole trace.

This chapter has given you the complete desk checking discipline: setting up trace tables, tracing all three pseudocode structure types, choosing test data that covers normal, boundary, and erroneous categories, and following the full bug-finding workflow when an error is identified. Chapter 8 brings every tool from this book together in a single, complete design-to-code worked example.

Chapter Summary

- A desk check is a manual, step-by-step trace of pseudocode using specific test data, recorded in a trace table. It confirms correctness, completeness (no uninitialised variables), termination (no infinite loops), and boundary accuracy — all simultaneously and before any code is written.
- A trace table has one column per variable, one step description column, and one output column. Set up the complete table structure (all headers and row labels) before filling in any values. A blank cell in the first data row of any column flags an uninitialised variable.
- Tracing sequential pseudocode: record each SET or OUTPUT statement as one row. Verify that every variable has a value before the first step that uses it. The final values in the table must match the expected output for the test data.
- Tracing conditional logic requires at least one test case per branch. Record the condition check as a step labelled with [TRUE] or [FALSE]. Skip the steps in unexecuted branches. Always include boundary test cases at every threshold.
- Tracing loops: show the condition check at each iteration, and record all variables that change within the loop body. For long loops, show the first two iterations (to establish the pattern), the last iteration (to verify termination), and any iteration where a conditional inside the loop changes state.
- Test data must cover three categories. Normal: typical, in-range inputs that should produce standard outputs. Boundary: values at and immediately adjacent to every threshold. Erroneous: invalid inputs that should trigger error handling. A desk check using only normal data may pass even when boundary and erroneous cases would fail.
- Equivalence partitioning groups inputs that the algorithm treats identically and tests one representative from each group, supplemented by boundary tests. This provides comprehensive coverage without testing every possible input value.
- The bug-finding workflow: run the normal test first (to confirm setup), then erroneous or boundary tests (to expose errors). When an error appears, identify the row where the trace first diverges from the expected output, trace back to the source of the error, correct the pseudocode, and re-trace from the beginning with both test cases to confirm the fix.

Guided Exercises

Complete all five exercises before moving on to Chapter 8. Draw trace tables on paper or in a spreadsheet for exercises that require tracing. Each exercise includes a hint to help you get started.

Exercise 1

Set up (but do not yet fill in) a trace table for the following pseudocode. Identify every variable, draw the column headers, and write a row label for each executable step. SET base_price = 120.00 SET discount_rate = 0.15 SET discount = base_price × discount_rate SET final_price = base_price − discount SET gst = final_price × 0.10 SET total = final_price + gst OUTPUT 'You pay: $', total

Hint: List every variable that appears in a SET statement: base_price, discount_rate, discount, final_price, gst, total. Add a Step column and an Output column. Write one row label per executable step (SET or OUTPUT). Do not fill in values yet.

Exercise 2

Complete the trace table you set up in Exercise 1, using the given values (base_price = 120.00, discount_rate = 0.15). Then perform a second trace using base_price = 200.00 and discount_rate = 0.20. Verify that both traces produce the correct expected output by computing the answer independently.

Hint: Trace one step at a time. For each SET row, compute the right-hand side using the current values in the table. Show — for any variable that does not change in a given step. For the output step, record the formatted value. Check: 120 − 18 = 102, 102 × 1.10 = 112.20.

Exercise 3

Perform a complete conditional desk check for the pseudocode below, using three test cases: (a) hours = 35, rate = 25.00; (b) hours = 38, rate = 30.00 (boundary); (c) hours = 45, rate = 20.00. Show a separate trace for each test case. IF hours <= 38 THEN SET pay = hours × rate ELSE SET standard = 38 × rate SET overtime = (hours − 38) × rate × 1.5 SET pay = standard + overtime END IF OUTPUT pay

Hint: Your trace table needs columns: hours, rate, standard, overtime, pay, Output. Test case (b) is the boundary: hours = 38 means the condition hours <= 38 is TRUE (no overtime). Test case (c) should show all three SET statements inside the ELSE branch executing.

Exercise 4

Perform a complete loop desk check for the following pseudocode using test data = [3, 7, 2, 9, 5]. Show every iteration. Then state what changes would be needed if the loop were required to find the minimum rather than the maximum. SET maximum = data[1] FOR i FROM 2 TO COUNT(data) DO IF data[i] > maximum THEN SET maximum = data[i] END IF END FOR OUTPUT maximum

Hint: Your columns: i, data[i], condition, maximum, Output. The loop starts at i=2 (not i=1) because maximum is initialised to data[1]. For each row, evaluate data[i] > maximum using the current value of maximum in the table. For the minimum version, think about what the condition and initialisation would need to change to.

Exercise 5

Design a complete test data set for a program that accepts a user's age (must be a whole number between 0 and 120) and returns: 'Child' (0–12), 'Teenager' (13–17), 'Adult' (18–64), or 'Senior' (65–120). Include at least three normal test cases, boundary test cases at every threshold (0, 12, 13, 17, 18, 64, 65, 120, plus one value each side of each boundary), and four erroneous test cases. Present your test data in a table with columns: Category, Test Value, Expected Output, What It Tests.

Hint: There are four grade bands, so you need four normal test cases (one per band). There are four boundaries (12/13, 17/18, 64/65, and the outer limits 0 and 120), each requiring two boundary values. Erroneous inputs include: negative age, above 120, a decimal, and a non-numeric string.

Challenge Tasks

These tasks have no hints. They require independent thinking and are suitable for extension or assessment. Complete the Guided Exercises before attempting these.

Challenge Task 1

The pseudocode below is intended to calculate the median (middle value) of a sorted list of five numbers. Perform a complete desk check with two test cases: (a) data = [2, 5, 7, 10, 14] and (b) data = [8, 8, 8, 8, 8]. The pseudocode contains one logic error that is revealed by one of the test cases. Identify the error, state which test case reveals it and why, correct the pseudocode, and confirm the fix with a re-trace. SET n = COUNT(data) SET mid_index = n / 2 SET median = data[mid_index] OUTPUT 'Median:', median

Challenge Task 2

Write a pseudocode algorithm for the following problem: given a list of student names and their three assignment marks (each out of 100), calculate the weighted average (assignments are each worth 33.3%) and assign a grade (HD >= 85, D >= 75, C >= 65, P >= 50, F otherwise). Then perform a complete desk check with: one normal test case; boundary test cases at each of the four grade thresholds (both sides of each); and two erroneous test cases (one negative mark, one mark above 100). Produce a properly structured trace table for each test case, and state which test cases (if any) reveal errors in your pseudocode.

Challenge Task 3

This challenge asks you to trace an iterative algorithm for a real computational problem: binary search. The algorithm searches for a target value in a sorted list by repeatedly halving the search range. PSEUDOCODE: SET low = 1 SET high = COUNT(data) SET found = FALSE WHILE low <= high AND found = FALSE DO SET mid = (low + high) / 2 (integer division) IF data[mid] = target THEN SET found = TRUE ELSE IF target < data[mid] THEN SET high = mid − 1 ELSE SET low = mid + 1 END IF END WHILE IF found THEN OUTPUT 'Found at index', mid ELSE OUTPUT 'Not found' END IF Trace this algorithm with: (a) data = [3, 7, 12, 19, 25, 31, 44], target = 19 (normal: found); (b) data = [3, 7, 12, 19, 25, 31, 44], target = 20 (erroneous: not found). Show every iteration with columns for low, high, mid, data[mid], condition result, and found. Explain in your own words why binary search is more efficient than linear search, using your trace tables as evidence.

From Design to Code — A Complete Worked Example

> This chapter is the capstone of this book. A single, realistic problem is taken from a plain-English description all the way through to a tested, working Python implementation — applying every planning tool introduced in the preceding chapters. You will see how the Understand stage shapes the design, how a structure chart guides decomposition, how pseudocode specifies each function's logic, how a UML class diagram documents the object-oriented structure, how a desk check verifies correctness before coding, and how the Python code emerges as a direct, faithful translation of the plan. The chapter closes with a reflection on what the planning process prevented, and a guide to applying the same process to your own projects.

1 The Problem and the Process

Every chapter of this book has introduced one planning tool in isolation. Pseudocode in Chapter 2, flowcharts in Chapter 3, UML in Chapter 4, decomposition in Chapter 5, logic errors in Chapter 6, desk checking in Chapter 7. In real design work, these tools are not used in isolation. They are applied in sequence, each one building on the previous, each one answering a question that the others cannot.

This chapter demonstrates that integrated practice. A problem is stated, and then the design-first workflow from Chapter 1 is followed from start to finish: Understand, Plan, Design, Code, Test, Refine. Every step is shown explicitly, with a planning reflection at the end of each one that identifies what the planning caught — or would have caught if skipped.

The problem chosen is a Quiz Program: a practical, self-contained application of the kind that appears in Digital Technologies assessments, that has enough complexity to require all the planning tools, but is small enough for its design to be readable in a single chapter. Read each step actively: do not just follow the design — think about why each decision was made and what would have gone wrong without it.

Example 1.1 Introduction — The Problem Statement

The problem is stated exactly as it might be given in a classroom assessment or a client brief. It is intentionally somewhat vague — as real specifications almost always are — and the Understand stage will resolve that vagueness before any design begins.

```
PROBLEM STATEMENT

Build a quiz program for secondary school students.
The program presents a series of multiple-choice questions on
```

```
a topic of the programmer's choice. Each question has four
options (A, B, C, D). The student selects an answer for each
question. After all questions are answered, the program displays
the student's score, a percentage, and a grade.
The program should tell the student which questions they got
wrong and what the correct answer was.
Questions should be loaded from a file so that the quiz content
can be updated without changing the code.
```

At first reading, this specification leaves many questions unanswered. How many questions? What grade boundaries? What is the file format? What should happen if the file is missing or malformed? What constitutes a valid answer? These questions are all answered in the Understand stage — not by guessing, but by making explicit, documented decisions before any design begins.

Example 1.2 Variation — The Six-Step Workflow Applied to This Problem

```
THE DESIGN-FIRST WORKFLOW - applied to the Quiz Program

STEP 1:  UNDERSTAND   Restate the problem. Identify all inputs,
                      outputs, and constraints. Make decisions
                      about anything the specification leaves open.

STEP 2:  PLAN         Decompose the problem top-down. Draw the
                      structure chart. Write function signatures.

STEP 3:  DESIGN       Write pseudocode for each function. Produce
                      a UML class diagram for the Question class.
                      Draw a flowchart for the most complex logic.

STEP 4:  DESK CHECK   Trace the core algorithm with normal,
                      boundary, and erroneous test data.

STEP 5:  CODE         Translate pseudocode to Python, function
                      by function, following the design exactly.

STEP 6:  REFLECT      Identify what the planning process caught
                      before it became a bug in the code.
```

Example 1.3 Real-world application — Why This Sequence Matters

The temptation with a problem like this is to open a Python file and start writing a list of questions. Within twenty minutes, the programmer discovers that the question data structure is incompatible with the answer-checking logic, that the score calculation produces the wrong grade at boundary values, that the file format was not designed carefully enough to parse, and that the results display shows the wrong question numbers. Each of these problems — and they are all real problems that arise from this exact approach — is identified and resolved in the planning stages that follow.

The planning process does not make programming easier by making it simpler. It makes it easier by front-loading all the thinking. By the time the first Python function is written in Step 5, every design decision has already been made, verified, and documented. Coding becomes translation, not invention.

> ▶ **NOTE** Follow each step in the sequence shown. Resist the urge to skip ahead to Step 5. The value of this chapter lies not in the finished Python code — which is only a few dozen lines — but in the planning decisions that produced it and in seeing clearly what each planning stage contributes to the final result.

2 Step 1 — Understand

> **STEP 1**
>
> **Understand**
>
> Restate the problem. Identify inputs, outputs, and constraints. Make explicit decisions about anything left open.

The Understand stage begins by restating the problem in precise terms, then listing every input, every output, and every constraint. For anything the specification leaves open, an explicit decision is made and documented. These decisions form the foundation of the design — changing them later requires revisiting every downstream stage.

Example 2.1 Introduction — Restating the Problem

```
RESTATED PROBLEM (precise version):

Build a command-line quiz program that:
1. Loads multiple-choice questions from a CSV file.
   Each question has: a question text, four options (A-D),
   and the correct answer letter.
2. Presents each question to the student in sequence.
3. Accepts answers A, B, C, or D (case-insensitive).
   Re-prompts if the answer is not one of these.
4. After all questions: displays the score (e.g. '7 out of 10'),
   the percentage, and a grade (HD/D/C/P/F).
5. Lists every question the student answered incorrectly,
   showing the question text and the correct answer.
6. If the quiz file cannot be found or is empty,
   displays an error message and exits gracefully.

DECISIONS MADE (filling in specification gaps):
  - Number of questions: determined by the file (flexible).
  - Grade boundaries: HD >= 85%, D >= 70%, C >= 55%,
                      P >= 40%, F below 40%.
  - File format: CSV, one question per row:
    question_text,option_A,option_B,option_C,option_D,answer
  - Invalid file rows (wrong column count) are skipped
    with a warning.
  - Score is always out of the number of valid questions loaded.
```

Example 2.2 Variation — Inputs, Outputs, and Constraints

```
INPUTS:
  File:     A CSV file containing quiz questions (path hardcoded
            as 'quiz.csv' or passed as an argument).
  User:     Answer to each question (one character: A, B, C, or D).

OUTPUTS:
  For each question:  The question text and four labelled options.
  After each answer:  'Correct!' or 'Incorrect.'
  Final summary:      Score (e.g. 7/10), percentage, grade.
  Incorrect list:     Question text + correct answer for each
                      question the student got wrong.
  Error (if needed):  Clear message if file is missing/empty.

CONSTRAINTS:
  - Valid answers: A, B, C, D only (case-insensitive).
  - Re-prompt until a valid answer is given.
  - Grade boundaries as decided above.
  - Skip malformed rows in the file (not crash on them).
  - Handle FileNotFoundError and empty file gracefully.
  - Percentages displayed to one decimal place.
```

Example 2.3 Real-world application — What the Understand Stage Prevented

✍ **Planning reflection**

At the end of Step 1, five things are now explicit that were not in the original specification:

Grade boundaries — without these, the calculate_grade() function cannot be written.

File format — without this, the load_questions() function cannot be written.

Invalid row handling — without this decision, a malformed file would crash the program.

Answer validation rule — without this, invalid answers (like 'E' or 'yes') have no defined behaviour.

Re-prompt behaviour — without this, the get_answer() function has no defined loop structure.

Each of these would have been discovered during coding — forcing mid-implementation design decisions and possible rework of already-written code.

▶ **NOTE** The Understand stage is complete when every function you will need to write has all the information required to specify its parameters, return values, and logic. If any function's specification is still ambiguous, the Understand stage is not yet finished.

3 Step 2 — Plan

STEP 2	**Plan** Decompose the problem top-down. Draw the structure chart with data couples. Derive function signatures.

With the problem fully understood, the next step is to decompose it into manageable functions and document the decomposition as a structure chart. Top-down design is applied in two passes. The first pass identifies the major operations of the program. The second pass refines any operations that are still too complex to implement directly.

Example 3.1 Introduction — Two-Pass Decomposition

```
PASS 1 — Major operations:

  1. Load questions from file
  2. Run the quiz (present questions, accept answers)
  3. Display the final results

PASS 2 — Refine each major operation:

  1. load_questions(filename)
     1a. Open file and handle FileNotFoundError
     1b. Read and parse each CSV row
     1c. Validate row structure (skip malformed rows)
     1d. Return a list of Question objects

  2. run_quiz(questions)
     2a. For each question: display it (display_question)
     2b. Accept a validated answer (get_answer)
     2c. Check the answer, update score and wrong list

  3. display_results(score, total, wrong_list)
     3a. Calculate percentage
     3b. Determine grade (calculate_grade)
     3c. Display score, percentage, grade
     3d. Display list of incorrect answers

LEAF FUNCTIONS (all simple enough to implement directly):
  load_questions, parse_csv_row, display_question,
  get_answer, calculate_grade, display_results
```

Example 3.2 Variation — The Structure Chart

The structure chart below documents the full decomposition with data couple annotations. Read it top-down: main() calls load_questions() and run_quiz() and display_results(). Each of those calls further sub-functions. The loop marker (○) on display_question and get_answer shows they are called once per question.

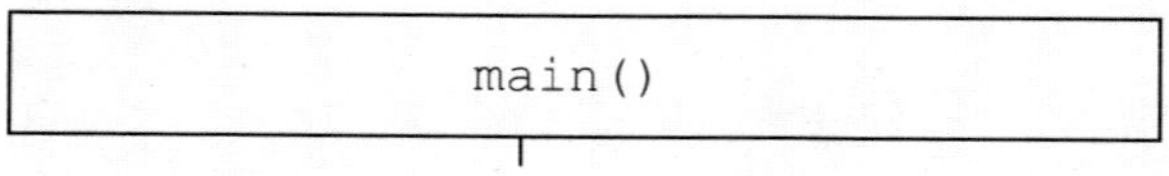

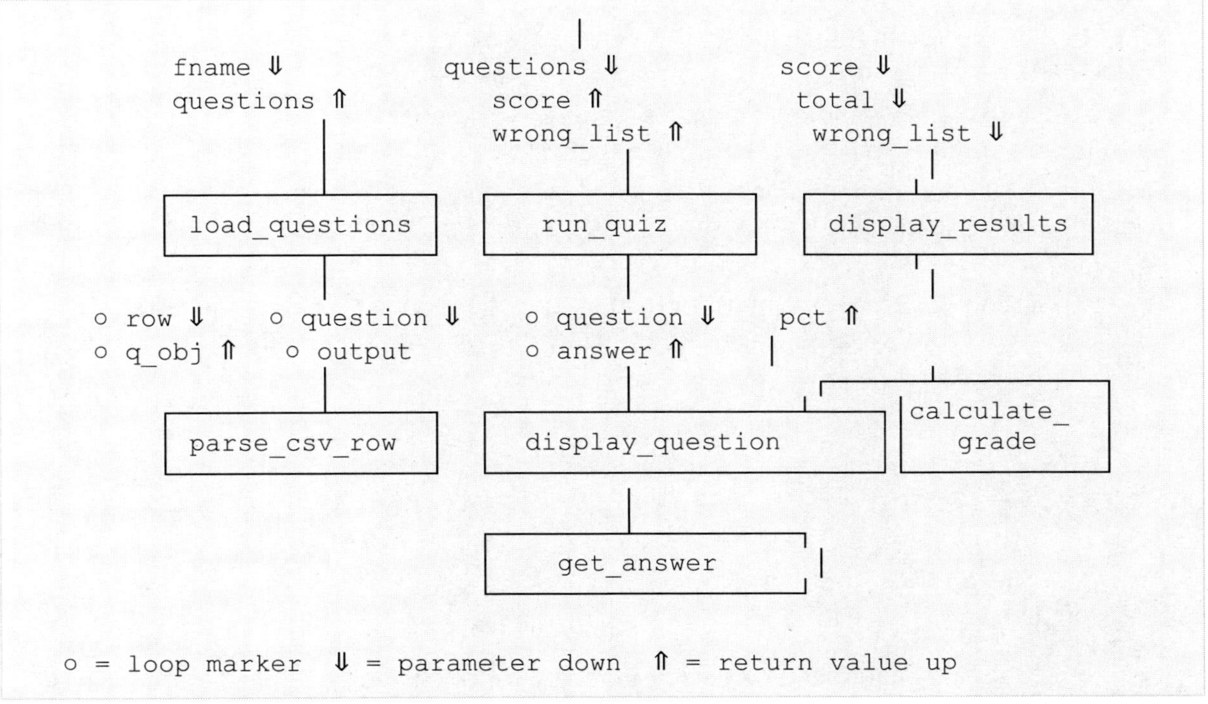

Example 3.3 Real-world application — Function Signatures from the Chart

Every function signature is derived directly from the structure chart. Parameters come from data couples with downward arrows; return types come from data couples with upward arrows.

Function	Parameters	Returns
main()	(none)	(none)
load_questions()	filename: str	list of Question
parse_csv_row()	row: list	Question | None
run_quiz()	questions: list	score: int, wrong_list: list
display_question()	question: Question, number: int	(none)
get_answer()	(none)	answer: str
calculate_grade()	percentage: float	grade: str
display_results()	score: int, total: int, wrong_list: list	(none)

```
Python function skeletons (all ready to fill in):
def main():                             ...
def load_questions(filename):           ...
def parse_csv_row(row):                 ...
def run_quiz(questions):                ...
def display_question(question, n):     ...
def get_answer():                       ...
def calculate_grade(percentage):        ...
def display_results(score, total, wrong_list): ...
```

✍ **Planning reflection**

Step 2 produced eight function signatures before any logic was written. Every function's interface is now agreed:

The Question class was identified as necessary — run_quiz() and display_question() both need structured question data that a plain list cannot cleanly provide.

The wrong_list parameter in display_results() was identified here, not in Step 3. Without decomposition, this would have been discovered mid-implementation, forcing a rewrite of run_quiz().

The separation of parse_csv_row() from load_questions() was a design decision: loading is a different responsibility from parsing. Each is independently testable.

4 Step 3 — Design

STEP 3

Design

Write pseudocode for each function. Produce a UML class diagram. Draw the flowchart for complex control flow.

With function signatures established, the Design stage fills in the logic. Pseudocode is written for each function, the Question class is documented as a UML class diagram, and a flowchart is drawn for the most complex control flow: the answer validation loop inside get_answer().

Example 4.1 Introduction — UML Class Diagram for Question

The Question class stores the data for one quiz question. It has five attributes (one for the text, four for the options, one for the correct answer) and two methods: one to display the question, one to check an answer. The class diagram specifies this before the class is written in Python.

```
Question
--------------------------------------------------------
-  __text      : str
-  __options   : dict    (keys: 'A','B','C','D')
-  __answer    : str     (one of 'A','B','C','D')
--------------------------------------------------------
+  __init__(text: str, options: dict, answer: str)
+  display(number: int)
+  check_answer(response: str) : bool
+  get_text() : str
+  get_answer() : str
```

```
Note: get_text() and get_answer() are getters used by
display_results() to access the private attributes when
building the incorrect-answers report.
```

Example 4.2 Variation — Pseudocode for the Core Functions

Pseudocode is written for each function. The most important functions are shown in full; the simpler ones are summarised.

```
FUNCTION load_questions(filename):
  SET questions = empty list
  TRY
    OPEN filename FOR READING
    FOR EACH row IN file DO
      SET q = CALL parse_csv_row(row)
      IF q IS NOT None THEN
        ADD q TO questions
      END IF
    END FOR
    CLOSE file
  EXCEPT FileNotFoundError
    OUTPUT 'Error: quiz file not found:', filename
    RETURN empty list
  END TRY
  IF COUNT(questions) = 0 THEN
    OUTPUT 'Error: no valid questions found in file.'
  END IF
  RETURN questions
END FUNCTION

FUNCTION parse_csv_row(row):
  SET parts = SPLIT row BY ','
  IF COUNT(parts) ≠ 6 THEN
    OUTPUT 'Warning: skipping malformed row.'
    RETURN None
  END IF
  SET options = {'A': parts[1], 'B': parts[2],
                 'C': parts[3], 'D': parts[4]}
  RETURN new Question(parts[0], options, parts[5].UPPER())
END FUNCTION

FUNCTION run_quiz(questions):
  SET score = 0
  SET wrong_list = empty list
  FOR i FROM 1 TO COUNT(questions) DO
    SET q = questions[i]
    CALL q.display(i)
    SET answer = CALL get_answer()
    IF q.check_answer(answer) THEN
      OUTPUT 'Correct!'
      SET score = score + 1
    ELSE
      OUTPUT 'Incorrect. The correct answer was:', q.get_answer()
      ADD q TO wrong_list
    END IF
  END FOR
  RETURN score, wrong_list
END FUNCTION

FUNCTION get_answer():
  INPUT response
  SET response = response.UPPER()
  WHILE response NOT IN ['A','B','C','D'] DO
```

```
      OUTPUT 'Invalid. Please enter A, B, C, or D.'
      INPUT response
      SET response = response.UPPER()
    END WHILE
    RETURN response
  END FUNCTION

  FUNCTION calculate_grade(percentage):
    IF percentage >= 85 THEN RETURN 'High Distinction'
    ELSE IF percentage >= 70 THEN RETURN 'Distinction'
    ELSE IF percentage >= 55 THEN RETURN 'Credit'
    ELSE IF percentage >= 40 THEN RETURN 'Pass'
    ELSE RETURN 'Fail'
    END IF
  END FUNCTION

  FUNCTION display_results(score, total, wrong_list):
    SET pct = (score / total) * 100
    SET grade = CALL calculate_grade(pct)
    OUTPUT '────────────────────────────────'
    OUTPUT 'Score:', score, 'out of', total
    OUTPUT 'Percentage:', pct, '%'
    OUTPUT 'Grade:', grade
    IF COUNT(wrong_list) > 0 THEN
      OUTPUT '────────────────────────────────'
      OUTPUT 'Questions answered incorrectly:'
      FOR EACH q IN wrong_list DO
        OUTPUT '  •', q.get_text()
        OUTPUT '    Correct answer:', q.get_answer()
      END FOR
    END IF
  END FUNCTION
```

Example 4.3 Real-world application — Flowchart for get_answer()

The get_answer() function contains the most complex control flow: a validation loop that re-prompts until a valid letter is entered. A flowchart makes the loop structure unambiguous.

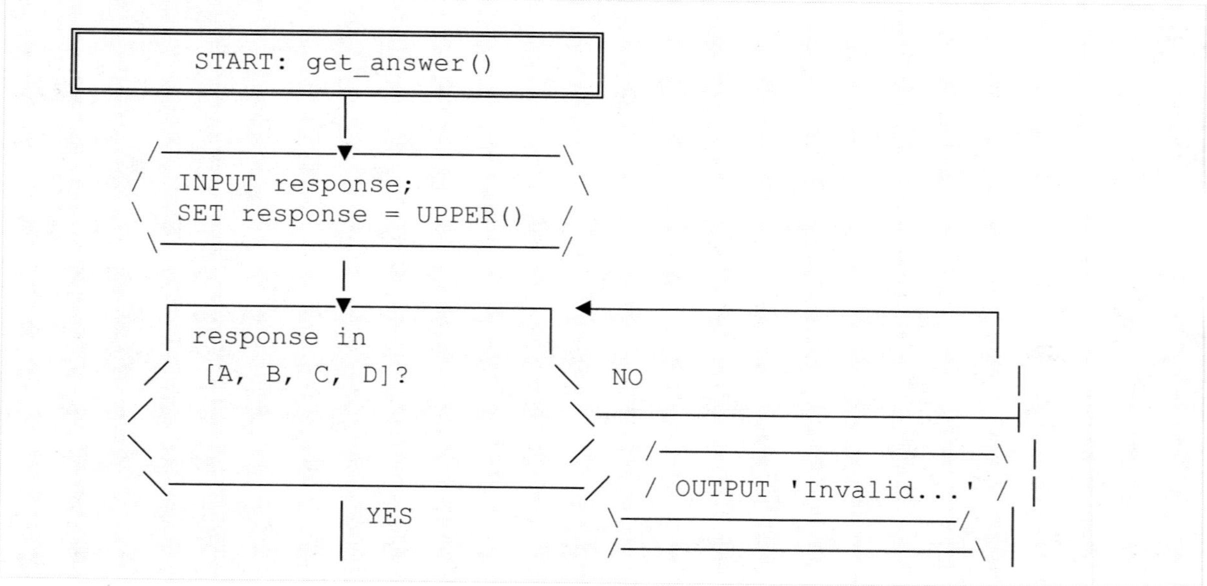

```
                 |                    /  INPUT response;        \ |
                 |                    \  SET response = UPPER() / |
                 |                     \------------------------/ |
                 |                             |__________________|
                 |
 ================▼=====================
 ||   RETURN response                ||
 ||   STOP: get_answer()             ||
 ======================================
```

The back-arrow on the right side of the flowchart shows the validation loop. The YES branch exits the loop and returns the validated response. The NO branch re-prompts and loops back to the condition diamond. This structure confirms that the loop is a WHILE (pre-test): if the first input is valid, the loop body never executes again.

> **✍ Planning reflection**
>
> Step 3 produced three planning artefacts: pseudocode for all eight functions, a UML class diagram for Question, and a flowchart for get_answer().
>
> The pseudocode for display_results() revealed that get_text() and get_answer() getters are needed on the Question class — without pseudocode, these would likely have been discovered mid-implementation.
>
> The flowchart for get_answer() confirmed the WHILE (not REPEAT...UNTIL) loop is correct: if the first response is valid, the validation message should never appear. A REPEAT...UNTIL would always show it at least once.
>
> The UML diagram revealed that check_answer() returns a bool — making run_quiz() cleaner than if it had to compare strings directly.

5 Step 4 — Desk Check

> **STEP 4**
>
> **Desk Check**
>
> Trace the core algorithm with normal, boundary, and erroneous test data before writing any Python.

Three desk checks are performed: one for calculate_grade() (boundary test at each threshold), one for run_quiz() (normal trace with three questions), and one for get_answer() (erroneous input followed by valid input). Together these three traces cover all three test data categories and all three control structures (sequential, conditional, iterative).

Example 5.1 Introduction — Boundary Test: calculate_grade()

The grade boundaries are: HD >= 85%, D >= 70%, C >= 55%, P >= 40%, F below 40%. The desk check traces six boundary values: one just below each threshold, and the maximum value of 100%.

Boundary test — calculate_grade() with values at and around each threshold

percentage	Condition path taken	grade returned
100.0	>=85? YES → first branch	'High Distinction'
85.0	>=85? YES → first branch	'High Distinction'
84.9	>=85? NO, >=70? YES → second branch	'Distinction'
70.0	>=85? NO, >=70? YES → second branch	'Distinction'
69.9	>=85? NO, >=70? NO, >=55? YES	'Credit'
55.0	>=85? NO, >=70? NO, >=55? YES	'Credit'
54.9	>=85? NO, >=70? NO, >=55? NO, >=40? YES	'Pass'
40.0	>=85? NO, >=70? NO, >=55? NO, >=40? YES	'Pass'
39.9	All NO → ELSE branch	'Fail'
0.0	All NO → ELSE branch	'Fail'

All ten boundary values produce the expected grade. The >= operators are confirmed correct: a score of exactly 85.0 is a High Distinction, exactly 70.0 is a Distinction, and so on. The desk check also confirms there are no gaps: 84.9 correctly falls into Distinction, not Credit.

Example 5.2 **Variation — Normal Trace: run_quiz() with Three Questions**

This condensed trace uses three questions to verify the score accumulation, the wrong_list update, and the correct final values returned by run_quiz(). The test data is: Q1 correct (answer C, student gives C), Q2 wrong (answer A, student gives B), Q3 correct (answer D, student gives D).

Normal trace — run_quiz() with 3 questions, 2 correct answers

Step	i	answer	correct?	score	wrong_list
Initialise	—	—	—	0	[]
Q1: answer=C, give C	1	C	check_answer: [TRUE]	1	[]
Q2: answer=A, give B	2	B	check_answer: [FALSE]	1	[Q2]
Q3: answer=D, give D	3	D	check_answer: [TRUE]	2	[Q2]
RETURN	—	—	—	2	[Q2] ✓

The trace confirms: score = 2 (two correct answers out of three); wrong_list contains Q2 only. These are the correct expected values. display_results() will receive score=2, total=3, wrong_list=[Q2] and should output: 2/3, 66.7%, Distinction.

Example 5.3 **Real-world application — Erroneous Input: get_answer()**

This trace verifies that get_answer() correctly re-prompts when the user enters an invalid response. The test sequence is: 'E' (invalid), 'yes' (invalid), 'B' (valid).

Erroneous trace — get_answer() with invalid inputs before a valid answer

Step	`response (raw)`	`response (upper)`	Output / Return
INPUT response	`'E'`	—	—
SET response = UPPER()	—	`'E'`	—
'E' in [A,B,C,D]? → FALSE	—	—	—
OUTPUT 'Invalid...'	—	—	`Invalid...`
INPUT response	`'yes'`	—	—
SET response = UPPER()	—	`'YES'`	—
'YES' in [A,B,C,D]? → FALSE	—	—	—
OUTPUT 'Invalid...'	—	—	`Invalid...`
INPUT response	`'B'`	—	—
SET response = UPPER()	—	`'B'`	—
'B' in [A,B,C,D]? → TRUE	—	—	—
RETURN 'B'	—	—	`returns 'B'` ✓

The trace confirms that the WHILE loop re-prompts exactly twice (for 'E' and 'yes') before exiting with 'B' on the third input. The UPPER() conversion on line 2 would have handled 'b' (lowercase) equally — the desk check with 'B' also implicitly confirms case-insensitivity.

> **✍ Planning reflection**
>
> Three desk checks, covering all three test data categories and all three control structures, were completed in approximately 20 minutes.
>
> The boundary trace of calculate_grade() confirmed all five grade thresholds use >= correctly. A common error (using > instead of >=) at any threshold would have been visible as a wrong grade at the exact boundary value.
>
> The normal trace of run_quiz() confirmed that wrong_list accumulates correctly and that score is incremented only when check_answer() returns TRUE.
>
> The erroneous trace of get_answer() confirmed the WHILE loop structure: the function loops correctly and exits as soon as a valid input is received. No infinite-loop risk was found.

6 Step 5 — Code

STEP 5

Code

Translate pseudocode to Python, function by function. Follow the design. Do not improvise.

With the design verified, the Python code is written by translating pseudocode line by line. Each function is implemented in the order it appears in the structure chart, from the bottom up: leaf functions first (parse_csv_row, calculate_grade, get_answer), then mid-level functions (load_questions, display_question, display_results), then the orchestrators (run_quiz, main). This bottom-up implementation order means each function can be tested as soon as it is written, before the functions that call it are complete.

The translation is mechanical and fast. Every design decision was made in Steps 1 through 4. During coding, the only decisions remaining are Python-specific ones: which string method to use for validation, how to format the percentage output, how to structure the CSV parsing. These are minor, low-risk decisions that do not affect the program's architecture.

Example 6.1 Introduction — The Question Class

The Question class is translated directly from the UML class diagram. Private attributes use double underscores (Python name mangling); public methods map to the + symbols in the diagram.

```
class Question:
    """Represents one multiple-choice quiz question."""

    def __init__(self, text, options, answer):
        self.__text    = text
        self.__options = options    # dict: {'A': '...', 'B': '...',
...}
        self.__answer  = answer     # one of 'A', 'B', 'C', 'D'

    def display(self, number):
        """Print the question and its four options."""
        print(f'\nQuestion {number}: {self.__text}')
        for letter, option in self.__options.items():
            print(f'  {letter}. {option}')

    def check_answer(self, response):
        """Return True if response matches the correct answer."""
        return response.upper() == self.__answer

    def get_text(self):   return self.__text
    def get_answer(self): return self.__answer
```

Example 6.2 Variation — Core Functions Translated from Pseudocode

The five core functions translate directly from their pseudocode. Annotations on the right show which pseudocode line each Python line came from.

```
def load_questions(filename):
    """Load and return a list of Question objects from a CSV file."""
    questions = []                                  # SET questions = empty
list
    try:
        with open(filename) as f:                   # OPEN filename FOR
READING
            for line in f:                          # FOR EACH row IN file
DO
                row = line.strip().split(',')
                q = parse_csv_row(row)              # CALL
parse_csv_row(row)
                if q is not None:                   # IF q IS NOT None THEN
                    questions.append(q)             # ADD q TO questions
    except FileNotFoundError:
        print(f'Error: quiz file not found: {filename}')
        return []                                   # RETURN empty list
    if not questions:                               # IF COUNT(questions) =
0
        print('Error: no valid questions found.')
    return questions

def parse_csv_row(row):
    """Parse one CSV row into a Question, or return None if
malformed."""
    if len(row) != 6:                               # IF COUNT(parts) ≠ 6
THEN
        print('Warning: skipping malformed row.')
        return None                                 # RETURN None
    options = {'A': row[1], 'B': row[2], 'C': row[3], 'D': row[4]}
    return Question(row[0], options, row[5].strip().upper())

def get_answer():
    """Prompt until the user enters A, B, C, or D. Return
uppercase."""
    response = input('Your answer: ').upper()   # INPUT response;
UPPER
    while response not in ['A', 'B', 'C', 'D']:# WHILE not in list DO
        print('Invalid. Please enter A, B, C, or D.')
        response = input('Your answer: ').upper()
    return response                                 # RETURN response

def calculate_grade(percentage):
    """Return grade string for a percentage score."""
    if   percentage >= 85: return 'High Distinction'
    elif percentage >= 70: return 'Distinction'
    elif percentage >= 55: return 'Credit'
    elif percentage >= 40: return 'Pass'
    else:                  return 'Fail'
```

Example 6.3 Real-world application — Orchestrators and main()

The orchestrating functions — run_quiz(), display_results(), and main() — are written last. They contain almost no logic of their own; they simply call the functions defined above them in the hierarchy.

```
def run_quiz(questions):
```

```
        """Present each question, collect answers. Return score and wrong
list."""
        score, wrong_list = 0, []
        for i, q in enumerate(questions, start=1):   # FOR i FROM 1 TO N
            q.display(i)                              # CALL q.display(i)
            answer = get_answer()                     # CALL get_answer()
            if q.check_answer(answer):                # IF check_answer
THEN
                print('Correct!')
                score += 1                            # score = score + 1
            else:
                print(f'Incorrect. Correct answer: {q.get_answer()}')
                wrong_list.append(q)                  # ADD q TO
wrong_list
        return score, wrong_list

    def display_results(score, total, wrong_list):
        """Display final score, percentage, grade, and incorrect
answers."""
        pct   = (score / total) * 100                # SET pct
        grade = calculate_grade(pct)                  # CALL
calculate_grade
        print('\n' + '-' * 35)
        print(f'Score:      {score} out of {total}')
        print(f'Percentage: {pct:.1f}%')
        print(f'Grade:      {grade}')
        if wrong_list:                                # IF COUNT > 0
            print('-' * 35)
            print('Questions answered incorrectly:')
            for q in wrong_list:                      # FOR EACH q IN
wrong_list
                print(f'  • {q.get_text()}')
                print(f'    Correct answer: {q.get_answer()}')

    def main():
        """Entry point: load, run, display."""
        questions = load_questions('quiz.csv')        # CALL
load_questions
        if not questions:
            return                                    # Exit if no
questions
        score, wrong_list = run_quiz(questions)       # CALL run_quiz
        display_results(score, len(questions), wrong_list)  # CALL
display_results

    if __name__ == '__main__':
        main()
```

> ✍ **Planning reflection**
>
> Step 5 produced approximately 75 lines of Python from eight functions. The average function is fewer than 12 lines.
>
> Every function's name, parameters, and return type exactly match the structure chart from Step 2. No function was added or removed during coding.

The most complex implementation decision — using enumerate(questions, start=1) for the loop index — was a Python-specific detail that did not affect the design. The pseudocode's FOR i FROM 1 TO N structure translated cleanly.

No design decisions were made during Step 5. All decisions were made in Steps 1 through 4.

7 Step 6 — Reflect

STEP 6

Reflect

Review what the planning process caught. Identify what would have gone wrong without each stage. Apply this workflow to your own projects.

The final step in the design-first workflow is reflection: a structured review of what each planning stage contributed. This is not a formality. It is how planning habits are built — by connecting specific planning decisions to the specific errors they prevented. Over time, this connection becomes instinct: a programmer who has reflected on enough desk checks eventually performs them mentally and automatically, just as the experienced programmers in Chapter 1 were described as doing.

Example 7.1 Introduction — What Each Stage Prevented

```
  PLANNING STAGE    WHAT IT PRODUCED          WHAT IT PREVENTED
  ______________    ________________          _________________

  Step 1: Understand  Grade boundaries,         Mid-coding design
                      file format, validation   decisions; rework of
                      rules, error behaviour    already-written
functions

  Step 2: Plan        Structure chart with      Discovery of wrong_list
  (Decompose)         8 signatures before       parameter mid-
implementation;
                      any code was written      untestable monolithic
code

  Step 3: Design      Pseudocode revealing      Missing getters on
Question;
  (Pseudocode/UML)    get_text() and            REPEAT loop error in
                      get_answer() getters;     get_answer(); untested
                      WHILE confirmed correct   grade logic

  Step 4: Desk Check  All boundary grades       Incorrect >= vs > at any
                      verified; run_quiz        grade threshold; silent
                      accumulation confirmed;   wrong_list bug; infinite
                      get_answer loop proven    loop in validation

  Step 5: Code        75 lines, all functions   Improvised architecture;
```

```
                        matching the design       mid-implementation
rewrites;
                        exactly                   inconsistent naming
```

Example 7.2 Variation — How to Apply This Workflow to Your Own Projects

The six-step workflow is not specific to quiz programs. It applies to any programming task of any size. The proportions change — a simple two-function script needs only a brief Understand and a short pseudocode sketch; a complex multi-class application needs all six steps in full — but the sequence never changes.

```
APPLYING THE WORKFLOW TO ANY PROJECT:

Problem size            Suggested planning depth
────────────────        ─────────────────────────────────────────
Simple script           Understand (1 paragraph) + pseudocode for
(1-2 functions)         main logic + desk check with 3 test cases

Moderate program        All of the above + structure chart +
(5-10 functions)        function signatures + boundary desk checks

OOP project             All of the above + UML class diagram +
(2+ classes)            sequence diagram for key interactions +
                        flowchart for complex logic

Large system            All of the above + use case diagram +
(many modules)          activity diagram for workflows + complete
                        test data set for every module

The minimum planning for any project:
  1. Restate the problem in your own words
  2. Write pseudocode for the most complex function
  3. Desk check with at least one boundary test case
Even this minimum prevents a significant proportion of logic errors.
```

Example 7.3 Real-world application — Planning as a Habit, Not a Requirement

The programmers who plan most effectively are not the ones who follow a checklist because they are required to. They are the ones who have reflected enough on their own errors — and on the planning decisions that would have prevented them — that planning has become automatic. They reach for pseudocode before they reach for a keyboard, not because a teacher told them to, but because experience has taught them that it is faster.

This chapter has shown you every stage of that process applied to a single concrete problem. The quiz program was not particularly complex — it was chosen because its complexity is enough to require all the planning tools without being so large that any stage becomes overwhelming. Take the same six steps and apply them to the next program you write. Then the one after that. The habit builds with repetition.

This book has been about thinking before coding. Not instead of coding — thinking before coding. The tools in this book — pseudocode, flowcharts, UML diagrams, structure charts, desk checks, and the logic error prevention checklist — are not obstacles between you and the keyboard. They are the path from the problem to a correct, working, maintainable solution. Use them.

▶ **NOTE** Keep your planning documents. A pseudocode listing, a structure chart, and a desk check trace are not temporary scribbles to be thrown away when the code is written. They are the documentation of your design thinking — exactly the kind of evidence that assessment tasks, code reviews, and professional practice require. File them with the code they describe.

Chapter Summary

- The design-first workflow has six steps applied in sequence: Understand (restate the problem, identify inputs, outputs, and constraints, resolve all ambiguity); Plan (decompose top-down, draw the structure chart, derive function signatures); Design (write pseudocode, produce UML diagrams, draw flowcharts for complex logic); Desk Check (trace with normal, boundary, and erroneous data); Code (translate pseudocode to Python, function by function, following the design); Reflect (identify what the planning caught and what would have gone wrong without it).
- The Understand stage is complete when every function's specification is unambiguous: its inputs, its outputs, its validation rules, and its error behaviour are all defined before design begins. Unresolved ambiguity at the end of Step 1 becomes a mid-implementation design decision in Step 5.
- The structure chart documents the decomposition and becomes the direct source of Python function signatures. Every box becomes one function; every data couple annotation becomes a parameter or return value. No function should be written in Step 5 that does not appear in the structure chart from Step 2.
- Pseudocode written in Step 3 specifies logic at the right level of abstraction: precise enough to desk-check, relaxed enough to express design decisions without Python syntax. UML class diagrams specify the OOP structure. Flowcharts verify complex control flow (especially validation loops and nested conditionals).
- Three categories of test data cover the full input space: normal (typical values confirming standard behaviour), boundary (values at and adjacent to every threshold), and erroneous (invalid inputs confirming validation). A desk check that uses only normal data will often pass even when the algorithm contains boundary or validation errors.
- Code is written bottom-up from the structure chart: leaf functions first (they can be tested immediately), then mid-level orchestrators, then main(). Every function name, parameter list, and return type should exactly match the structure chart. If they do not, the design and the code have diverged.
- Planning habits are built through reflection: connecting each planning decision to the specific error it prevented. Over time, this connection becomes instinct

— the same rapid, automatic reasoning that experienced programmers perform mentally before coding.

- The minimum planning for any project is: restate the problem in your own words; write pseudocode for the most complex function; desk check with at least one boundary test case. Even this minimum prevents a significant proportion of the logic errors that appear in programs written without planning.

Guided Exercises

Complete all five exercises before attempting the Challenge Tasks. These exercises ask you to extend and apply the Quiz Program design from this chapter. Each exercise includes a hint to help you get started.

Exercise 1

The Quiz Program currently hardcodes the filename 'quiz.csv'. Using the six-step workflow (abbreviated: Understand, pseudocode, desk check only), extend the program so that the filename is provided as a command-line argument (using sys.argv), with 'quiz.csv' as the default if no argument is given. Produce: a one-paragraph Understand stage describing the change; updated pseudocode for main() only; and a desk check of two cases (argument provided and argument omitted).

Hint: The change is confined to main(). The Understand stage needs to answer: what happens if two or more arguments are given? What happens if the argument is not a valid filename? Keep the change minimal: use sys.argv[1] if it exists, otherwise default to quiz.csv.

Exercise 2

Extend the Question class with a new method: get_option(letter) that returns the text of the option for the given letter (A, B, C, or D). Update display_results() so that the incorrect-answers list shows both the correct letter and the full text of the correct option (e.g. 'Correct answer: B. Canberra'). Produce a UML class diagram showing the updated Question class, and updated pseudocode for display_results().

Hint: Add get_option(letter) to the bottom compartment of the UML class diagram with + visibility. Its signature is: + get_option(letter: str) : str. Update the pseudocode for display_results() to call q.get_option(q.get_answer()) to retrieve the full option text.

Exercise 3

The current program presents questions in the order they appear in the file. Design an extension that shuffles the questions into a random order before the quiz begins. Produce: updated pseudocode for main() showing where the shuffle occurs; a desk check demonstrating that the shuffle does not affect the total question count or the correctness of answers. Hint: Python's random.shuffle() shuffles a list in place.

Hint: The shuffle is a single line added to main() between load_questions() and run_quiz(). In the desk check, show that COUNT(questions) before and after the shuffle is the same, and that each Question object is still present (just in a different order). The pseudocode change is minimal.

Exercise 4

The current load_questions() reads all rows regardless of whether they are headers. If the CSV file has a header row (e.g. 'question,option_a,option_b,option_c,option_d,answer'), it will be parsed as a question and either skipped (wrong column count) or cause an error. Design a fix: add a parameter has_header to load_questions() that, when True, skips the first row. Produce: updated pseudocode for load_questions(); updated function signature; and a desk check with a file that has a header row, confirming the header is skipped.

Hint: Add has_header: bool = False as a parameter with a default value. In the pseudocode, add an IF has_header THEN skip first row before the FOR EACH loop. In the desk check, use a two-row file (one header, one question) and show that only one Question object appears in the returned list.

Exercise 5

Perform a complete planning reflection on a program you have previously written — from this book, from the Think, Code, Create foundation text, or from your own work. Apply the structure of Example 7.1: for each planning stage (Understand, Plan, Design, Desk Check), identify one specific thing the stage would have produced for your program, and one specific error or design problem the stage would have prevented. Present your reflection in a table with four columns: Stage, What it would have produced, What it would have prevented, Was this actually a problem in your original code?

Hint: Choose a program that you remember having bugs in, or that you had to rewrite part of. The most valuable reflections connect a planning decision to a real error that you actually encountered. If the program was short, the reflection will be short too — even a two-row table is valuable if the connections are genuine.

Challenge Tasks

These tasks have no hints. They require independent thinking and are suitable for extension or assessment. Complete the Guided Exercises before attempting these.

Challenge Task 1

Apply the complete six-step design-first workflow to the following problem: build a Student Gradebook program that reads a list of student names and five assessment marks (each out of 100) from a CSV file, calculates each student's weighted average (marks are equally weighted), assigns a grade, displays a formatted class report (name, average, grade for each student), identifies the highest and lowest scoring students, and calculates the class average. Produce a complete planning document: Step 1 (restated problem, inputs, outputs, constraints, decisions made), Step 2 (structure chart with data couples), Step 3 (pseudocode for every function, UML class diagram if any classes are used), Step 4 (desk check with normal, boundary, and erroneous test data for at least three functions), Step 5 (complete Python code). Close with a Step 6 reflection identifying what each planning stage contributed.

Challenge Task 2

The Quiz Program in this chapter is a purely sequential quiz: every question is presented, every answer is accepted, and the score is calculated at the end. Design and plan (Steps 1–4 only — no code required) an extended version that supports the following additional features: a time limit per question (if the student takes longer than 30 seconds, the question is counted as wrong); a difficulty rating for each question (Easy / Medium / Hard, stored in the CSV file); a bonus scoring system where Hard questions are worth 2 points, Medium questions 1.5, and Easy questions 1 point; and a leaderboard that saves the top 5 scores (name + score + date) to a separate file and displays it at the start of each session. Your planning document must include: a full Understand stage for the extended specification; a structure chart showing all new and modified functions; pseudocode for the three most complex new functions; and at least two desk checks for the new logic.

Challenge Task 3

This challenge is a design critique task. Review the Quiz Program design produced in this chapter — specifically the structure chart, the UML class diagram, and the pseudocode for run_quiz() and display_results(). Identify at least three design improvements that could be made, each addressing either cohesion, coupling, extensibility, or error handling. For each improvement: state the current design decision and why it is suboptimal; describe the improved design; produce a revised structure chart fragment, pseudocode block, or UML diagram showing the change; and explain what problem the improvement solves and what new benefit it provides. The improvements must be genuine design improvements — not cosmetic or stylistic changes — and must be justified with reference to the principles introduced in this book.

Made in United States
Cleveland, OH
06 November 2026

47640856R00095